1—

✳ A MONTH OF SUNDAYS ✳

✳ A Month of Sundays ✳

✳ Kent Biffle ✳

University of North Texas Press

10 9 8 7 6 5 4 3 2 1

Requests for permission to reproduce material
from this work should be sent to:
Permissions
University of North Texas Press
P. O. Box 13856
Denton, TX 76203

The paper used in this book meets the minimum requirements
of the American National Standard for Permanence of Paper
for Printed Library Materials, Z39.48.1984.

Library of Congress Cataloging-in-Publication Data

Biffle, Kent.
    A month of Sundays / Kent Biffle.
            p.   cm.
    Includes index.
    ISBN 0-929398-56-4
    1. Texas—History—Anecdotes. I. Title.
F386.6.B54 1993   93-7882
976.4—dc20   CIP

TABLE OF CONTENTS

✳   **TABLE OF CONTENTS**   ✳

(With date of publication in *The Dallas Morning News*)

✳ PART I—TEXAS HISTORY ✳

MARCH 2, 1836: AMID CHAOS, TEXANS FORM NATION 3
    (3-2-86)
POLITICIANS OF OLD RELIED ON LOW BLOWS 12
    (5-22-88)
TEXANS PLOTTED INDIAN-MEXICAN CONFLICT 15
    (12-14-86)
SINS OF SAM: HOUSTON LED A WILD LIFE 18
    (3-27-86)
CROCKETT SURRENDER? DEBATERS OF THE ISSUE JUST WON'T GIVE 23
    (11-9-86)
SAN JACINTO BATTLE EARNED RANK IN BOOK 25
    (4-16-89)
PORCINE INTRIGUE REVISITED 34
    (10-15-87)
YELLOW ROSE STORY LOSES ITS BLOOM 37
    (11-17-85)
INDIANOLA—NOTHING LASTS ON THE COAST'S SHIFTING SAND 41
    (8-25-85)
THE RIDE OF TEXAS' PAUL REVERE 49
    (2-26-89)
KIOWA CHIEF REVERED IN LIFE AND DEATH 53
    (4-28-91)
TRUE STORY OF 1860 FIRES AND LYNCHINGS 56
    (3-12-89)
CONFEDERATE GRAVES REVIVE TALES OF BATTLE 60
    (7-19-87)
CUSTER WAS A POPULAR MAN DURING HIS TEXAS STAY 64
    (1-1-89)
FORT CHADBOURNE—A MONUMENT TO THE OLD WEST 67
    (4-24-88)
A FRONTIER SOLDIER'S LOT WAS NOT A HAPPY ONE 71
    (4-19-87)

OLD "BUFFALO SOLDIERS" RECALL HORSEBACK DAYS .75
    (8-11-85)
COURAGE EARNED BLACK SEMINOLES A PLACE IN HISTORY 79
    (7-1-84)
HOW THE VOTE WAS WON 82
    (3-15-87)

✳ PART II—TEXAS OUTLAWS ✳

OLD TEXAS LAWS GAVE DEATH MORE OFTEN THAN LIBERTY 89
    (4-5-76)
PICTURING THE BAD GUYS 91
    (8-21-99)
ON THE TRAIL OF THE TRUE TALE OF A GUNFIGHTER 96
    (7-15-84)
WHO WERE THE REDHEADED WARRIORS? 98
    (3-29-92)
LET THE RECORD SHOW JANE WAS HANGED FIRST .102
    (12-13-87)
WRITER TURNED DETECTIVE TO TRACE BLOODY FEUD 105
    (6-16-85)
BESSIE'S DEATH IN 1877 STILL CAUSES DEBATE 107
    (4-30-89)
OUTLAW'S CAPTURE WAS AN INSIDE JOB 111
    (8-7-88)
NO KIDDING, BILLY MAY HAVE DIED IN TEXAS IN 1950 114
    (7-27-86)
THE HANGING OF WILD BILL LONGLEY 119
    (9-27-87)
DARING TRAIN ROBBER GOT THE GOODS, NOT THE GLORY 122
    (8-31-86)
BILL DALTON SHOT STRAIGHT IN BANK NOTE 126
    (3-5-89)
PINK FLOWERS MARK A BADMAN'S GRAVE 131
    (1-3-88)
OLD-STYLE BANDITS HAD PANACHE 134
    (5-1-88)
RICHES WERE EASY COME, EASY GO FOR TRAIN ROBBER 137
    (5-19-85)
THE DAY SANTA BROUGHT A LITTLE CHRISTMAS FEAR 141
    (12-9-84)

BONNIE-CLYDE TEAM ECLIPSED BONNIE'S ROY 146
    (1-15-89)
IN OLDEN DAYS, THE OUTLAWS OUTDREW 'EM ALL 149
    (1-20-85)
TELLING IT STRAIGHT 152
    (4-22-84)
LAST MEALS: INMATE ORDERS RARELY EXOTIC 156
    (2-26-92)

❋ PART III—TEXAS FOLK AND FOLKLORE ❋

WHAT'S IN A NAME? 163
    (8-24-84)
PHANTOMS PLY TWILIGHT ZONE IN CADDO LAKE'S PAST 165
    (10-19-86)
BELL COUNTY WITCHCRAFT LEGEND LIVES 171
    (10-30-88)
GRAVES SERVE AS REMINDERS OF WILD WACO 174
    (8-30-87)
UT HOLDS "SMOKING PISTOL" TO PA FERGUSON 177
    (3-15-81)
WEST TEXAS' HALLIE STILLWELL IS AN ORIGINAL 184
    (9-1-91)
THE LEGEND OF DAREDEVIL ROY BUTLER 187
    (10-25-87)
"CONAN" CREATOR'S LIFE DIDN'T MATCH TALES 192
    (6-22-86)
MURPHY'S WAR DIDN'T END IN THE ARMY 196
    (2-28-88)
OLD SALTS REMEMBER SAM DEALEY'S VALOR 201
    (5-28-89)
MEMORABILIA REVEALS THE LIPSCOMB LEGACY IS ALIVE 205
    (5-24-81)
THEY'RE PICKIN' GRASS IN NACOGDOCHES 207
    (2-7-88)
CHEROKEE JACK LOOKS THE PART, AND HE'S APT TO PLAY IT 210
    (12-6-87)
STALKING THE ELUSIVE BUCKAROO 213
    (6-18-89)
"DOVE" STILL RUFFLING A LOT OF FEATHERS 216
    (2-19-89)

ACE REID COULD ALWAYS DRAW LAUGHS 222
    (11-17-91)
JOHN HENRY FAULK LOOMS TALL OVER TEXAS 225
    (7-30-89)
J. EVETTS HALEY: "SORT OF AN ALAMO" 232
    (4-12-81)
CHILI VS. STEAK FEUD COULD GET POWERFUL HOT 237
    (6-4-89)
TEXAS' CARL HERTZOG: TYPOGRAPHY AS FINE ART 240
    (10-21-79)

✳✳✳

Preface

I have been waterlogged in San Antonio, snowbound in El Paso, afoot and helpless in several of the 254 counties of this 267,000-square-mile state. I have outlucked hurricanes and seen a couple of tornadoes up close.

I have been stuck in sand, ice, mud, and something in Jefferson County that must have been epoxy. It was unfazed by two runs through a carwash. Once in Big Spring, I watched in disbelief as the blazing Texas sun peeled the chrome-finished brightwork off my car.

In Lubbock, I got lucky. I caught a ride back to the hotel in the tow truck. At Brownfield Highway and Salem, my rented Tempo was rammed amidships by a blonde showboat from Texas Tech. She was steering, loosely speaking, a Mustang convertible the color of a red M&M. The top was down and four guys were aboard when she hit me with an expensive noise.

No one was scratched. The Mustang wasn't dented. But when the Tempo finally quit windmilling in the crossroads, it was an undrivable mess. A cop was writing the showboat a ticket when the tow truck driver told me to get in. I wished her happy trails until we intersect again.

And there was the time in Leon County when my Chevy began billowing smoke. I coasted nearly a mile into Buffalo and found a fire extinguisher.

See, these misadventures are out-takes from a column I write about Texas. It is called "Texana." My work—and I call it that with an almost straight face—carries me to the four corners, well, the eight or ten corners of Texas.

Nearly a decade ago, editors at *The Dallas Morning News* concluded that I needed a column. You know, something to keep me busy and preferably out of town. That is how I fell into the world's best job. Prowling Texas for columns is flat out fascinating. I've had experiences I will never forget, no matter how hard I try.

The rumor that I live in the car, I guess, can be blamed on my impaired packing genes or my permanently unpressed clothes. Truth to tell, I have not slept in the car since Ronald Reagan slept in the White House. When I travel, I try to get at least thirty-five dollars worth of sleep every night, plus hotel tax.

Now and then, be it said, I have put up in lodgings with fewer amenities than the car afforded. In contrast, I have unwittingly stayed in a few places that—we can talk here—offered more amenities than the law allows. Invariably, I get suspicious about a tourist court only after I have signed my right name.

Actually, I am not put off by motel rooms that are merely ugly. I use them only for sleeping, and I sleep with my eyes closed. Every traveler knows there are more urgent problems—small daily crises, deadlines, and hot pursuits. I have chased down fugitive luggage and chased off thieves. I have whined at overcharges and smiled with all my teeth when a motel chain awarded me a free night for being a good customer. My life in vagabondage has keenly honed my diplomatic and survival skills. (I hate the word "coward.")

My diet has been varied. I have eaten fajitas in Lajitas (Brewster County), apples in Eden (Concho County), New York cheesecake in New York (Henderson County) and the most outré, experimental chili throughout a state that is bigger, more cantankerous, and better dressed on Sunday than all of New England, New York, Pennsylvania, Ohio, and Illinois combined (an odious thought).

I have supped low in the food chain, the fast food kind. And I have dined exotically and quixotically, swallowing fried pit vipers, glands of ruminants, and bits of small burrowing animals with strong claws and bony protective plates. I have consumed the famous tripes of Caen in France, where I uncovered a Texas story, and in South Texas, the infamous tripes of San Antonio (aka menudo). In behalf of my readers, I have masticated these and other only slightly sought after delicacies. I have eaten things posing as other things (most of them trying to be chicken fried steak or barbecue.)

To travel Texas is to heighten one's awareness of what the food writers call "greasy mouthfeel." One and a half centuries ago Allen White, the father of William Allen White, late editor of the Emporia, Kansas *Gazette*, tried to settle in Texas but fled after ninety days because everything was fried. In Texas, only the brave deserve the fare. Texans prefer their vitamins fried, when not refried. Granted, not all things fried are *ipso facto* tasty, but Texas cuisine is informed always by the wisdom of the great Texas chefs who declare: "Sometimes you bites the honey and sometimes you bites the bee." My culinary rule of the road is simple; it is correct to eat with your fingers if the food is clean.

Now, leaping from the frying pan to the sublime, I will say that I find Texas endlessly alluring. Driving through the Hill Country at dawn is an experience to be revered. Aesthetic seizures may similarly strike in the Big Thicket, on South Padre Island, in the Big Bend and in a dozen other places. Personally, I am a pushover for Lovers' Leap in Waco. I submit that wherever you happen to be in Texas, you are less than half a tank away from breathtaking scenery. As show people say, the visuals are stunning.

And Texas history is gripping. No other state comes close to the color and drama of our state's past. Once a nation, Texas has encompassed kingdoms—oil, cattle, cotton, and the Dallas Cowboys. As the littérateur Lon Tinkle once put it: "There is a Texas character, a Texas caricature, a Texas myth, a Texas mystique, a Texas legend, a Texas tradition, and then there is a Texas reality. The latter is not easy to pin down." I never tire of trying to pin it down and I never tire of Texans, however much they are maligned by inferior species such as non-Texans.

Whether Texans be city slickering or country reveling, the vitality and variety of their sayings, doings, and poses are, I contend, captivating. Texans' dispositions are diverse and, at times, perverse. A political consultant observed that running a statewide race in Texas is "like campaigning at the United Nations." I hope I have bottled some of that quirky quality in this book, which offers pieces rescued from a steamer trunk filled with "Texana."

Careful readers will find here more than a month of Sunday pieces. There is no extra charge. That is just the kind of guy I am.

Along about here an author thanks those who helped him put the book together. They were countless and many of them are named in the following pages. I have scrupulously tried to cite those whose scholarship and research I have used, but columnists are pathetic victims of unconscious recall. Some cynic cited the columnists' creed as "all work and no plagiarism makes dull reading." Some cynic. I forget who.

But I will not forget to thank Fran Vick, director of the University of North Texas Press, for envisioning this book. Managing Editor Bob Mong of *The Dallas Morning News* liked her idea out loud. A blessing came also from Ab Abernethy, who fills J. Frank Dobie's big boots for the Texas Folklore Society.

From Fink (Grayson County or Bell County or both) to Fodice or Four Dice or Fordyce (Houston County), from officially misspelled Motley County to long abolished Foley County, from Abbott (old Willie Nelson's hometown in Hill County) to Zephyr (knocked down but not out by a Brown County tornado), Texans get my thanks for being Texans. And please do not erase the names of men and women who have helped me out of various ditches:

Ralph Langer, Bill Evans, Stu Wilk, Donnis Baggett, Lowery Metts, Mike Kingston, Bob Compton, Mary Crawford, Howard Swindle, Margaret Henson, Don Carleton, Laurence McNamee, Jim Byrd, Archie McDonald, James Ward Lee, Charles Link and Ernestine Sewell, Fred Tarpley, Mike Cox, Elmer Kelton, Bill O'Neal, Lawrence Clayton, Clay Reynolds, A. C. Greene, Don Graham, Max Lale, Ron Tyler, Joyce Roach, John Edward Weems, Ellen Murry, Roger Conger, Leon Metz, Dale Walker, Larry L. King, Robert Pierce, Greg and Gail Beil, Randolph Campbell, Margaret Rambie, Lewis Rigler, Alwyn Barr, Linda Hudson, George Ward, Al Harting, Tom Simmons, J. Evetts and Ros Haley, Bill Hughes, Patrick Bennett, Hugh Aynesworth, Jim

Lehrer, Darwin Payne, Jim Goodson, Wally Chariton, Cactus Pryor, Gene Wilson, Kenneth Davis, Sam Attlesey, the late Blanche Barrow, Ace Reid, John Henry Faulk and C. L. Sonnichsen.

UNT Press editors Marie Schein and Charlotte M. Wright have earned my gratitude and a share of my lottery winnings.

My purty wife Suzanne inspires my work, forever insisting that I hold a job. She used to ride with me from San Saba's shore to Lavaca's tide, but the birth of our son Patrick modified her travels. My other kids, Laurie Brodeur and Jeff Biffle, are not kids anymore, or so they claim.

Here, I must bow deeply to the memory of my old amigo Frank X. Tolbert whose *Dallas Morning News* columns on Texas through three decades set high standards for all who follow.

Kent Biffle
The Dallas Morning News

✳ PART I ✳

✳ TEXAS HISTORY ✳

***

March 2, 1836: Amid Chaos, Texans Form Nation

Part One: The Creation

Washington-on-the-Brazos, Texas—March 2, 1836. In a rickety room in this new town, polished gentlemen and raw frontiersmen are convening to legitimize an infant nation, the Republic of Texas.

A Declaration of Independence of the Republic of Texas will be speedily adopted. Time is precious. The delegates fear for their families. The Mexican army, recently driven from Texas soil, has returned, rampaging, swollen in strength and scary as smallpox.

The Texans' military hopes are pinned on Sam Houston, the big, battle-scarred soldier and erstwhile governor of Tennessee. Indian friends and Anglo enemies alike call him "Big Drunk." A crony of President Andrew Jackson, Houston was formally delegated to this convention from Refugio, after a defeat for delegacy from Nacogdoches.

The Republic hasn't taken its first breath, but politics is alive and kicking. Delegate Houston and Delegate Robert Potter from Nacogdoches, the winner in Houston's losing race, glare daggers across the crude table. Politics. Ayuntamientos. Municipalities. Comisarios. Consultations. Conventions. Committees of Safety. Peace Party. War Party. Politics. The proposal for this Convention of 1836 was vetoed by Henry Smith, impeached governor of the provisional government of Texas. Politics.

Now, Houston impatiently awaits his commission as the Republic's commander-in-chief. Naturally, Potter wants no part of an army commanded by Houston. Potter is a one-time U.S. congressman from North Carolina, where he was jailed for emasculating two in-laws. (He made Potterizing

3

a verb in the Carolinas.) Potter will hold out for secretary-
ship of the Texas Navy. The feud simmers. Houston knows
a new Texas army must be quickly raised and trained. The
old one is being blown to bits by Mexicans.

Commanding the Mexican soldiers is Antonio Lopez de
Santa Anna, the Mexican dictator. He has sworn to kill
these rebels, these traitors. "Foreign devils," he calls the
Anglos. He will legally execute prisoners as "pirates." In
the eyes of Santa Anna, the rebel colonists have viciously
betrayed Mexico, a country that had befriended them. He
has a point. In several ways, Anglo colonists once fared
better under Mexican rule than they had back in the U.S.A.
Then Presidente Santa Anna anointed himself dictator.

Santa Anna, the self-styled "Napoleon of the West,"
rightly suspects that the umbilical cord of the rebels' infant
government is attached to the U.S.A. Indeed, volunteers,
arms, supplies and money have been rushed into desperate
Texas from the U.S.A. There, many officials and citizens
envision a nation that will reach from sea to shining sea.
Annexation of a vast, independent Texas would be a supreme leap toward that goal. But slavery, although outlawed by Mexico, is a Texas institution. That's trouble.
Equally troubling, annexation would mean certain war
between the United States and Mexico. The flow of aid into
bleeding Texas is not sufficient to win a rebellion. Politics.

Santa Anna's thousands of troops are massed in San
Antonio, 150 miles to the southwest. Within a week, after
an expectedly expensive, but predictably successful major
assault, Santa Anna plans to butcher the handful of Texans
who defend the Alamo church. The defenders—under command of Colonel William B. Travis, Colonel Jim Bowie and
"High Private" David Crockett—manfully await the show-
down.

Meanwhile, as delegates to the Texas Convention of
1836 talk of liberty and laws, another Mexican column,
1,000 strong, under Gen. Don Jose Urrea, is far to the south,
but on the move. Having overrun San Patricio, a Texan

garrison, Urrea's cavalry is on this day sporting with Texans scattered in the wilderness, riding them down and lancing them like wild pigs.

Urrea's thrust is toward Presidio La Bahia at Goliad, where the main body of the Texan army is commanded by a West Pointer named James Walker Fannin, Jr., who isn't moved by pleas for help from Travis at the Alamo. Fannin is a riddle of incompetence. A pointless surrender by Fannin to the Mexicans would surprise no one. Sam Houston must count Fannin's 400 men as utterly lost.

Washington-on-the-Brazos isn't idly named. It is one more indication of how ambitiously and longingly the Texas patriots look to Washington, D.C., for cooperation and recognition. At this moment, empresario Stephen F. Austin, the bachelor "father of Texas," is in the District of Columbia with two other commissioners from Texas, Branch T. Archer and William Wharton, both dedicated revolutionaries. They are seeking, reportedly with some promise, recruits and arms to fight the Mexicans.

Of gentle and reasonable instincts, Austin for years sought accommodation with mercurial Mexico, whose officials responded by high-handedly imprisoning him for months. Austin finally lost patience and now urges rebellion against Mexico, stating: "I am tired of their government. They are always in revolution and I believe always will be." The Washington in Texas, where delegates talk while heroes die, sits on the west side of the Brazos River, opposite the mouth of the Navasota. In its single year of existence, the town has been whooped along as the future capital of Texas. In reality, it is no more than a dozen cabins and shanties staggered along a single street. Chopped from the woods, the street is still studded with stumps. William Fairfax Gray, a traveler who likely will settle in the Republic, describes the place:

"We stopt at a house, called a tavern, kept by a man named John Lott, which was the only place in the city at which we could get fodder for our horses. It was a frame house, consisting of only one room, about forty by twenty feet, with a large fire place at each end, a shed at the back, in which the table was spread. It was a wretchedly made establishment, and a blackguard, rowdy set was lounging about. The host's wife and children, and about thirty lodgers, all slept in the same apartment, some in beds, some on cots, but the greater part on the floor. I fortunately lodged on a good cot with a decent Tennessean named H. S. Kimble (now secretary of the convention), who is looking for land, but says the state of anarchy is such that he is afraid to buy and is waiting to see the course of things after the meeting of the Convention."

A Virginian, Gray complains of the monotony of "coarse and dirty" cornbread, fried pork and "miserable coffee." He says the delegates must depart from this town "promptly to avoid starvation." Of the frigid convention hall, he notes: "An unfurnished house, without doors or windows. In lieu of glass, cotton cloth was stretched across the windows, which partially excluded the cold wind."

Delegates sit around a long, rough table that extends down the room. It is heaped with papers. Richard Ellis of Pecan Point on the Red River, president of the convention, is at the head of the table.

Ellis personifies these fast and chaotic times. A Virginian who helped write Alabama's Constitution in 1819 and served on that state's supreme court, Ellis moved to an alluring area claimed by both Arkansas and Mexico—and now by the Republic of Texas. He was elected a delegate to the Arkansas constitutional convention a few months earlier, but was too ill to serve. His long-suffering wife may have typified the wives of these Texas adventurers when she wrote from Alabama in September 1827 seeking information about Ellis, who had come to Texas on a business trip in 1826. She sent the query to empresario Austin: "Dear Sir I am the wife of Judge Ellis from Alabama he went to Texas to Collect a debt due from Col Pettus which debt he was security for and Pettus ran away from here and left him to pay and I wish you to state to Judge Ellis if he dont Come home directly he will have his property sold. . . . I have not herd from my husband since the 30 of may for God sake let me know what has become of him since that time and whare he is if he is thare."

Ellis, who will eventually move his family from Alabama to Texas, is now trying to keep order in the ramshackle hall. This is a public meeting. Onlookers wander in and out, some of them making a show of respectfully tiptoeing around the long table.

Inevitably, the document adopted here will be compared with another signed sixty years earlier by English colonists in America who declared their independence from Britain. The Texas declaration will suffer in comparison. Be mindful, this assembly is far from cosmopolitan Philadelphia and is convened in an area not famous for its distinguished intellectuals. This poor town of about one hundred souls has neither a library nor a printing press. Moreover, the Republic of Texas has no Thomas Jefferson to write a brilliant rationale for revolution.

The Texas declaration is mostly the work of George Childress, a thirty-two-year-old lawyer and land speculator from Tennessee who has lived in Texas less than three months. A melancholy streak in Childress is so marked that his suicide before many years may be anticipated. To more than 300 words runs the first sentence of the catalog of grievances. The declaration is an indictment accusing the Mexicans of crimes that range from "piracy" to inciting "the merciless savage, with tomahawk and scalping knife, to massacre the inhabitants of our defenseless frontiers."

Declaring "our connection with the Mexican nation forever ended," the document closes with the boast: "We fearlessly and confidently commit the issue to the decision of the Supreme Arbiter of the destinies of nations." This is a bold assertion from signatories who plan to dash off a quick constitution for their new republic and then "fearlessly and confidently" take to their heels.

Beginning in front of the Mexican troops is a retrograde maneuver by unsettled settlers that will be styled a "Runaway Scrape." Texan families, non-combatants and even some soldiers will be thrown together in this disorderly eastward retreat. The delegates, however, know that their work must be completed.

The Republic of Texas must have a government, a new beginning. Signers will ultimately number fifty-nine. Only two will be native Texans—Francisco Ruiz and Jose Antonio Navarro, delegates from Bexar. Only ten signers will have lived in Texas for as long as six years.

After adopting the declaration, delegates will give several days to hammering out a Texas Constitution. This document will be a medley of provisions copied from the constitutions of several states and from the Constitution of the U.S.A. No one expects the Texas Constitution to be more than quick carpentry. And, without doubt, it will be as eccentric as some of the personalities at this convention. For instance, approval is certain for an article that will forbid ministers of the gospel from holding public office in the Republic of Texas. Slavery will be legalized, but slave-running will be outlawed.

Speed is more essential than the creation of a timeless document. At the first signal that a windy speech is beginning, delegates suppress a speaker. The eloquent delegate Lorenzo de Zavala of Harrisburg can get no further into an oration than: "Mr. President, an eminent Roman statesman once said. . . ." He is told sharply that the pressing problem isn't dead Romans, but live Mexicans. Zavala is an able statesman. One may forecast that the delegates will elect him vice president of the Republic, to serve with conservative President David G. Burnet of Liberty.

The war has overtaken Houston. He cannot linger to await completion of a constitution. Options are few for the commander-in-chief. He must ride toward San Antonio. He must torch the Anglo settlements in front of Santa Anna, denying the Mexicans any remaining supplies or shelter.

Houston must raise troops and train them as the panicky Runaway Scrape reels eastward. Surely, for now, he will resist all impulse and all urging to battle the Mexican army. Houston's retreat must draw Santa Anna into East Texas, where the Anglo population is concentrated. The best Houston can hope is that Santa Anna will make a strategic mistake—such as impulsively splitting up his forces while in hostile territory. If that should happen and if the Texas army isn't driven into the sea and if the Supreme Arbiter smiles on this new Republic, Houston may even have an outside chance. He may catch that Napoleonic egomaniac napping.

Part Two: Where Did the Declaration Go?

Somehow the Texans won the war. Then somehow they lost their Declaration of Independence.

It was missing in action for about 60 years.

Historians knew the document was approved on March 2, 1836, and signed the following day at Washington-on-the-Brazos (Washington County). Five so-called *fair* (or legally exact) copies were sent to scattered settlements. But these apparently were lost forever. Luckily, about 1,000 handbill versions of the Declaration of Independence were printed in San Felipe (Austin County). But, these were not fair copies. To some people they were downright *unfair*. The defective handbills omitted the names of nine of the fifty-nine signers.

The original declaration traveled with other documents to Washington, D.C., where Texans were seeking statehood or at least formal recognition of their republic. Colonizer Stephen F. Austin, the bachelor Father of Texas, was in Washington, seeking U.S. recognition for his baby republic, when on June 10, 1836, he wrote to David G. Burnet, interim president of Texas:

"Nothing is wanting in Washington to procure an acknowledgment of our independence but *official information. . . .* All this should be sent immediately in an official form to the representatives of Texas in Washington (George C. Childress, Robert Hamilton, and William Wharton)."

On November 18, 1836, Texas President Sam Houston appointed William Wharton minister plenipotentiary to the United States. At that time, Austin, by then the republic's secretary of state, sent Wharton a package of credentials and official papers. Austin wrote, "You already have the Declaration of Independence."

By the way, you have noticed that everyone mentioned here has a Texas county named in his honor. Perhaps a county should have been named too for Louis Wiltz Kemp, a businessman who became a Texas historical sleuth. Kemp ultimately qualified for an honored grave in the Texas State Cemetery in Austin. Kemp tried to unravel the mystery of the missing document. He correctly figured the original Declaration of Independence was presented to Washington officials by Wharton. When the document was finally found it was marked, "Left at the Department of State, May 28, 1836, by Mr. Wharton, the original." But that date looks wrong. Evidence suggests that Wharton deposited the document later.

Kemp concluded, "When and by whom the notation was made is not recorded. The author [Kemp] believes that Wharton left the document with the state department subsequent to Nov. 18, 1836, when President Houston appointed him minister plenipotentiary to the United States. It is true that he was in Washington on May 28, but there is no evidence, other than the notation, that he left the Declaration with the State Department at that time." What happened to it in the hands of Washington bureaucrats is anyone's guess. Perhaps not much.

For about sixty years, the whereabouts of the Declaration of Independence was a riddle without an answer. Until 1896, puzzled officials and historians guessed the document may have been destroyed in one of the Texas Capitol's fires. But in May of that year the document turned up.

Seth Shepard, a native Texan and associate justice of the court of appeals for the District of Columbia, was talking with a Washington friend named William Hallett Phillips. Knowing that Judge Shepard was a historian, Phillips casually mentioned that in a file in the State Department he had seen a document that appeared to be the Texas Declaration of Independence.

They dug it up. At first, Shepard assumed it was one of the fair copies. But investigation revealed that—bingo—it was the original. Within a few days, U.S. Secretary of State Richard Olney wrote Shepard that because the document was the property of Texas, he would return it in exchange for a receipt from Texas Governor Charles A. Culberson.

Shepard hastily wrote to Culberson, who responded on June 11 with the receipt as requested. This Shepard presented to the

U.S. Department of State. The Texas Declaration of Independence was then returned to Texas.

A front page story of the *Austin Evening News* indicates that Culberson received the document on July 1, 1896.

It promptly disappeared again for about 30 years.

Enter a remarkable woman.

Jane Y. McCallum, darling of the feminists, had been chosen Texas secretary of state by Governor Dan Moody. Journalist and suffragette leader, Ms. McCallum had been reluctant to accept the post. Finally, she had decided, "I wanted to do something for women and for myself too."

Beginning her duties in early 1927, she was doing some, well, housecleaning, when she came across a rusty tin box containing a scroll of paper that was ragged with decay. Carefully unrolling it, she gazed on what is considered the state's most important historical document.

Hello, Declaration of Independence. Long time, no see.

Ms. McCallum gave it the best of care. She studied for a couple of years to determine the best way to restore and display it. University of Texas experts preserved it, although the paper now remains dangerously fragile. The process scared Ms. McCallum, who wrote: "When the time came to take it out to the University, I called Dan [Moody] and Claud Teer—he was chairman of the [Texas] Board of Control then—and the three of us took it out. I died a thousand deaths when they gave it a bath—took the dust off."

The document was placed in a specially built shrine in a niche of the Texas Capitol. It remained on display until 1940, when officials moved it downstairs to the Texas State Library. As office space shrank, the document was shuffled about—to the Highway Building in 1951 and to a Quonset hut in a Highway Department storage yard in 1956.

Saddened, Ms. McCallum, a year before she died, spoke out.

"The Declaration and the other wonderful documents should be displayed to give the people inspiration. It is shameful to kick Texas' history from place to place."

The reaction of concerned citizens ultimately led to the Texas

State Library's construction in 1962 of the structure now known as the Lorenzo de Zavala State Archives and Library Building. The document's traveling days are about ended. Its 1986 sesquicentennial appearance at the Hall of State in Dallas may have been its final tour.

That the Texas Declaration of Independence kept its date with the sesquicentennial showing is a near miracle. Consider the alternative to its being lost for sixty years after Wharton deposited it with the U.S. State Department. If Wharton had tried to return it to Texas in his hip pocket, the document would have certainly been destroyed or seized by the Mexican government.

I'll explain. After the recognition of the Republic of Texas by the United States, Wharton was eager to return home. On April 10, 1837, he boarded the *Invincible* of the Texas Navy. Off the coast of Texas, almost in sight of Wharton's plantation in Brazoria county, the *Invincible* was captured by the Mexican brigs of war *Vencedor del Alamo* and *Libertador*.

As prisoners, Wharton and the other passengers were taken to Matamoros. Although Wharton survived, his belongings didn't. As the brigs were closing with the *Invincible*, he destroyed some of his Republic of Texas papers. The remaining ones were captured by the Mexicans.

In either event the Texas Declaration of Independence would have become a memory.

✳✳✳

POLITICIANS OF OLD RELIED ON LOW BLOWS

Presidential campaign speeches were hard-hitting in the Republic of Texas, 1836-1845. Stumping candidates and their speech writers didn't wear twelve-ounce gloves. Political speechification—as Texans then called it—was caustic enough to unclog drains.

Take the 1841 election. Sam Houston was seeking a second presidential sitting, after skipping a term as the law demanded.

His opponent was David G. Burnet, who'd been war-time provisional president during the revolution. Burnet hammered a time-worn theme he'd been sounding since independence. He raged that Houston was a cowardly incompetent and a drunk.

On the other side, Houston's pet name for Burnet was an Indian term—wetumpka, meaning hog thief. (Be mindful, all over the state today we have have counties, cities and schools named for both gentlemen.) They happily hated one another. Some of their remarks were unprintable. Some were, barely. Take the following newspaper exchanges.

Burnet on Houston: "When the whole truth shall be known, then this reputed hero (of the Battle of San Jacinto) will be despoiled of his furtive laurels; and be depicted as a quailing, irresolute braggadocio who fled by instinct and fought by compulsion. . . . Oh, fugitive fame, got by accident, retained by fraud, and merged in bestial debaucheries . . . with his robes of office dabbled in intoxication and the foul and most bloated blasphemies trembling on his tongue."

Houston on Burnet: "Even some of the soldiers facetiously remarked that the letter G. in your name stood for Grog. . . . You prate about the faults of other men while the blot of foul unmitigated treason rests upon you. You political brawler and canting hypocrite whom the waters of Jordan could never cleanse from your political and moral leprosy."

Houston's eventual victory prompted this left-handed kindness from one editor: "Old Sam H. with all his faults appears to be the only man for Texas. He is still unsteady, intemperate, but drunk in a ditch is worth a thousand of . . . Burnet."

Ellen Murry from the Star of the Republic Museum at Washington-on-the-Brazos in leafy Washington County told me about the warm Houston-Burnet feud. As educational curator of the museum, Ellen has wagon-loads of information on every aspect of life in the Republic of Texas. She told me that mud-slinging was often a crowd-pleasing show in elections during the time of the Republic. The show sometimes led to violence.

In 1839, Ben McCulloch, a hero of San Jacinto, got into a duel because of statements made in the heat of a congressional election. His opponent, Col. Alonzo Sweitzer, a physician and educated man, apparently thought he would have the advantage over a backwoodsman like McCulloch in a debate. McCulloch allowed he didn't want to debate Dr. Sweitzer because Dr. Sweitzer was—sad for McCulloch to mention—nasty when drunk.

Sweitzer began calling McCulloch a "moral coward" and "sneaking skulker." McCulloch burned. After winning the election, McCulloch bided his time, and several weeks later, at a time of his choosing, challenged the doctor to a duel.

When Sweitzer at first declined, McCulloch fumed: "As you will not fight when you have a fair and honorable opportunity, I cannot afford to shoot you down like a dog. I must content myself by pronouncing you a black-hearted cowardly villain, and in every respect beneath the notice of a gentleman."

They back and forthed like that. Because McCulloch could no longer recognize Sweitzer as his gentlemanly equal, he finally ended up dueling Sweitzer's second, Col. Reuben Ross. The duel was with rifles at 40 paces. Ross was spared but McCulloch was wounded in the arm, which he carried in a sling throughout the congressional session.

A favored way for a popular hero to win office with a minimum of slung mud and blood—then as now—was to be drafted. Since there were no primary elections or nominating conventions during the Republic period, a candidate's name could be put forward at a meeting of voters, usually his friends. For example, in 1836, the first public nomination of Sam Houston for president came at a meeting in San Augustine County.

Often a resolution of this sort nominating a candidate and detailing his qualifications would be adopted, with copies sent to other towns and newspapers. The nominee could then make a sacrificial response to the demands on his good citizenship. He would modestly announce that he had yielded to the solicitations of his friends and would run for the good of the country.

A candidate was expected to "canvass"—as old-timers called it—his district. Francis Lubbock described his initiation into politics when he sought the clerkship of Harris County in 1840. Unknown outside Houston, he accompanied a deputy sheriff as he made tax assessments throughout Harris County. Lubbock carried a large supply of tobacco to distribute to prospective voters. He noted that a candidate had to attend every ball and wedding in the county. Some of the balls were protracted. A young girl described a barbecue and ball at a polling station for the election in 1836. "The ladies spent the day quilting, and the younger people began dancing at three o'clock and kept it up until the next morning."

Dispensing of free booze was common. Too often such treats were exchanged for votes. Francis Lubbock noted that it was customary for a candidate to place a barrel of whiskey at the local country store. A barrel cost eight to ten dollars in those days.

A customer was told who bought the barrel, then offered a drink. That is to say, he was offered a drink if he were a white, male customer—the only kind who could vote. If the customer drank from a candidate's barrel, he was expected to support him.

The system had drawbacks, but, by all accounts, it was more amusing than today's primaries.

✳✳✳

TEXANS PLOTTED INDIAN-MEXICAN CONFLICT

In the days of the Texas Republic, a daring covert military scheme by the president's men could flop without a blush.

A plot by Texans to pit Indian warriors against Mexico during a time of putative peace has surfaced. The scheme was revealed in a letter from Thomas Jefferson Rusk to Sam Houston. The newly published letter—marked "private and confidential"— appears in *Most Excellent Sir*, a collection of letters to President Houston, edited by historian James L. Haley.

A Texas brigadier general and twice secretary of war, Rusk (ancestor of Dean Rusk, secretary of state to U.S. Presidents John Kennedy and Lyndon Johnson) dated the letter January 30, 1837. He was in Nacogdoches, attending to his neglected affairs and

preparing a successful campaign for the Texas Congress, when he
wrote to Houston, who was based at the old capital in Columbia
(Brazoria County). I added some punctuation:

Dr Genl,

Mr. Harper, whom you know very well, visits Columbia for
the purpose of obtaining permission for four Indian Chiefs of the
Creek tribe to visit Texas in order to have a talk with you on the
subject of procuring a settlement on the frontier between the
settlements of Texas and Mexico or the wild Indians & aiding in
defending the Country.

This is a delicate & highly responsible business and one
which, taking into view the peculiar attitude in which those
Indians stand, ought to be managed with the greatest caution and
prudence. I have had considerable conversation with Mr. H. He
states that the Creeks would be willing to the number of five
thousand to engage in an active war against Mexico.

I am thoroughly convinced that we need not expect permanent peace with the Mexican nation until they are fully convinced
of our ability to do them great harm at home & I would like to see
five thousand Indian warriors turned loose upon them west of
Rio Grande if they can be prevented from killing women &
children.

Five thousand Creeks could destroy the northern part of
Mexico & frighten the others into whatever term[s] might be
dictated to them. But your better knowledge of the Indian character could make me distrust my own opinion if not in accordance
with your views of the matter.

I am sorry I had not more time to reflect upon a matter of so
much importance before writing to you but Mr. H. just called as
he was leaving town & requeste[d] me to write. If the four Indian
chiefs are permitted to come, I think it would be well to call
Congress together the latter part of March or first of April.

This last matter I think is of great importance anyhow from
the fact that some of the action or rather want of action of the
Congress when in session has given considerable dissatisfaction
to the people & is really injuring us in the United States. . . .

I need not write you any of the news we have from the U. S. as you always have it there in advance of us.

I am truly your friend,

Tho J Rusk

The letter was one of more than 4,000 Sam Houston documents in the Andrew Jackson Houston Collection, presented to the Texas State Library in 1973 by Houston heirs. Haley is one of the few researchers who has examined the heap of raw correspondence.

Interviewed in Austin, where he lives, Haley spoke of the Rusk letter:

"Later on, in a letter, I found that Sam Houston did meet with those four Creek chiefs. He told them he had no objection to their settling in Texas. It wasn't recorded, however, that he told them, 'By the way, if you want to raid across the river, it's fine with us.' But apparently when the Indians went off and held a council of their own, they decided not to move to Texas."

The failed scheme joined others afoot about that time. For example, a few months earlier, after the Battle of San Jacinto, there was a recurring Texan plot to invade Mexico and capture Matamoros. Both Houston and Rusk were favorably intrigued by that idea, but later reconsidered and defused the plan.

In his letter of January 30, 1837, Rusk drew a distinction between the Creeks, an Eastern civilized tribe, and the wild Indians of the Southwest. The "wild Indians"—including Apaches and Comanches—were far too intractable to be assigned cat's-paw roles in the Texans' strategies against Mexico.

If the Texans' proposal to use Indians in the struggle with Mexico fell within the category of dirty tricks, it was one repeatedly attempted against the rebel Texans by the Mexicans.

Haley said, "The Mexicans tried all the time to provoke the Indians against Texans." Neither side had notable success in launching Indian raids against the other.

Of the Rusk proposal, Haley explained, "It often slips the attention of casual students of Texas history that virtually all of Texas' political concerns during this period were colored by an expected re-invasion from Mexico. This didn't ultimately occur until spring of 1842, but throughout the Columbia period the possibility was a weight that Houston had to place on the balance of each of his decisions."

Rusk's suggestion to turn loose 5,000 warriors upon Mexico would have provided a fascinating complication to Mexican relations. Rusk's willingness to defer to Houston's "better knowledge of the Indian character" had dissipated by 1839, when Rusk played a role in the Cherokee War, which resulted in the death of Chief Bowl and the expulsion of that tribe from Texas. That act axed a rift between Rusk and Houston that lasted until shortly before Rusk's death in 1857.

Throughout most of his life, Houston had been amiably close to the Cherokees. On the other hand, his experience with the Creeks had been violent. Twenty-two years before entertaining Rusk's plan for employing the Creeks against Mexico, Houston had become a hero in the Battle of Horseshoe Bend in Alabama during the Creek War.

Distinguishing himself, Houston won the enduring friendship of General Andrew Jackson, who would later as president befriend the Texans' cause.

At Horseshoe Bend, the Creeks gave Houston three severe wounds, one of which never completely healed. Rumor persists that the wound affected Houston's love life. Haley's looking into it.

✳✳✳

SINS OF SAM: HOUSTON LED A WILD LIFE

Brothers and Sisters, our discussion today might be called "The Sins of Sam."

Yes, if he were alive, Sam Houston would be the darling of the supermarket tabloids.

He was star stuff. And his private life was wild and woolly. Moreover, there was that mysterious opium thing.

On April 6, 1836, just a couple of weeks before the battle of San Jacinto won him lasting glory and won Texas independence,

General Houston wrote: "I am sorry that I am so wicked, for the prayers of the righteous shall prevail. That you are so, I have no doubt."

Indeed, Houston had no doubt. He was writing to the noisily righteous David G. Burnet, interim president of the struggling republic. Burnet was a revolutionary conservative, a prig and a leading Houston-hater. Burnet detested Houston's cussing and his reputation for hell raising.

Beyond that, Houston's command of the Texas army lifted Burnet into towering rages. Houston wouldn't take advice and Burnet failed to comprehend what the general was doing. Burnet couldn't find a safe place to open up his office.

Today Houston's strategy seems brilliant. Avoiding a costly battle until the proper moment, he drew Santa Anna and his Mexican troops ever deeper into rebel territory. Burnet didn't see it that way.

Throughout Houston's retreat from Gonzales to the Gulf of Mexico, Burnet fumed and wrote scalding letters. Burnet accused Houston of stupidity for sure, cowardice most likely, and treason perhaps.

No doubt, Burnet had heard the stories about Houston's delinquent boyhood in Tennessee and his almost killing a man in a duel. And he had perhaps been titillated by rumors surrounding Houston's fractured marriage to a young southern belle that ended his Tennessee political career, a career that had included two terms in Congress and one as governor.

Burnet had heard about Houston's living with the Cherokees in Indian Territory and taking a Cherokee wife while still legally married in Tennessee. (The Indian girl, Tiana Rogers Gentry, came from the same family as did 20th-century humorist Will Rogers.)

Anyhow, Burnet, along with nearly everyone else in North America, had heard about Houston's return visit to Washington, D.C., and the scandal he created. In the April 3, 1832, *National Intelligencer* appeared an account of a speech made by Congressman William Stanberry of Ohio: "Was the late Secretary of War (John Eaton) removed in consequence of his attempt fraudulently to give to Governor Houston the contract for Indian rations?"

As everyone and Burnet knew, Houston had assaulted Stanberry in the street, disarmed him and thrashed him with a cane. Houston had been cited for contempt and tried before the House of Representatives.

As the tale ran, on the night before closing arguments, Houston and some pals got drunk with the speaker of the House, who was acting as presiding judge in Houston's case. When Houston's attorney—Francis Scott Key, no less—was too hungover to function, Houston had relied on his own oratory and charm to escape punishment.

More grist for Burnet's mill was coming. On April 9, 1836, a strange young man—part adventurer and part clergyman—wrote a letter at Houston's camp on the Brazos.

He was James Hazard Perry, twenty-five, a New Yorker and a former West Pointer who'd been working as a volunteer aide to Houston, or so it seemed until Houston, a random censor, opened Perry's letter.

The letter revealed Perry as a spy—not for the Mexicans but for Texas Navy Secretary Robert Potter, an all-around scoundrel who was in cahoots with Burnet.

Perry described the poor shape of the Texas army. "We have now about 300 men sick and not more than twice that number reported for duty. In the manner affairs are at presently conducted the men are not likely to become better disciplined than an ordinary mob. Indeed, in an election riot in the United States I have seen the contending parties much better organized . . . ."

And he ripped Houston:

"We are in striking distance of the enemy and there are no signs of moving. Our men are loitering about without knowing more of military tactics at evening than they did in the morning.

"While the general either for want of his customary excitement (for he has entirely discontinued the use of ardent spirits) or as some say from the effort of opium is in a condition between sleeping and waking which amounts nearly to a constant state of insanity."

Houston complained about the spy in a letter to Burnet two days later:

"At this crisis the shafts of envy or malice should rest in the quiver ... I am worn down in body by fatigue, and really take my rest most in the morning, for I watch nearly all night, instead of being in a state of insanity I fear I am too irritable for my duties."

Houston reprimanded Perry. When Perry walked off from the army, Houston had him arrested, but restored his arms in time for him to fight at the battle of San Jacinto.

That Houston didn't directly address the opium charge may have been a political mistake.

The first detailed account of the revolution, preceded only by Houston's official report of his campaign, was a savage defamation of the general. It was titled *Houston Displayed: Or Who Won the Battle of San Jacinto?*

Written according to the 1837 pamphlet's cover, "By a Farmer in the Army," the attack on Houston was known to be the work of another of the general's aides, Major Robert M. Coleman.

The little book, in reprint editions, haunted Houston for years, along with Perry's repeated charges. (The latest reprint was in 1964 by the Brick Row Book Shop in Austin, edited by John H. Jenkins of Jenkins Publishing Co. The Dallas Public library has a copy.)

Houston Displayed was filled with dirty lies and just enough truth to keep a reader wondering.

For example:

"[Houston's] whiskey and opium gave out, and none could be procured; so that, from disappointment and the want of those stimulants, he became deranged. In one of his moments of delirium he drew a pistol and attempted to blow out his brains, but was prevented by the untimely interference of [Jim] Bowie ...."

And:

"The commander-in-chief of the army of Texas was spending his nights in the grog-shops of Washington [on-the-Brazos], in company with the gamblers and dissipated multitude which the session of the convention had collected at that place; and his days were devoted to sleep. ..."

And:

"[Houston] had the unblushing impudence to acknowledge to the bystanders that he did not recollect to have set out from any place sober or free from intoxication during the last five years; but on that occasion he considered himself sober. . . ."

The booklet is filled with trash, but some of it does *sound* like Houston. Most of the stuff—accusations of cowardice and adoration of Santa Anna—are preposterous.

Now, take Santa Anna. There was an opium user. After his capture, the Texans had to give him a fix before he could parley.

Historical consultant Margaret Henson of Houston has noted that opium was a common military treatment for pain and "camp fever" or diarrhea. Besides, its use was perfectly legal in the nineteenth century.

Among reports of Houston's opium use is that of Anson Jones, surgeon for the Texas army, who noted in an 1855 letter that Houston was "stupefied and stultified with opium" during the San Jacinto campaign.

Dogging the popular politician for years were the charges in *Houston Displayed*. The booklet outlived its author, Coleman, who, weeks after its publication, drowned while trying to bathe in the Brazos. (Coleman County was named for him.)

The Reverend Perry continued to hurl charges at Houston from New York pulpits. Eventually Perry joined the Union Army and in 1862 died of apoplexy.

By then, Houston had become a hard target for scandal.

In 1840—after a Tennessee divorce and the death of his Cherokee wife—Old Sam married a preacher's daughter, a pretty poet from Alabama, Margaret Lea.

Margaret dried him out and cleaned up his act.

On November 19, 1854, in a stream called Rocky Creek, the Reverend Rufus Burleson baptized Houston into the Baptist Church.

Assured by Dr. Burleson that all his sins had been washed away, Houston glanced down the creek and said, "God help the fish."

※※※

CROCKETT SURRENDER?
DEBATERS OF THE ISSUE JUST WON'T GIVE

Davy Crockett's name in inch-high letters made the cover of *Texas Monthly* magazine above the headline: "Hero or Hype?" A lower deck demanded: "Should we all still believe in a man who wasn't born on a mountaintop, hardly ever wore a coonskin cap, and surrendered at the Alamo?"

Well, nobody gives a rat's tail about Davy's altitude at birth. And his fans could probably adjust to the notion of Davy in a tractor hat or a Bosox cap. But the surrender part warms them to incandescence.

Even Paul Andrew Hutton—who wrote the *Monthly* piece, but not its headlines—approaches the subject as if he were undressing in public. He is one of the few academics who isn't afraid to write about the Alamo.

A Texan who teaches history at the University of New Mexico, Hutton was a boyhood believer in Crockett's going down clubbing heads with Old Betsy. But he grew up and surrendered to the revisionists. To be fair, Hutton is not treading new ground with this subject. Controversy has shrouded Crockett's final moments ever since the smoke cleared on that terrible March morning in 1836. Various Mexican eyewitnesses report Crockett among several men captured in the battle's final moments. Because of certain inconsistencies in some of the testimonies, it is the memoirs of one Jose Enrique de la Pena that are usually drawn upon when discussing Davy's demise. De la Pena, a lieutenant colonel in the Mexican army, took part in the final storming of the Alamo and later recorded the event in his private diary:

"Some seven men had survived the general carnage and, under the protection of General Manuel Castrillón, they were brought before Santa Anna. Among them was one of great stature, well proportioned, with regular features, in whose face there was the imprint of adversity, but in whom one also noticed a degree of resignation and nobility that did him honor. He was the naturalist Davy Crockett, well-known in North America for his exploits. . . . "

The question of Crockett's death is not that simple. In fact, other credible testimonies indicate that Tennessee's favorite son did indeed live up to the legends he spawned and went down swinging.

De la Pena states Crockett and the other captives were brought before Santa Anna then executed. Three other eyewitnesses report that the Tennessean was already dead when Santa Anna, who observed the battle from a considerable distance, first entered the Alamo compound.

Apolinario Saldigua, a sixteen-year-old fifer in the Mexican army, and Francisco Ruiz, the alcalde (or mayor) of San Antonio, both accompanied Santa Anna into the Alamo after the battle had ceased. Santa Anna's cook, Ben, also rode in this party.

Ruiz's express purpose on this mission was to point out to the Mexican dictator the bodies of Crockett, William B. Travis and Jim Bowie. Ruiz had known these men in San Antonio in the days preceding the siege and could easily identify them.

According to Ruiz: "Santa Anna sent one of his aides-de-camp with an order for us to come before him . . . and to accompany him, as he was desirous to have Col. Travis, Bowie and Crockett shown to him. On the north battery of the fortress lay the lifeless body of Col. Travis. . . . Toward the west . . . we found the body of Col. Crockett. Col. Bowie was found dead in his bed, in one of the rooms of the south side."

Saldigua offers similar testimony. Santa Anna, Saldigua writes, "had employed three or four citizens of San Antonio to enter with him, and to point out the bodies of several distinguished Texans." The general "was then conducted to the body of [Crockett]. This man lay with his face upward; and his body was covered by many Mexicans who had fallen upon him. His face was florid, like that of a living man; and he looked like a healthy man asleep. Santa Anna viewed him for a few moments, thrust his sword through him, and turned away."

Saldigua's testimony, like Ruiz's, states that Crockett was already dead when Santa Anna first laid eyes on him, rendering de la Pena's story implausible.

Ben, Santa Anna's cook, reported finding Crockett's body surrounded by "no less than 16 Mexican corpses," and that one lay across his body with the "huge knife of Davy buried in the Mexican's bosom to the hilt." As with Ruiz's and Saldigua's accounts, Ben's testimony refutes de la Pena's recollections. An additional riddle can be found in Saldigua's and Ben's descriptions of Crockett's final posture: How could a man who had surrendered, been tortured and then been executed be found with the bodies of fallen foes lying atop him?

Even more puzzling is why the testimonies of these three men have never found their way into the works of so-called revisionist historians.

According to Hutton, the Crockett surrender story has for years been ignored because it came from Mexican sources. Yet Hutton has extended the same discourtesy to Ruiz, Saldigua and Ben, two Mexicans and a black slave, by ignoring their reports.

Perhaps the best argument against the Crockett surrender story comes from the battle reports of Santa Anna himself. In his official communique to Mexico City, the Mexican dictator specifically mentions seeing the "cadaver" of Crockett. No mention is made of Crockett's surrendering, and no records have ever been found in which Santa Anna says Crockett did surrender.

Given the dictator's well documented disdain for Americans and his braggadocio nature, it seems certain that if so famous an American as Davy Crockett had indeed surrendered, the generalissimo would have felt compelled to comment upon it.

In the end, the question of Crockett's death is unimportant: Whether Davy surrendered or went down fighting, he died a martyr for Texas freedom.

✳✳✳

SAN JACINTO BATTLE EARNED RANK IN BOOK

Texans are mighty fond of the Battle of San Jacinto. They spent less than twenty minutes winning it and they've been celebrating the victory for 155 years.

On the shores of the San Jacinto River in 1836, Sam Houston's out-numbered rag-tag army whipped Santa Anna's troops in about eighteen minutes. Then frenzied Texan soldiers spent several hours bloodily avenging the Alamo and Goliad massacres. Decisive is the adjective most often used to describe the battle. But how decisive was it?

Military historian James W. Pohl of Southwest Texas State University posed that question at a meeting of the Texas State Historical Association. Pohl, who practiced Marine tactics as a young shavetail in Korea before switching his zone of action to academia, has made a career of reviewing history's most brilliant campaigns in much the way that chess players reprise the games of the masters.

"The view that the battle was decisive comes from Clarence Wharton's book entitled *San Jacinto: The Sixteenth Decisive Battle*, published in 1930. By the time of the centennial celebration in 1936, Wharton's book had been read by Texas teachers and history buffs. His contention had become the conventional wisdom of the day."

Mr. Pohl continued, "The idea of a sixteenth decisive battle came about because of another book published seventy-nine years earlier. In 1851, Sir Edward Creasy published his *Fifteen Decisive Battles of the World*, an enormously popular book that went through many editions." Mr. Pohl noted that Sir Edward's list, beginning with the victory of the Athenians over the Persians at Marathon in 490 B.C., listed seven decisive engagements before the Battle of Hastings in 1066. "By Hastings, he had reached the eighth battle," said Mr. Pohl, who added that of the final eight battles in Mr. Creasy's count, Britain was directly involved in six. "The book obviously has something of a local bias," he said, smiling.

Mr. Pohl's own book, titled *The Battle of San Jacinto*, features a fine new battle map. And the action looks decisive to me.

"Was San Jacinto decisive simply because Wharton said it was?" Mr. Pohl asked. "It would be hard to deny that it was tactically decisive. Santa Anna's command was wiped out. Its men were dead, captured or running.

"But after San Jacinto, there remained in Texas a Mexican army still strong, still capable of continued campaigning, and a

Texan force still tiny, still vulnerable, and easier to find than at any time before.

"If San Jacinto has any claim at all to strategic decisiveness, it would be in the fact that Santa Anna was captured and his orders to the Mexican army to withdraw from Texas were obeyed by his subordinate commander, Vicente Filisola."

Mexicans criticized Filisola for obeying a prisoner of war. "But for what it's worth, and I confess that it's simply my opinion, the Mexican army was still able to carry on the campaign," said Mr. Pohl.

"The Battle of San Jacinto, therefore, was more decisive in appearance than in fact." But for Mexican troops at San Jacinto, the battle was decisive enough. Dr. Margaret Henson of Houston, author and historical consultant, researched the fate of Mexican prisoners.

"Texas Secretary of War Thomas Jefferson Rusk estimated that 600 Mexicans had been killed and over 600 captured. Both figures are too high but, given the strain and excitement, who could count?" she stated.

The *Texas Almanac*, published by *The Dallas Morning News*, estimates that Houston had 900 soldiers, while Santa Anna had between 1,100 and 1,300. Dr. Henson said the Texans ringed the prisoners with guards and bonfires except for Santa Anna and his aides, who were kept in a tent close to that of Sam Houston. Texans separated Mexican officers from enlisted men. Severely wounded Mexican officers were treated—along with Texan casualties—by Texas surgeons in the nearby vacant residence of Texas Vice President Lorenzo de Zavala. But food and medicine soon became scarce.

"Sam Houston made an agreement with Santa Anna to protect the captured president if he would order General Filisola and the large Mexican force on the Brazos to retreat," said Dr. Henson, author of *Samuel May Williams: Early Texas Entrepreneur* and other works on early Texas.

"In other words, the prisoners were held as hostages. Treating captured officers reasonably was time-honored," she said, "to assure the safety of your associates held by the enemy." She noted that common soldiers, with little protection, were usually assigned to labor gangs. Santa Anna and his aides were permitted some comforts and a change of clothing. They were envied by other captive officers. Colonel Pedro Delgado, for example, had lost his boots in the quicksand of Peggy's Slough. Barefoot and without even a blanket, he watched sadly as his only boots and clothing were auctioned off by the Texans on April 26.

"On April 30, the Texans moved their camp and the prisoners away from the increasingly noxious odors borne by the wind from the battleground where Mexican dead lay unburied. The Texans settled three miles up Buffalo Bayou on the farm of George M. Patrick, where Santa Anna and his aides occupied one of the small buildings while General Houston and his officers appropriated others," said Dr. Henson.

Texas President David G. Burnet and his Cabinet arrived from Galveston Island to negotiate a treaty with Santa Anna. And on May 7, the dignitaries and the Mexican officers boarded a steamer for Galveston. Santa Anna and his aides occupied one cabin and Texan officials the other.

On May 7, about forty Mexican officers were crowded on the deck by guards, who threatened to blow their brains out. On May 10, President Burnet and Cabinet members escorted their prisoners to Velasco at the mouth of the Brazos. The hostages were held in a hut infested with flies. An officer complained about being robbed of $125 one night.

The presidential prisoner of war, in return for protection from those Texans who demanded his death, obligingly signed treaties favorable to Texas. Mid-June found his party lodged in a two-room house near Columbia. Their time was devoted to dominos and cards. When some Texans tried to kill Santa Anna, he and the others were moved to an isolated plantation ten miles away.

Dr. Henson said, "These moves also foiled an attempt to rescue Santa Anna, a scheme concocted by a wine shop owner in Velasco and financed by friends and kinsmen of Santa Anna." Involved in the plot was Ramon Martinez Caro, Santa Anna's secretary. He was deported in August to New Orleans, where he took a ship to Mexico, becoming the first known prisoner from San Jacinto to return to his homeland.

For trying to escape, Santa Anna wore a ball and chain for two months. "Correspondence was opened between Santa Anna and U.S. President Andrew Jackson concerning possible mediation by the U.S. President Jackson's negative response reached Santa Anna on Oct. 23, one day after Sam Houston was inaugurated as president of Texas," Dr. Henson stated.

"Nevertheless, Santa Anna wanted to go to Washington, D.C. And President Houston's new administration, viewing him as a useless burden, wanted him out of Texas. Houston overrode senatorial objections to releasing Santa Anna (some Texans still wanted him dead), and on November 26, Santa Anna, armed with letters from President Houston stating that he was a free man, left for Washington." He spent a week in Washington, meeting with officials and President Jackson. Mexican diplomats refused to recognize Santa Anna as their president.

A U.S. Navy frigate was ordered by President Jackson to return the toppled Mexican president to his country. Santa Anna sailed from Norfolk, Virginia, for Veracruz on January 31 with a twenty-one-gun salute.

Meanwhile, the other Mexican officers and enlisted men languished on Galveston Island, where there was no fresh water. Drinking water was collected during rains. Colonel James Morgan, commander of an unfinished fort on the island, set aside a fifty-yard square outside the walls for Mexican officers. Common soldiers were kept inside the fort.

"Until mid-August, they survived on the barren island, subjects of curiosity, vicious threats and outbreaks of disease," said Dr. Henson. Of 300 privates at the island fort on June 1, 1836, about 160 were hospitalized with various ailments and injuries. Three died.

"Texans realized that prisoner exchange was impossible and that they held a large number of prisoners who had little value," she said. In August, forty-six Mexican officers and their fourteen soldier-servants were moved from Galveston to Liberty, where the prisoners were guarded by the local militia. Two escaped during seven and a half months in Liberty.

At the end of April 1837, President Houston freed all the prisoners, possibly as a gesture to commemorate the first anniversary of the battle. He quickly rescinded the order after learning that the Mexican navy had seized the Texas schooner *Independence* and several passengers. The Texans sent thirty prisoners to Mexico in exchange for Texans aboard the *Independence*.

President Houston allowed a number of Mexican officers to go to New Orleans in mid-June. And by mid-September, he had allowed all the remaining officers, enlisted men and three women to return to Mexico.

Dr. Henson said, "During all this time, the ordinary soldiers had mixed experiences. Some were taken by civilians for use as laborers. For example, the Harris family of Harrisburg had four [prisoners] re-build a home burned by Santa Anna."

When word came that they'd been freed, prisoners held by private citizens started overland to Mexico. Those on Galveston Island accompanied returning officers as space on vessels permitted. All were gone by September 1837. "All in all, Mexican hostages in Texas were treated as well as prisoners of war were in most civilized nations," Dr. Henson said.

Three decades after the final shot, the battle was still being fought in the courts. Unheroic issues were raised. Did a Texan officer wantonly kill prisoners, including a Mexican woman? Were Texan soldiers cheated when the spoils of war were divided?

Legalistically, the central issue was whether a Texan colonel had been libeled in an account of the fighting that appeared in the *Texas Almanac*. Old hatreds surfaced in sworn statements from a parade of aging Texan soldiers that included their fiery-tongued commander, General Sam Houston.

Max S. Lale of Fort Worth, a retired editor of newspapers that included the *Marshall News-Messenger*, and later President of the Texas State Historical Association, brought up this forgotten mess in a talk to the East Texas Historical Association. Lale, who knows a good story when he sees one, came across a time-yellowed collection of depositions in the case, discovered in an old law office in Marshall.

"Here is a version of what happened at San Jacinto that very few people are aware of. The general public is unaware of the brutality described by these veterans," he said.

Houston's quartermaster, Colonel John Forbes, was the target of murderous rumors and larcenous complaints in the Texans' camp. These reached such a pitch that Forbes asked Houston, a longtime friend, for a court of inquiry to clear his name.

On April 28, 1836, the court was presided over by Colonel Sidney Sherman, who concluded: "We find no evidence whatever in support of such charges or any grounds for censure against Colonel Forbes." The ruling resolved nothing. Questions still circulated twenty-two years later when Dr. Nicholas Descomps Labadie of Galveston, who'd been an army surgeon, wrote a first-person account of the battle for the 1859 *Texas Almanac*. Not only did Labadie criticize Houston's leadership, but he implied that Colonel Forbes had killed prisoners, including a woman, and, moreover, that he had stolen some of the $12,000 in the war chest of captured Mexican General Antonio Lopez de Santa Anna.

Claiming he'd been slandered, Forbes, mayor of Nacogdoches at the time, filed suit, seeking $25,000 from Labadie.

When Houston rose in the U.S. Senate on February 28, 1859, to make his farewell address, he devoted his speech to excoriating his critics in Texas and especially the *Almanac*. In its 1860 edition, the *Almanac* printed Houston's wrathful speech for its growing readership, which counted thousands of lovers of invective and conflict.

Meanwhile, from 1858 to 1860, lawyers gathered depositions from witnesses scattered from Corpus Christi to Cincinnati. General Houston's deposition is dated December 28, 1859. Lale noted, "Derisive and sarcastic as he frequently was, Houston's sworn version of the events is replete with . . . caustic comments about some of his associates."

He quoted Houston: "I have never read the Labadie sketch, nor do I believe it was written or seen by Mr. Labadie. I believe upon good information that the facts charged in it were fabricated by [Sidney] Sherman, [Mirabeau] Lamar [both revolutionary heroes] and other small fry. . . . I do not believe it contains one word of truth."

In reference to a Labadie statement about "drones" sharing the spoils of victory, Houston replied, "I cannot tell who the drones referred to were, unless they were the President ad interim [David G. Burnet] and Robert Potter, secretary of the navy. . . . As neither had rendered the country any service, they might be designated as drones."

Labadie had written that after routing the Mexicans "we found many had thrown themselves into the bayou, having only their heads above water. It was here that one or two women were killed by someone taking aim at their heads, and two or three others taken prisoner. Colonel Forbes of Nacogdoches was accused of the deed."

Equally bothersome to Forbes, Labadie described rescuing from a bog a Mexican colonel called Bertrand [probably Colonel Jose Batres], "when bang goes a gun, the ball entering the forehead of the poor Bertrand, and my hand and clothes were spattered with his brains, as he falls dead at my feet. Then comes up Colonel Forbes; he searches his pockets, in one of which he finds a fine gold snuffbox, saying: 'This I will take to Houston.' Disgusted with such acts, I walked away, but shortly after I again fell in with the same man, Colonel Forbes, and shortly afterward witnessed acts of cruelty which I forebear to recount. My heart sickened to witness such cruelties on the dead and dying."

More damning was the deposition of Private Thomas F. Corry, long an acquaintance of Forbes. On the shore of San Jacinto Bay, where the Texans were shooting at swimming Mexicans, Corry testified that he walked away "as this work did not suit my feeling. I left them and soon after met the plaintiff, who was alone on foot and apparently coming from our camp. He had his drawn sword in his hand.

"Almost instantly there came from the timber into the prairie where we stood, two men in the uniform of Texas regulars, bringing with them two prisoners—a man and a woman. Barely had they joined us when Colonel Summerville [Alexander Somervell] or Colonel [Edward] Burleson, I do not remember which, who was galloping at two or three hundred yards distance, cried out: 'Kill them . . . damn them. Remember the Alamo.'"

Corry testified, "The two regulars immediately attacked the man with their bayonets. There was a momentary struggle in which I tried to save the man's life. At the same time Colonel Forbes thrust his sword through the woman's breast, the blade entering in front, and coming out her back. As the sword was withdrawn she fell forward upon her face, quivering, [and] died without a groan. This dreadful deed paralyzed me, and the man was killed."

Although "two or three hundred yards" is an unlikely distance for even a colonel's voice to be heard, the rest of Corry's statement tended to be supported by others. Colonel Sherman recalled, "After my regiment had defeated the division opposed to us...there I saw lying dead a woman. I asked: 'Who killed her?' Several answered at the same time, 'Colonel Forbes.' I asked why. The same men replied that he [Colonel Forbes] was anxious to bloody his sword."

In the *Almanac*, Labadie wrote that the $12,000 (sometimes said to have been $18,000) in the money chest "had been counted so often, and by so many, that it naturally stuck to their fingers .... The drones got the best of the food in the camp, and at the last, they seized on all the money they could touch, whilst the hard workers fared the worst. I got nothing."

Sherman recalled that he, Burleson and Forbes were named "on a committee to count the money. I had nothing further to do with it. I think $3,000 of it was voted to the Texas Navy. I do not remember the amount of the spoils but my impression was that each man was to receive about $11. I know that I ne'er received any share of it. Commissary General Forbes was the principal man in keeping and distributing the money."

Houston said, "I never saw a dollar of the money. I appointed Colonel Sherman and other officers to divide the spoils and had nothing further to do with it.... That a number of the spoils were purloined I have no doubt."

Houston was stung by Labadie's account of the gold snuffbox: "I never heard of a gold snuffbox on the battleground. General Santa Anna had one, and retained it, after he was discharged and some days thereafter. Dr. Branch T. Archer presented me, I believe, the same snuffbox, and said he was requested to do so by General Santa Anna. I accepted it, and have it yet.

"I immediately wrote to Colonel Harkley, who accompanied General Santa Anna to the United States, to procure for Santa Anna a handsome one, which he did in Philadelphia, amounting to $280 in value, which amount I refunded to Colonel Harkley. This is all I know about the far-famed snuffbox."

Forbes vs. Labadie languished in the district court in Nacogdoches throughout the Civil War. But legal skirmishes resumed when the war ended. Then Labadie signed a statement admitting that his *Almanac* article had been "hastily" written and that he didn't intend to accuse Forbes of conduct "unworthy of a soldier or a man of honor." Forbes introduced a certified copy of the proceedings of the 1836 court of inquiry. With that, Forbes moved to drop the lawsuit, with the stipulation that each litigant pay his own legal costs. And so it ended.

✳✳✳

Porcine Intrigue Revisited

Every diplomat knows Pig Wars are dirty, no matter which side you root for.

On October 15, 1987, former Governor William Clements and former French Prime Minister Jacques Chirac commemorated France's 1839 recognition of the newborn Republic of Texas. That came just a year after the United States (and a year before Britain) agreed that Texas diplomats could exchange lies with their diplomats.

Clements dedicated a plaque at the site of the Texans' old legation in the Place Vendome, a pretty good neighborhood even after 140-odd years. The Place is home (and there's no Place like Vendome) to some of the world's biggest spenders at the Ritz and the U.S. Embassy.

A deluxe address was an absolute necessity to the Republic of Texas. After all, the Texans were in France to try to float a loan. Their loan proposal sank.

The Pig War is sometimes blamed for the French refusal to guarantee a hard-sought loan of five million dollars for Texas.

The truth is—Pig War or Pig Peace—that loan just wasn't in the cards. Still, the Pig War muddled international affairs.

The Kingdom of France, ruled by His Majesty Louis Philippe of Orleans, had appointed Comte Alphonse Dubois de Saligny to be chargé d'affaires in Texas. Never mind that the comte wasn't a genuine French count. Never mind that he was a transcontinental liar. It was likely on the strength of Saligny's glowing—if phony—reports about Texas that French officialdom recognized the ragamuffin Republic.

Despite defects in character, Saligny was, for a time, a social success, a strutting dandy who dazzled the elite of Austin, the backwoods capital.

Early in 1840, Saligny revealed his plans for a colonizing corporation that would bring French settlers to Texas. He framed an act titled the Franco-Texienne Bill, which he hoped to get rushed through the Texas Congress. The bill proposed that Texas grant Saligny's corporation three million acres of western land. On the land, the company was to locate at least 8,000 French immigrants. As an inducement, the immigrants were to enjoy freedom from taxes and a right to import whatever they chose free of duty.

In return, the French company was to establish a line of at least twenty forts along the savage frontier from the Red River to the Rio Grande. Clearly, Saligny was cutting a good deal for himself and for France. The Franco-Texienne Bill was the equivalent of a French invasion without casualties.

Still, Sam Houston and other Texas patriots and politicos, under the influence of the lavish lobbyist's imported chef, cigars and wines, tended or pretended to favor Saligny's project. Although arguments were dutifully sounded in favor of Saligny's bill, which spent a lot of time lying on tables, it never quite made it through the Texas Congress. Saligny was mad enough to kick a pig.

The chargé d'affaires had initially set up shop in February 1840 at the Austin hotel of Richard Bullock at what is now Sixth and Congress, site of a high-rise office building.

As I understand the layout, Bullock may have invented the motel. Near his hotel, he owned several cabins that he rented out.

Trouble started in 1841 when Saligny moved his legation from the hotel to one of the cabins. Soon he was writing angry letters like this one to the Texas government:

"I have for a long time suffered from the many hogs with which this town is infested. Every morning one of my domestics (Note: he had three imported ones) spends two hours in putting up and nailing the palings of the fence, which these animals threw down for the purpose of eating corn of my horses; 140 pounds of nails have been used for this purpose. One day these hogs entered even to my chamber, and ate my towels and destroyed my papers."

Saligny ranted that the pigs belonging to Bullock had ruined the diplomat's garden and that Saligny's servant, who had killed several pigs, had been attacked by Bullock.

It got into a New Orleans newspaper, *The Bee*, that Bullock had assaulted the "unlucky murderer" of the pigs, "bunging up his eyes and phlebotomizing his nose in a manner to appease the ghosts of the slaughtered innocents."

In his correspondence, Saligny failed, of course, to mention Bullock's grievance: Saligny's failure to pay his hotel bills. Outraged, the diplomat charged that the honor of France had been traduced and demanded that Bullock be punished for "the enormity of the offense."

It was, cried Saligny, "an odious violation of the law of nations." After some discussion, Texas officials decided they couldn't punish Bullock without some kind of trial. And Saligny refused to attend a trial on the grounds that it was beneath his official dignity.

Huffily, Saligny gathered up his passport, his servants, cigars and remaining wines and left Austin to its pigs. He moved to New Orleans, where he spent months sending off expense vouchers for such items as 140 pounds of nails and writing unflattering things about Texas.

But Texans must applaud Saligny for one thing. In the fall of 1840, he purchased a tract of land in Austin and began building on it the structure that would be known as the Legation de France and, today, as the French Legation Museum.

One day recently, John Cleary, the director, took me on a tour of the museum at 802 San Marcos, just east of Interstate 35. Cleary said the place is "designed in the Louisiana Greek Revival bayou style. This is the oldest surviving building in Austin," he said. "When other buildings were being constructed from logs, the lumber for this one was milled from Bastrop pine." The property, acquired from Saligny by the Catholic Church, passed through several owners before being bought by the state of Texas and placed in the care of the Daughters of the Republic of Texas.

That Saligny would part with his fancy new quarters, featuring imported glass windows, is an indication of how seriously wounded he was in the Pig War. In his last official correspondence as Texas chargé d'affaires, the diplomat reported that Richard Bullock, his tormentor in the Pig War, had died. Saligny never returned to Austin.

Saligny was in Mexico for that breakdown of diplomacy known as the short fatal reign of Emperor Maximilian. Saligny married a young but wealthy Mexican woman—after subtracting seven years from his age on the marriage papers, returning to his forties from his fifties.

With her money, he retired to France and lived out his remaining years in a feudal castle fit for a genuine count.

※※※

Yellow Rose Story Loses its Bloom

Today, right here, we're going to debunk the Yellow Rose of Texas. You know the story about the beautiful young slave girl, Emily Morgan. She had long midnight-colored hair, eyes dark as war headlines, and a complexion like a pony of cream with a dollop of bourbon in it.

The Yellow Rose. She was the heroine of San Jacinto and the savior of the Republic of Texas. Remember?

His Mexican Excellency Santa Anna—that opium-eating egomaniacal Napoleon of the West—had led his overdressed officers and overofficered troops across Texas, killing and plundering the uppity Anglo settlers. And he was busily driving the republican pests into the Gulf of Mexico when he espied Emily, invited her into his candy-striped tent at siesta time, and as the story goes, Texas patriot Emily surrendered her virtue to save the Republic. She dallied with, ugh, Santa Anna. As he made his move, the Texans prepared to make theirs. Meanwhile, with the help of a fellow slave, Emily unerringly advised Texan commander Sam Houston on the best strategy for whipping the Mexicans.

Her duty done, Texas-loving Emily promptly disappeared into the mists of Buffalo Bayou, but not without inspiring a musical tribute, "The Yellow Rose of Texas." The ballad became a Confederate marching song. It kept Mitch Miller in razor blades for years. And it provided background music for Rock Hudson to stomp bigots by in the movie *Giant*. OK, you know all that.

Well, hold the phone. Margaret Henson's on the other line.

How's that, Margaret?

So, the name of The Yellow Rose wasn't Emily Morgan. It was Emily D. West. And there is no link connecting her with the old song, "The Yellow Rose of Texas." And she wasn't a slave. And there is no evidence she was in Santa Anna's tent.

Emily D. West was—what?—a New Yorker who visited Texas and then returned to New York. "Whether she was young or beautiful isn't known," says Margaret. Margaret is a Texas historian who teaches at the University of Houston and writes serious history books (*Anglo American Women in Texas; Juan Davis Bradburn, A Reappraisal;* and *Samuel May Williams, Early Texas Entrepreneur*).

I met Margaret when she lectured in Austin on causes of the Texas revolution. That was at a cram course on Texas history for the media. Conceived by George Christian, it was conducted by the UT College of Communication. Margaret has investigated the case of the Yellow Rose. Her findings jolt me. Listen. "Eyewitnesses who had reason to criticize Santa Anna fail to mention his dallying with a woman."

For example, Romon Caro, Santa Anna's secretary at San Jacinto, wrote a vindictive exposé of the dictator in 1837. "Caro was ready to denigrate the dictator and certainly would have happily mentioned that a woman delayed him. Caro didn't."

Another eyewitness, Colonel Pedro Francisco Delgado, was no admirer of Santa Anna. He wrote in his diary about the Mexican Napoleon's foolishly rushing about wringing his hands when the Texans attacked. But the colonel mentions no woman. He surely would have, if one had been there. Santa Anna had plenty of detractors in his camp. None recorded anything about a woman in his tent. "No contemporary at the battle said anything about Santa Anna in the tent with Emily. The closest remark was that of George Erath (a Texan soldier who later gave his name to a county), who spoke of Santa Anna's 'voluptuousness,' which in the nineteenth century might as well refer to his opium habit as the sexual interpretation by twentieth-century historians," says Margaret. (Note: After his capture, Santa Anna was allowed by the Texans to eat opium to calm his strung-out nerves.)

"The story of a woman in the tent was a popular ribald tale told by men who wanted to believe that about Santa Anna," she remarks. "William Bollaert [an English ethnologist] was the first to mention Emily, and that in a footnote in 1842. In the original manuscript in the Newberry Library in Chicago, Bollaert says that he heard the story from an officer who had been at San Jacinto. The Bollaert note fixed the myth: 'the battle was lost,' said Bollaert, 'because of the influence of a mulatto girl [Emily] belonging to Colonel [James] Morgan, who was closeted in the tent with General Santa Anna.'"

Emily did not belong to Morgan or to anyone else. But on the strength of Bollaert's gossipy item, generations of Texas writers took up the tale and ran with it, embroidering it, and romancing it. Martha Anne Turner wrote a book about Emily, *The Yellow Rose of Texas*, in 1976. Margaret says the book "is based on popular folklore and lacks reliable documentation."

She adds, "The story that a black woman (or white) could plot and carry out such a strategic delay is preposterous. Only the Sons of the Knights of the Yellow Rose of Texas, who meet occasionally in Houston, like to perpetuate such fantasies.

"Emily D. West was born in New York, possibly in the area of Albany. She had free papers when she arrived in Texas in December, 1835. She left New York City for Galveston Bay November 2, 1835, in company with the wife of Lorenzo de Zavala (Lorenzo would be Texas' first vice president) on board the schooner *Flash*. James Morgan, the agent for the New Washington Association, a group of New York investors who had purchased land on the San Jacinto River, dispatched the ship along with another company-owned vessel, the *Kosciusko*. Both schooners arrived at Morgan's warehouse on the San Jacinto River about December 15.

"Emily probably lived with the Zavalas on Buffalo Bayou until April 13, 1836, when the family fled to Lynchburg upon learning about the approach of Santa Anna's troops. It is possible that Morgan employed Emily as a housekeeper because his wife was in North Carolina. She must have been at Morgan's place on April 16 when Colonel Juan Almonte and a company of dragoons rode down from Harrisburg. She could have been helping Texas President David G. Burnet and his family store their goods in Morgan's warehouse before boarding the *Flash* anchored in the river. While the Burnets and two men escaped to the schooner, Emily was captured.

"Santa Anna arrived at Morgan's house on April 17 and perhaps acquired Emily's services. She accompanied the Mexican army to the battleground on April 20, and was able to escape during the battle the next day but lost her free papers." Margaret found Emily D. West's application for a Texas passport that would get her back to New York. Although her free papers were lost, Emily was described in it as "a free woman."

I shall add a historical footnote: The name of the schooner *Kosciusko*, was obviously a corrupted spelling of Kosciuszko, which is harder to spell.

Tadeusz Kosciuszko was George Washington's adjutant, a colonel of artillery in the Continental Army, and a revolutionary firebrand back in Poland. Early in this century, there was an undocumented story about an unfortunate New York policeman who found a dead horse in Kosciuszko Street. When he took out his notebook to write a report, he couldn't spell "Kosciuszko." The cop had to drag the horse to Third Avenue.

✳✳✳

INDIANOLA—NOTHING LASTS ON THE COAST'S SHIFTING SAND

Just off the beach road, a big smoky gray heron was working the slate-colored waves that hide whatever is left of the once lively town. I watched the bird's hungry passes for a couple of minutes, then I drove on down the spit, Matagorda Bay on the left and Powderhorn Bayou on the right. "Powderhorn" was an early name of the long gone town.

Passing a cluster of shacks, I pulled up at a sign that said, "Indianola Fishing Center." A woman was frying something for supper. Pushing back a damp curl, she smiled when I asked about Indianola.

"Sorry," she said. "Indianola's gone."

"All gone?"

"There's a piece of an old concrete cistern. You can see it from the road."

"That's all?"

"Yes. Just about."

"What else?"

"Well, some graves."

The woman, Sue Fowler, was right. Nothing much remains of Indianola, a deep water port that was once heir apparent to the riches of the Texas Coast. Indianola was the teeming gateway to San Antonio and all points west and south, a city too vital to die. But Indianola did die. And then, spectacularly, she died again, in the manner of an operatic tragedienne who rises to sing one last aria before the final curtain.

Brief notes on the Matagorda marine charts tell the tale. They describe shorelines "subject to continual change" and "subject to continual shifting." Nothing is forever on the coast.

Hurricanes in 1875 and 1886 wrecked Indianola. The shifting shorelines finished the job, hiding every recognizable vestige of the promising city. The hurricane season has cursed this pleasant coast since the first footprint marked its shifting sand.

"We are overdue," admitted George Fred Rhodes, in the midst of another of his many hurricane seasons. He talked to me about major storms as we sat in his office building in Port Lavaca, seat of Calhoun County, a political designation once enjoyed by Indianola.

"I'd like to get through a season, June through September, without being concerned about what might happen. But I can't do it. My wife and I are thinking of moving inland. Every hurricane season we think about it."

A nearly retired lawyer, George writes historical pieces for the *Lavaca Wave*. He was born on the coast and he has weathered numerous hurricanes. He isn't among those coastal bon vivants who believe that a bottle of gin will get you through one. His brick building has walls one foot thick and no windows. The silver-haired chairman of the Calhoun County Historical Commission is a fifth-generation Texan; historically, five generations is but a wink on this venerable coast.

Spaniards explored the shoreline in the early 1500s and named Calhoun County's Espiritu Santo Bay. In 1685, René Robert Cavalier Sieur de la Salle planted a French colony on the coast. It perished. The Spaniards planted a camp of their own on La Salle's site. It vanished.

The Ranger Cemetery in Port Lavaca is crowded with history. H. Oram Watts is buried there. He was killed in the Comanche raid on Lavaca Bay's Linnville in August 1840. The flaming attack was so fierce that Linnville, three or four miles northeast of Port Lavaca, was not rebuilt. At least ten Yankee soldiers are buried in the Ranger Cemetery, silent reminders of the Civil War, a time when Yankee forces dominated the middle Texas Coast. They remained a bullying but pitiable presence through the period of Reconstruction. Union belt buckles, I'm told, are yet found with skeletons unearthed in Calhoun County.

Originally identified as "Powderhorn," the natural port on the west shore of Matagorda Bay was called "Carlshaven" by the German immigrants who were landed there in 1843 by colonizer Prince Carl of Solms-Braunfels. Indianola stole its name from an earlier ephemeral encampment a few miles up the coast. The older "Indianola" or "Indian Point" died as surely as a beached fish when Powderhorn, or Powder Horn, as it was then spelled, revealed coin-clinking symptoms of prosperity. Later Indianolans were happy to inherit the name. Their leaders recognized that "Powder Horn" might fall rudely on refined ears, in the unlikely event that any refined ears were within earshot of the place.

From 1842, when it began as an Indian trading post, to 1875, with time out for Civil War skirmishing, Indianola grew steadily in commercial importance. Texas was a busy importer of manufactured goods and an eager exporter of raw materials. Among Indianola's biggest exporters were several slaughterhouses where longhorn cattle were stripped of their marketable hides and tallow. For years, Indianolans gorged on such unprofitable byproducts as rib roasts and steaks.

In 1856, Egyptian camels disembarked in Indianola to begin their overland march to the Texas Hill Country for experimental use as U.S. cavalry mounts. They proved no threat to the status of the horse. Meanwhile, Indianola prospered as a military depot for frontier forts in Texas. In 1849, Charles Morgan had chosen Indianola as a key landing point for ships of his Morgan line. A decade later, the Indianola Railroad, among the state's first, began making short runs.

Bartenders in Indianola's sophisticated saloons served juleps chilled with imported ice. Great quantities of winter ice cut in New England were shipped in for packing oysters, fish, and dressed wild turkeys. On that note, several Indianola factories canned the meat of giant sea turtles. The stuff was said to be delicious.

Indianola's population reached about 6,000, give or take an ever present mob of sailors and transients. The city was a popular port of call for rowdy cowpunchers and gravely-notched gunmen like John Wesley Hardin. Still, the community affected shock when the gun-happy violence of DeWitt County's Sutton-Taylor feud exploded on the Indianola docks.

On March 11, 1874, William Sutton, his young wife, and a pal, Gabriel Slaughter, boarded a steamer bound for New Orleans with one stop at Galveston Island. Gun-heavy cousins Jim and Billy Taylor of the opposing faction rode up to the docks and alit. As the steamer prepared to get under way, the Taylors began blazing away. Sutton, twenty-seven, fell dead and Slaughter, twenty-one, fell dying on the deck. The Taylor boys rode away like the sea breeze.

As it happened, William Sutton, a tall, blue-eyed, curly-haired cowman, had been the only person actually named "Sutton" among the warriors on his side of the dispute. Still, folks had to call his faction something, so "Sutton," it became. His men were commonly called "Suttons." The other warring party counted a multitude of Taylors with names recorded in that way in family Bibles.

Shortly before the shooting, William Sutton and Laura, his wife, had moved to Victoria County from bleeding DeWitt County. Some say that when Sutton was killed he was trying to leave Texas and the feud behind him. Others insist he was merely traveling on business. Whichever, the grieving widow placed an ad in the June 4, 1874, *Victoria Advocate*, published in Victoria County, next door to Calhoun and DeWitt counties.

"On the eleventh of March last, William Sutton, my husband, and Gabriel Slaughter, while engaged in getting their tickets for Galveston, on board the steamer *Clinton*, at Indianola, were murdered by James and Bill Taylor, in my presence, without warning or notice, James Taylor shooting my husband in the back with two six-shooters. One of the murderers, Bill Taylor, has since been arrested by Marshal Rube Brown of Cuero (DeWitt County), and is now in Galveston jail. James Taylor, the murderer of my husband, is still at large, and I offer to anyone who will arrest and deliver him inside the jail of Calhoun County, Texas, one thousand dollars in addition to the reward of $500 offered by the governor of Texas. Marshal Brown of Cuero can say whether the governor's has been promptly paid, as he is the man that arrested the murderer Bill Taylor. As to my ability to pay the $1,000 I refer to Brownson's Bank, Victoria, Texas. Description of James Taylor, age twenty-three years; weight 165 or 170 pounds, very heavy set; height five feet and ten inches; complexion dark; hair dark; round features; usually shaves clean about a week; wears no whiskers, beard rather heavy, talks very little, has a low dull tone, and very quiet in his manners. —Mrs Laura Sutton."

The hefty reward was never claimed because within months Jim Taylor was in no condition to go to jail or to face early trial. With two companions, he was mortally gunned down in a furious shootout with Sutton partisans. The battle was in Clinton, the busy seat of DeWitt County until the courthouse was moved in 1876 to railroad-blessed Cuero (sealing Clinton's fate as a ghost town).

Before the DeWitt County records arrived in Cuero, however, Cuero Marshal Rube Brown, who had arrested Bill Taylor after the Indianola killings, had himself become a fatal casualty in the Sutton-Taylor war. On the night of November 17, 1875, a gang of gunmen shoved into Cuero's Exchange Saloon and killed the Marshal as he sat playing cards.

By then, to be sure, Indianola was in ruins. The hurricane had savaged Matagorda Bay, wiping out three-fourths of Indianola in mid-September, 1875. For nearly two weeks before striking Indianola, the storm had raised hell out in the Atlantic, kicking up squalls, dismasting sailing vessels, and ripping smokestacks off steamers. As the hurricane matured, ships began disappearing at sea. Surging from the Atlantic into the Caribbean, the hurricane cut a devastating swath across Barbados, the lesser Antilles, Haiti, Jamaica, and Cuba. At Key West, the storm tossed vessels ashore, among them the steamer *City of Waco*. In the Gulf of Mexico, big ships went down. Schooners *Witch of the Wave* and *Mabel*, for example, were never heard from again.

Weather predicting was sadly primitive. A hindsight weather map by the War Department, which ran the Signal Service weather stations in those days, chronicled that stormy September. Historian and Gulf Coast native Brownson Malsch of Edna in Jackson County studied the map. He tells me that the map's barometric lows reveal that as late as September 15—the eve of Indianola's ruin—the eye of the hurricane, moving west northwest across the Gulf of Mexico, was headed for the Texas coast in the neighborhood of Rockport, fifty miles south-southwest of Indianola.

"Then the high pressure area that had forced the storm on a west-northwest course began to slide rapidly to the east. With the removal of the blocking action, the hurricane swerved due north and drew a bead on hapless Indianola." He noted, "In time, cause and effect would be understood, but not in 1875."

Malsch's 1977 book *Indianola—the Mother of Western Texas* reflects the fascination with the old port. When I asked how long he'd researched the book, Louise Malsch, the author's wife, put in: "When we were married fifty-two years ago, he had a whole box of material on Indianola. He told me, 'If there's a fire, get the children, get your jewelry—and, Louise, get that box.' He'd been researching Indianola all his life."

A retired railroad man, Brownson Malsch called his book "a labor of love." Who on this coast can resist the story of Indianola? The historian's given name honors the family identified with the bank mentioned in Laura Sutton's offer of a reward for fugitive Jim Taylor.

As the hurricane bore down on the Texas coast, the captive Billy Taylor sat in an Indianola jail awaiting trial for the Sutton and Slaughter killings. Billy's presence had packed Indianola with visitors who'd come to watch the sensational trial.

All day on September 15, the wind grew, screaming at the Indianolans. On the following day, fine buildings crumpled like cardboard as great seas smashed the town. Three other prisoners and Billy Taylor watched with interest the water rising in their cells. At last, District Attorney William Crain got the jailer's keys and escorted them to the relative safety of Calhoun County Courthouse, which was built of stone and sat on a slight rise.

In a 1951 book, *I'll Die Before I'll Run*, the late historian C. L. Sonnichsen reported on Billy Taylor's legendary heroism:

"In the midst of that horrible uproar and overwhelming danger, Bill Taylor proved himself a man. He sallied out into the waves again and again to bring back a man or woman struggling in the shadow of death. When about three A.M. of the seventeenth, the wind suddenly shifted to the northwest and blew the water back into the Gulf faster than it had come in, there were almost a hundred people on the little hill, and many of them owed their lives to Bill Taylor."

But when Calhoun Sheriff Busch managed to ride up to the courthouse, one of the freed prisoners snatched the sheriff's six-gun, threw down the lawman, climbed aboard his horse, and rode away with Billy Taylor clinging behind. Looking back, the fugitives would have seen that surrounding the sturdy court-house was a flattened town.

Between two hundred and three hundred people weren't as lucky as the freed prisoners; they drowned or were hammered to death in the wreckage. Corpses were found many miles inland and scattered for miles up and down the coast. The mechanics of the destruction are clear now, as Sonnichsen suggested. The incoming storm shoved monstrous seas inland over the coastal plain. Then, with the passage of the eye of the hurricane, the explosive wind shifted. The effect was of a dam bursting, releasing a pent-up flood to crush Indianola one more time, and from a new direction.

Malsch reported: "The actual volume of water that had been built up miles inland behind Indianola is almost beyond calculation. At the bay shore, the maximum level above normal high tide was fifteen feet. That same height was reached over Powder Horn Lake and the marshlands to the rear of the city. A single cubic yard of salt water weighs slightly in excess of 1700 pounds, 1728 pounds to be exact. With the passage of the storm's eye, the weight force of the tens of millions of tons of flood water was pulled back to the bay by gravity, its speed of movement accelerated by the overwhelming pressure of the hurricane winds veering to the northwest." The enormous power of the rapidly returning wall of water swept much of Indianola out to sea, where it remains.

Marion Rhodes, George's wife, showed me an unpublished account of the storm by one of two brothers who were washed out of Indianola and then remarkably reunited on a smashed and drifting sailing vessel that finally ended up on dry land more than a mile from its original dock. After the storm the brothers took up residence far inland. So did almost everyone else.

Indianola still had its deep water port, but much of the city, never more than two or three feet above sea level, was now in the bay. A few buildings still stood that were occupied by diehards, determined to continue business as before. Indeed, it was to what remained of Indianola that Billy Taylor was ultimately returned after his arrest by Texas Rangers in the far-inland, West Texas county of Coleman in April, 1877. In June, 1878, he was tried at Indianola for killing William Sutton and—as sure as Justice is blind—was acquitted. In 1878, on a change of venue to Jackson County, he was called to trial on the Slaughter charge in the courthouse in Texana (another county seat destined to become a ghost town). Prosecutors, complaining of absent wtnesses, finally asked the case to be dismissed. The judge granted the request, although Billy Taylor oddly "demanded" a trial.

Historian Sonnichsen observed that how such legal goings on were possible "may well puzzle a non-Texan, but it was no surprise to anyone at that time. If a case dragged on long enough witnesses dropped out of sight, evidence was no longer easy to get hold of, and people got tired of having the old skeleton hauled out of his mortuary wrappings.

"A year later he was in more trouble. The Rangers arrested him again after a difficult chase and put him in the Cuero jail. According to Captain Lee Hall, his friends tried to burn the town in an attempt to free him, but did not succeed. Finding himself under indictment for horse theft, assault to murder, and forgery, he lost his nerve and told the Rangers everything they wanted to know. Somehow Billy got out of it all and lit out." At that point Sonnichsen lost his trail.

Billy Taylor rode right off the pages of history. Kinfolks later claimed that he went to Oklahoma where he eventually became a lawman and was killed by a desperado. No verification of that tale has surfaced.

Indianola's population dwindled to a few hundred. Most survivors of the great hurricane of 1875 had moved away. Town leaders were unable to rekindle the town's old confidence and commercial success. That was provident. On August 20, 1886, another massive hurricane finished off Indianola.

Winds and waters were worse this time. And a fire—caused by an exploding lamp in the weather station—spread through the wreckage of the commercial district. In the midst of the deluge, fiery splinters and boards rained on Indianola, an unbelievable scene. Some people thought it was the end of the world. For many it was. Brownson Malsch said 150 to 175 people were killed in coastal Calhoun County. An exact count is impossible. Certainly Indianola was depopulated by the storm. Survivors straggled away.

Calhoun County citizens dismantled the courthouse and moved the seat to Port Lavaca, fifteen miles to the northwest, more elevated and better shielded from storms.

Chief beneficiary of Indianola's violent death was the port of Galveston, a city that rapidly became the most populous and, by several standards, the most prosperous in Texas. Then on September 8, 1900, a hurricane swept the island, razing 2,600 homes and ruining another 1,000. More than 6,000 people died, about one-seventh of the population. After the catastrophe many industries were moved inland to Houston.

Nothing is forever on this coast.

✳✳✳

THE RIDE OF TEXAS' PAUL REVERE

George Masoner is best remembered on a historical marker, seven miles south of Gainesville at a roadside park on Interstate 35 in Cooke County: "On Jan. 5-6, 1868, Chief Big Tree and 150 to 200 Kiowas invaded Willa Walla Valley. . . . "

The State Historical Survey Committee's marker tells how the war party burned houses and killed thirteen people, including a woman who was scalped alive. Three captives escaped and two were later ransomed. The marker says: "More damage and deaths would have resulted if George Masoner had not become the 'Paul Revere' of the valleys and warned settlers of impending danger." It concludes: "Indian raids such as this one were in retaliation for loss of hunting grounds to settlers."

Indeed, the Kiowa plan for zero population growth among settlers on the frontier was effective for a time. Exploiting Civil War turmoil, the Indians held the line on settlements, even at times pushing the frontier eastward.

In the decade from 1860 to 1870, the population of Montague County rose from 849 to 885, a total of thirty-six brave or fool-hardy pioneers. Frontier families never knew when a raiding party would splash across the Red River from Indian Territory. Little was done militarily to curb these raids until the 1870s when, after continued raids, Big Tree and others were imprisoned. Big Tree later professed Christianity and lived a long life.

I learned about Masoner's ride from Michael L. Collins, a history professor at Midwestern State University in Wichita Falls. Collins had researched Big Tree's 1868 raid for the West Texas Historical Association.

Collins said, "Results of the raid would have been much worse had it not been for the courageous young Masoner, described by a contemporary as 'a mere boy.'"

"For example, a large Kiowa party encircled the home of J. C. 'Charlie' McCracken, who had been forewarned of the danger by the hard-riding Masoner. By the time the raiders arrived at the homestead, McCracken had already fled into a thicket, leaving his cabin door open. When the angry Kiowas found two Indian scalps hanging inside, they set fire to the house and surrounding crop fields, then rode off with McCracken's plow horse.

"Meanwhile, Masoner raced ahead, risking death in order to warn others. When told by young Masoner of the impending danger, George Washington (Wash) Williams and Alfred Williams led their families into the brush, leaving their homes to be ransacked by the raiders. Unfortunately, Masoner failed to arrive at the Carlton place in time. Reining up in front of the cabin, he learned that sixteen-year-old Perilee Carlton had been taken captive by Big Tree and his warriors.

"Not far away, near present-day Hardy, while young John Leatherwood was hurrying home to defend his family, Kiowa horsemen shot and killed him. Masoner's alarm did not frighten Austin Perryman and his wife into leaving their cabin. Quickly they barred their door, boarded up their windows, forted up, and waited with rifles protruding through small loopholes. The resourceful Mrs. Perryman even dressed in her husband's clothes and tucked her long tresses beneath his hat to help frighten away the Kiowas.

"Next Masoner rode his swift mount down Clear Creek to the farm of Nathan Long, arriving there soon enough to escort Mrs. Long and her children into the woods, concealing them in a dry stream bed before galloping away. But Nathan Long, unarmed and working in his fields, with only a slow-footed mule as a mount, was easily overtaken, slain and scalped.

"Meanwhile, Masoner continued rapidly down Clear Creek and found 'Chunky Joe' Wilson's five children alone in their farmhouse. Hurriedly, he ushered them into the thickets only minutes before the Kiowas looted and burned their cabin, nearby smokehouse, and surrounding corn fields."

Masoner rode off the wrong way and into history's mists when the Kiowas abruptly turned south toward present-day Rosston to continue their depredations. Casualties of the raid were mounting until a sudden norther plunged temperatures and blasted North Texas with sleet and snow. The blinding blizzard disoriented Big Tree's Indians. They retreated toward the safety of Indian Territory, leaving behind tracks but no damage in the outskirts of Gainesville.

And in Gainesville today, the Cooke County Heritage Society's Morton Museum is a good place to learn about the raid. Curator Shana Powell has the details. In Montague County, Veda Brogdon, longtime resident of Forestburg (formerly Horn Hill) near Willa Walla Creek, knows where five of the Kiowa victims are buried— in an abandoned graveyard on private property.

None of the historians I interviewed knew where George Masoner came from or where he went after his heroic ride. A Montague County historical commissioner, Mrs. Brogdon, and the commission chairman Melvin Fenoglio agree that Willa Walla

Creek (often spelled Willawalla) was named by Indians. But neither knew the meaning of the name of the creek that rises in eastern Montague County and flows southeast a dozen miles to join Clear Creek in the southwestern corner of Cooke County.

John Rydjord's *Indian Place-Names*, ignoring Willa Walla, says, "Wallawalla is the name of an Indian tribe living on the Walla Walla River where there was once a Walla Walla Fort in what is now Walla Walla County, Washington. It is said to be an Indian descriptive name meaning little river. . . . The Montague family, early residents in the Junction City (Kansas) area, had once visited Walla Walla in Washington Territory. They talked much about Walla Walla and loved the sound of its name. When they looked for a name for their Kansas community, Walla Walla was the answer."

Walla Walla became the name of a Kansas town that soon disappeared. Whether Walla Walla has any association with Willa Walla, I don't know. And whether Daniel Montague, the early Texas surveyor and Indian fighter for whom Montague County was named, has any link with the Kansas Montagues is another puzzler.

Oma Hartz lives with her father, C. W. Martin, in a brick house overlooking the mile-wide Willa Walla Valley near the Hardy community. Both have lived along the creek all their lives. Neither knows how the creek was named. When I asked if Willa Walla could be a corruption of Willow Wallow, Oma said, "You know, there used to be lots of willows on the creek. Back in the 1930s, a family pitched a tent on the banks of the creek and began cutting willows. The family made furniture to sell from the willows. They were there for more than a year, making willow chairs and tables."

She and her father agreed the family's name was "Louse." L-o-u-s-e? "That's right, like the bug," said Oma, who, with her father, recalled that a baby son was born to Mrs. Louse in that tent on the banks of Willa Walla Creek. They also agreed that the Louses named their son "Willie Walla."

Willie Walla Louse—now, there's a signature I'd bid on.

※※※

KIOWA CHIEF REVERED IN LIFE AND DEATH

Billy Horse blew on his hickory kindling until it blazed. He sprinkled into the flames a handful of cedar sprigs he'd brought from Oklahoma's Wichita Mountains. Swishing an eagle-feather fan, he scattered the white smoke over Peckerwood Hill in a Kiowa ritual of purification. Peckerwood Hill needs all the purification it can get. The sandy, pine-shaded hillside in Huntsville is a graveyard for Texas convicts.

It's the permanent address of a thousand guys so unpopular that their bones weren't claimed by the folks back home—if there were folks back home. Electric jolts or lethal injections landed a number of them in this necropolis of the misbegotten. Others were knocked off by fellow prisoners with sharpened spoons. Sharpshooting guards dropped a few as they hunted an exit. But many of the men on Peckerwood Hill just got sick and died. Suicide accounted for some of the graves. One of these was the focus of a ritual in April, 1991.

Billy Horse blew cedar and cigarette smoke toward Peckerwood Hill's biggest tombstone, which marks a grave unoccupied since 1963. The grave once sheltered an ancestor of Billy Horse, who'd brought his eagle-feather fan and ceremonial trappings from Apache, Oklahoma. The grave's former tenant was Kiowa War Chief Satanta, a convicted murderer whose freewheeling spirit was fatally at odds with confinement.

Satanta (or White Bear) was deeply hurt when guards told him to dig a ditch with a pick and shovel—woman's work by his light. Satanta first tried to kill himself by slashing his veins. Failing that, he flung himself from a second-floor window of the prison infirmary, bashing out his brains on the bricks of the courtyard below. That was in 1878. The traditional life of the Plains tribes was going the way of the buffalo. And Satanta, then past seventy, figured he'd never leave prison alive.

A few weeks before the chief's suicide, an Eastern journalist visiting the prison described him as "a tall, finely formed man, of princely carriage on whom even the prison garb seemed elegant." In better days he rode the plains in a U.S. Army officer's coat with epaulets, a gift from a general with whom he'd parleyed. Soldiers called Satanta "the orator of the Plains." He was among those who signed the Medicine Lodge treaty.

At the Medicine Lodge truce talks, he assured white emissaries: "Your people shall be my people, and peace shall be our mutual heritage." But he may have had his fingers crossed.

On the warpath, Satanta carried a red lance and rode a white horse marked by a bloody handprint. From his shield dangled the scalp of a blond woman. He prized an Army bugle that he blew in battle to signal his warriors and to confuse U.S. troops. At home, he blew bugle blasts to impose authority on his wife and children.

He was a determined raider, but his downfall came in 1871 when he was identified as leader of a band of warriors who destroyed Henry Warren's wagon train. Tribesmen killed and mutilated seven teamsters. "The Salt Creek Massacre," as it was known, happened in southeastern Young County as the wagons rolled between Fort Griffin and Fort Richardson.

General William Tecumseh Sherman, who was inspecting Texas posts, had passed that way with a small escort a few hours earlier. The warriors watched him pass. A shaman called Owl Prophet, after making medicine, had declared that the warriors should await a more profitable target than the general's party.

Days later at the Fort Sill reservation, General Sherman had Satanta, Satank (Sitting Bear) and Big Tree arrested as ringleaders in the massacre. He acted after Satanta began shooting off his mouth about the glorious raid. Nearby, soldiers rounded up forty-one mules taken in the raid.

In an unusual move, the Army chose to hand over the three chiefs to a civilian court for trial on murder charges. En route to trial in Jacksboro, Satank tried to kill himself, but Big Tree interfered. Still, Satank sang his death song. Then he desperately disarmed a guard, grabbing his carbine. Soldiers fatally riddled Satank before he could fire.

Satanta and Big Tree were convicted by a jury of armed cowboys in Jacksboro and sentenced to death by hanging. Reconstruction Governor E. J. Davis's scalp would be the first lifted by Satanta and Big Tree when they predictably hit the warpath

again. As the general expected, they soon were paroled and back
on the warpath. Satanta was arrested and returned to Huntsville
for violating his parole. Big Tree escaped, became a Baptist, and
lived until 1927.

Kiowas lionize Satanta. In 1963, Governor John Connally and
the Texas Legislature permitted them to return Satanta's remains
to Oklahoma for reburial on the old Kiowa reservation. Dr.
George Beto, who headed the Texas prison system at the time of
the exhumation, had watched the original purification. "I was
surprised they found any remains in that grave," he said. "In the
old days, they often just wrapped a dead convict in a blanket for
burial. But they did find a few bones."

Prison archivist Dr. Robert Pierce, president of the Texas
Prison Museum on the square in Huntsville, said that when
Kiowa gourd dancers were invited to Huntsville's Sam Houston
Folklife Festival, they expressed a wish to purify the old gravesite.
Several direct descendants of Satanta traveled to Huntsville.
Among them were Kiowas Betty Washburn of Carnegie, Okla-
homa, and Patsy Tehauno of Dallas. Mrs. Washburn's husband,
Kenneth, is a Choctaw, and Mrs. Tehauno's husband, Vernon,
calls himself a full-blooded Comanche, who was captured by a
Kiowa.

Billy Horse intoned a lengthy Kiowan prayer. In English, he
told the dozen people at the grave: "We are descendants of a great
man." He argues that Satanta was wrongly convicted. Kiowa
leaders Eagle Heart and Owl Prophet are to blame, he said.
"Satanta," he said, "was wrongly sentenced to life in prison here
in Huntsville." In a way, I think he's right. Satanta should have
have been a prisoner of war, not a felon.

Billy Horse said Satanta's descendants have organized with
a goal of clearing the old chief's name. Meanwhile, he is trying to
pin the wagon trail raid on Eagle Heart and the Owl Prophet.

"What about *their* descendants?" I asked. He grinned and
said: "They're not organized."

✳✳✳

True Story of 1860 Fires, Lynching Is Lost Chapter

Judge Lynch left no court records.

Dr. Donald Reynolds, a historian, faced that handicap in researching the Texas slave insurrection panic of 1860.

"In the two months or so that it took for the panic to run its course," he said, "vigilance committees in Texas hanged at least 30, and probably many more white and black men for alleged abolitionist activities."

The panic erupted in edgy Texas as the Civil War loomed. Lynch mobs rallied when unexplained fires on July 8, 1860, destroyed the entire business district of Dallas, half the town square of Denton, and a store in the village of Pilot Point.

In the week that followed, Charles Pryor, editor of the Dallas *Herald*, spread terror by blaming the fires on a conspiracy of abolitionist arsonists.

After losing his press in the Dallas fire, the editor dispatched blood-curdling letters to Texas newspapers and politicians. He declared that several slaves, under questioning, had confirmed a plot "to devastate with fire and assassination all of North Texas."

The slaves would rise up, he warned, aided by "white men of the North." In communities from the Red River to the Rio Grande, vigilantes began knotting nooses.

Meanwhile, fires broke out in Ladonia, Honey Grove, Milford, Fort Belknap, Henderson and elsewhere, spurring rumors of a widespread plot.

Dr. Reynolds emphasized that dry weather, with temperatures up to 110 degrees, had turned wooden structures into firetraps in Dallas and Denton counties, and other scenes of blazes.

"Fires which damaged stores in Ladonia, Honey Grove and Milford, for example, were eventually laid to the spontaneous combustion of the new and highly volatile phosphorous matches," he said.

Author of a book on southern newspapers during the secession crisis, *Editors Make War*, Dr. Reynolds quoted the Reverend

R. M. White, an early resident of Ellis County, which was shaken by abolitionist scares:

"It was thought the fires were the work of incendiaries, as in most instances no cause could be traced whereby the buildings could have taken fire from accidental causes, but finally matches in old Uncle Billy Oldham's store in Waxahachie took fire whilst lying on a shelf, right under the sight of the clerks and proprietor, in broad daylight. The explanation of all the mysterious and alarming conflagrations was plain spontaneous ignition."

On the Denton fire, Dr. Reynolds quoted C. A. Williams, a Denton resident at the time.

"The day was an oppressively hot one and there is no doubt in my mind but what the fires were all caused from the matches exploding by reason of the hot weather."

First accounts of the so-called conspiracy were roughly extracted from frightened slaves by threats and torture.

In the case of the Dallas fire, Dr. Reynolds said, Cyrill Miller, a farmer, supplied the initial so-called evidence:

"Miller lost his barn to fire a few days after Dallas had burned. Suspecting his slaves of setting fire to his property, he reportedly forced a confession from a small Negro boy by threatening to kill him if he refused to reveal the identity of the conspirators and warning him that if he died lying, 'The devil would get him sure.'

The youngster's confession led to the interrogation of other blacks, and there unfolded an incredible story of abolitionist-planned arson, murder, and rapine. By mid-July, the rest of the Southern people began to hear, via their newspapers, the horrifying details of the Dallas 'plot.'

A vigilance committee in Dallas lynched three slaves. Tales told by slaves to save their necks cost the lives of other slaves. Dallas lynchings stopped when owners concluded that hanging costly slaves was prohibitively expensive.

In an 1892 edition of *The Dallas Morning News*, Dr. Reynolds found a reporter's interview with one of the Dallas vigilantes from 32 years before:

"When the town was burned it was a hot day—so hot that matches ignited from the heat of the sun. Wallace Peak had just finished a new two-story frame building and in the upper story that day a number of men were lounging and smoking. Piled up near the building were a lot of boxes filled with shavings, and I think a cigar stump or a match was thrown into one of the boxes, and from that the fire started about 2 o'clock in the afternoon. . . . There was a great deal of excitement about the apprehended Negro uprising; somebody had to hang and the three Negroes went."

The head of ETSU's history department questions whether a slave conspiracy really existed. He focused his talk on one white victim—a reluctant martyr.

The Reverend Anthony Bewley was a northern Methodist minister who had conducted services in Johnson County for several years without winning many souls to his religion or his mildly Unionist views. A few years earlier, southern Methodists had broken away from the northern church over the slavery issue. And northern Methodists in Texas soon became suspected abolitionists. A pair had been run out of Dallas County a year before the big scare.

Tennessee-born Mr. Bewley, fifty-six, was moving his ministry from Johnson County to a more sympathetic German community on the Nueces when the cry of conspiracy went up. He gathered his family and headed north.

"The Bewleys didn't know that the Fort Worth and Sherman vigilance committees had offered a $1000 reward for the minister's capture and return to Texas," Dr. Reynolds said.

Arkansas vigilantes ordered the family to keep moving when they tried to rest in Fayetteville. And the Bewleys made it to Cassville, Missouri, before a hard-riding posse overtook them.

The father of eight wasn't allowed to visit with members of his family, but his captors allowed him to write a farewell letter to his wife.

Dr. Reynolds said, "It was a sad leave-taking for Mrs. Bewley. Her husband previously may have been naive about what could be accomplished by his missionary activities in the Lone Star State, but he was absolutely realistic now about his chances for survival in the hands of vengeful Texans. In his letter, dated September 5, 1860, he informed her that his fate had already been sealed."

The letter stated:

"Dear wife and children, who are big enough to know about these things. So far as I am concerned, all these things (conspiracy charges) are false. You have been with me, and you know as well as I do that none of these things have ever been countenanced about our house, but that we have repudiated such to the last."

After giving his wife assurances of his love and advising her on how to raise the children in his absence, he asked her to request that friends write of his good character to Captain "Daget" [Daggett], who was a leading citizen of Fort Worth.

Although conspiratorial evidence against Mr. Bewley was lacking, in Dr. Reynolds' view, the preacher was lynched a few hours after his arrival in Fort Worth.

He was left hanging all night from a large pecan tree from which an earlier abolitionist suspect had been suspended. The tree stood 300 yards west of the intersection of White Settlement Road and Jacksboro Highway.

The historian said:

"The next day the minister was cut down and buried without shroud or coffin. But to say 'buried' is to exaggerate, for he was placed in such a short and shallow grave that his knees poked through the earth for passers-by to see.

"The desecration didn't end there. About three weeks later, unnamed individuals unearthed the corpse, stripped its bones of their remaining flesh and placed them upon the roof of Ephraim Daggett's storehouse.

"This appears to have been the 'Daggett' to whom Reverend Bewley had asked his wife to direct letters attesting to his good character."

According to one source,

"The bones were 'in the care of a Dr. Peak,' who occasionally went up and 'turned them about.'

"Young boys made Daggett's roof a favorite place to play. They would set up the bones in a variety of attitudes by bending the joints of the arms and legs. And they'd mock the remains with cries of 'Old Bewley, Old Abolitionist.'"

In the 1930s, a survivor of those days told how he and his family had moved away from Fort Worth during the Civil War,

but found, on their return at war's end, the bones still atop
Daggett's building.

The elderly man recalled:

"After we got back—you know how kids will do—young
Eph Daggett and I crawled up and saw Old Bewley's bones, right
on top of the roof and bleached white."

✳✳✳

CONFEDERATE GRAVES REVIVE TALES OF BATTLE

Today it's hard to envision a Confederate States of America
reaching from sea to shining sea. But the vision was one southern
leaders kept alive until March 28, 1862, when their dreams died
at a place called Glorieta Pass.

As a Civil War battle, New Mexico's Glorieta Pass doesn't
rank mention in most encyclopedias. But it was there, in the
mountains of northern New Mexico, that Union forces demol-
ished Confederate hopes of capturing Colorado's rich gold fields
and annexing the long, blockade-resistant coast of California.

Now, news of the discovery of Confederate graves in New
Mexico has retrieved the battle from oblivion. For example, in a
parlor stacked with research documents, members of the Lee
Reid family in Plano sat talking like historians about the significance of the fight at Glorieta Pass. The family discussion has
progressed since a story in *The Dallas Morning News* told how a
team of diggers from the Museum of New Mexico has excavated
remains of Confederate soldiers killed in the fight.

Lee Reid is sure that one of the skeletons will prove to be that
of his great-great-granduncle, Ebenezer Hanna. "Ebenezer Hanna
lived in Brown County. There are still Hannas living around
there. You can see an old Hanna Cemetery there," said Reid, a
Texas Instruments engineer.

"The Confederates actually won that battle at Glorieta Pass,
but while they were winning it, the Yankees got around behind

them and burned their wagon train, destroying all their supplies and ammunition. That really ended the campaign," he explained.

Reid had been aware of his uncle's fate. But the surprising disclosure of a mass grave at the battlefield in New Mexico came as news from the front—a front almost forgotten in the passage of 125 years. Workers building a house near the pass found a human jawbone on June 22. More digging uncovered the common grave of thirty-two Confederate soldiers, buried in a double row, and the solitary grave of another, believed to be an officer.

Overnight at the Reids' place, Private Ebenezer Hanna became as familiar a household word as Lieutenant Colonel Oliver North. Reid's daughter, Barbara Littrell, unfurled a copy of a war journal in Uncle Ebenezer's handwriting. The original manuscript resides in the Texas State Library in Austin. Barbara sat up late a couple of nights translating the soldier's pinched antique script into readable copy.

Arkansas-born Private Hanna, only eighteen when he died, was elected his company's historian on February 10, 1862. His eleven-page journal describes movements and engagements of Company C, Fourth Regiment, Texas Mounted Volunteers, C.S.A. The last entry was made a day before the author's last battle.

The journal tells how the campaign of Brigadier General Henry Hopkins Sibley was stalked by hunger, exposure, and hostile Indians. Routine fatigue and suffering was intensified by occasional combat. On February 21, 1862, for instance, he wrote: "We marched five miles. The Yankees met us at the river five miles above Fort Craig. Commenced firing about 10 o'clock in the morning. The battle raged until about an hour by sun in the evening. We charged them, routed them, taken their artillery, routed and run them. The battle ceased at sunset. Our loss thirty-nine killed and about sixty wounded. Federals loss unknown. Only I know I seen plenty of them laying on the field and taken prisoners. We camped on the battlefield."

The following day, he added: "The most melancholy scene I ever witnessed was on the Valley of the Rio Grande where the Texas boys thrashed out the Yankees on the 21st day of February 1862. I have no name for this brave action but I think it would be very appropriately termed a young Manassas." He referred to the Virginia site of two important Rebel victories. His fight, however, would be called the battle of Val Verde.

On February 26, 1862, he mordantly wrote: "Moved fifteen miles. Camped four miles above San Antonio [New Mexico]. I had my horse killed in the battle of Peralta and I am now on foot and I now feel the pleasure of soldiering in New Mexico more plainly than I ever have before." He observed "the severity of the climate, the hardships of a march of a thousand miles over mountains such as is seen in no other country . . . without wood or water, but little food" was "worse than all the horrors that is witnessed on the battlefield."

When Sibley ultimately ordered the Fourth Regiment dismounted because of the heavy losses of horses, the young soldier worried about the other "Texas boys as they have never been accustomed to walking."

Given the hardships and fighting, C Company's luck was pretty good until the end of March. Private Hanna's final entry states: "Twas during the day of the 27th [March 27, 1862] that we had the trial of burying the first one of the members of Company C. The enemy did not make their appearance during the day."

About 2,000 Yanks and Rebels clashed in hand-to-hand battle twenty miles east of Santa Fe, at Glorieta Pass, a narrow cut through the mountains favored by travelers on the old Santa Fe Trail. The Rebs had a slight advantage in numbers and moved the Yankees before them throughout the day. But at the Rebel rear, the burning of nearly one hundred Confederate supply and ammunition wagons gave the Union an unexpected strategic victory.

Many guards of the wagon train, hearing the sound of battle, had run off to join the fighting, leaving the wagons vulnerable. Logistically, the Rebels were ruined. Loss of the supplies halted the determined advance of Sibley, a Texan and a man sometimes criticized for drunkenness but never for lack of ambition.

A West Pointer who had resigned his commission as major in the U.S. Army, Sibley in July 1861 proposed to Confederate President Jefferson Davis in Richmond, a grand plan for capturing the Southwest. Lieutenant Colonel John Robert Baylor, one of the Texas convention delegates who voted the state out of the Union, more recently had lain the groundwork for Sibley's bold scheme.

Baylor, of the Second Regiment of Texas Mounted Rifles had led his troops from El Paso to a series of easy wins against faltering Union forces in what is now the state of New Mexico. Baylor celebrated by appointing himself governor of the Confederate Territory of Arizona. Overly eager Southern sympathizers in Tucson were flying the Stars and Bars in the face of demoralized Union troops. And from Southern California came reports that secessionist-minded citizens were ready to revolt. An estimated 1,500 volunteers were ready to join the Confederate Army—or so the vague stories went.

Persuasive Sibley won Richmond's approval of his bright idea. Assembling a 3,700-man brigade, Sibley rode off to claim the Southwest. Hundreds of his men never made it back to Texas. As luck would have it, the Union Army commander responsible for halting Sibley's advance was U.S. Brigadier General Edward Richard Sprigg Canby, the husband of one of Sibley's sisters. Yes, the Civil War, known for pitting brother against brother, also pitted brother-in-law against brother-in-law.

Throughout the New Mexico campaign and especially during Sibley's agonizing retreat after the battle of Glorieta Pass, the two commanders were suspected of brother-in-lawing.

Canby eventually was accused of deliberately failing to capture Sibley's disabled force in one swoop. Canby explained—and it was probably true—that he lacked sufficient men and provisions to guard and care for Sibley's troops if they all surrendered at once. Sibley's retreat to Texas was a nightmare. Skirmishing with Yankees, ragtag Rebels straggled hundreds of miles without provisions. Some perished from thirst in the desert. Others died of exposure or were killed by Indians.

He showed me a memoir of the battle of Glorieta Pass written by one of Hanna's Confederate comrades, A. B. Peticolas:

"The battle began at ten minutes to eleven and ended about four o'clock. We had thirty-five killed and thirty-three wounded. They had from sixty to one hundred killed and from 100 to 300 wounded. [Note: some historians estimate Confederate losses were thirty-six or more killed, about sixty wounded, and twenty-five captured. Federal losses were about thirty-eight killed, sixty-four wounded, and twenty captured. Roughly half the wounded may have died.]

"All our killed (three in C Company) were shot in the very front of the battle. Abe [Eb] Hanna was shot down on the left in thirty yards of the enemy. Jake Henson, who was on the same side, coming along and seeing Abe down, went to him, gave him water, and began to pick the stones from under him.

"While in a kneeling position over his wounded friend he was shot and killed, the ball going in at the shoulder and ranging towards the heart.

"Abe Hanna died about an hour in[to] the night very easily. He was shot in the loins and bled inwardly. He said he felt no pain save that his limbs were numb and dead from his hips down."

※※※

Custer Was A Popular Man During His Texas Stay

In the wake of the Civil War, U.S. Army Major General George Armstrong Custer, vilified in recent years, was popular with Texans. Among the bluebellies and carpetbaggers who paraded into Texas to enforce Reconstruction, Custer was a rare exception. He made friends.

A decade after Custer's tour in Texas, when he was killed by Indians at the Battle of Little Bighorn in Montana in 1876, the Texas legislature remembered him fondly. Lawmakers expressed condolences to Custer's widow and family. The Texas resolution, unusual among the states, was read into congressional records. Meanwhile, rebel survivors of Hood's Texas Brigade, their ranks thinned and scarred by twenty-four battles, were meeting in Galveston when news of Custer's Last Stand reached Texas. Quickly, they adopted a tribute to the fallen cavalryman who had once been their foe.

With his pretty wife, Libby, Custer was in Texas a year, spring 1865 to spring 1866, headquartered first in Hempstead, the Waller County seat, and later in Austin, the state capital.

I got this information at an inconspicuous frame house in Brazos County. The six-room house is jammed to the rafters with books, documents, firearms, sabers, toys, games—all relating to Custer. The trove has been called the world's finest and largest collection of Custeriana. A daring and controversial career brought global attention to Custer, who won a brigadier general's star at age twenty-three and died at thirty-nine.

Historians John M. Carroll and his associate Bob Aldrich have spent decades assembling the priceless collection. Anything concerning Custer finds a place—an arrow from the Little Bighorn or a dire Italian comic book starring Calamity Jane and Custer, both out of uniform. Author of the 1975 book *Custer in Texas*, Carroll noted Custer's admiration for the state. "His letters home literally sang the praise of Texas as being the real future of America, and in each letter he advocated that members of his family settle here."

One did. His uncle George, the Custer for whom he was named, moved to Franklin (Robertson County), where, after a long and prosperous life, he was buried.

Texas has other ties to cavalryman Custer, a major general in the wartime volunteers who reverted to his regular rank of lieutenant colonel about the time he left Texas to join the 7th Cavalry. It was as a colonel he led his 7th's troopers to glory and death in the Indian Wars. Custer's chief of Crow Scouts at Little Bighorn, Luther Hare of Sherman (Grayson County), served as professor of military science at the University of Texas at Austin in 1918 and later as commander of the Students' Army Training Corps at Simmons College in Abilene (Taylor County). Texas was the final burial ground for three troopers who were with Custer at the Little Bighorn, two in Bexar County and one in Falls County. For most of this century, Texas has been home for Custer's 7th Cavalry—now part of the 1st Cavalry Division— first along the border bothering Pancho Villa, then Fort Bliss and later Fort Hood.

In the middle 1860s, the Custer family charmed Austin. Carroll explained: "The Custers' stay in Austin was highlighted by an enlightened administration which brought law and order to this frontier, this fiercely independent state of Texas. The population loved them, dined them and made them comfortable."

Earlier, on August 7, 1868, in Hempstead, Custer had issued an order that endeared him to Texans, although it cramped the style of some of his 4,000 troops, who were spoiling to begin harvesting the spoils of war. Custer issued General Order No. 15 from the Headquarters of the Second Cavalry Division of the Military Division of the Gulf:

"The command being about to march through a section of the country which has been beyond the control of the government for four years, and it being desirable to cultivate the most friendly feelings with the inhabitants thereof, all belonging to this command will be required to exercise the most scrupulous regard for the rights and properties of those with whom they may be brought in contact. . . . ."

That diplomatic policy marked Custer's administration in Texas. His gentle whip hand scarcely prepared Texans for the Reconstruction nightmares that would follow Custer's departure from the state.

Custer held his officers strictly responsible for the conduct of their men. He insisted that any lawlessness in his command be punished. Moreover, he ruled that no foraging parties would be permitted to prey upon the farms and populace of Texas.

This picture of an even-tempered administrator does not jibe with the villainous portrait of an egomaniacal squaw killer sketched by excitable writers of the 1960s and 1970s. To the squaw killer charge, Carroll replies: "Because General Eisenhower directed the forces in Europe does not make him a *fraulein* killer. There is no morality in war, so don't look for it or manufacture it. Emotional history is also flawed history."

Custer's headquarters in Austin, a handsome old stone building, can still be seen. The building is now the University of Texas Visitors' Center.

Exploring the collection, I wondered how Custer came to be outgeneraled at the Little Bighorn. "He wasn't outgeneraled," protested Aldrich. "You see, Major Reno was drunk. . . ."

The Battle of Little Bighorn will never end.

✳✳✳

Fort Chadbourne—A Monument to the Old West

At first glance, there's not much left standing. But if you poke around a little, these ruins will suggest the fort that was. That long building with the crumbling rock walls and collapsed roof was a barrack. You can find 130-year-old graffiti carved in the sandstone. Look, here's a name: "Albert Haneman, Co. B, 1858."

Soldiers came here in October 1852 to show the U.S. flag to the hard-riding Indian warriors. The Indians didn't salute. So, the outnumbered troops erected these stone buildings and settled in for a warm truce or a hot war. At that time, Texas had a frontier of more than 1,200 miles, protected by roughly two soldiers per mile. That open space yonder was the parade ground.

Before the astonished garrison, a Kiowa once contemptuously rode across the parade ground flashing a blond woman's scalp from the point of his spear. Nobody shot him because of an uneasy truce in effect at the time. That was in the early days of the fort.

Fort Chadbourne, with five companies of the 8th Infantry, was the deepest permanent military intrusion into Indian country. Why infantry? Well, the original plan called for light cavalry, but you know the Army.

That rock house over there must have been a colonel's quarters. In 1856, a young cavalry officer named Robert E. Lee used Fort Chadbourne as a base for his patrols. His wounded were treated in the fort's hospital. Over there is what's left of the hospital. Lee's gallantry had earned him the battlefield rank of colonel in the Mexican War, a war that had claimed the life of

Lt. Theodore Chadbourne, whose name was ultimately given to the fort.

Another colonel from the Mexican War was Joe Johnston, circuit-riding paymaster for Chadbourne and several other frontier forts. In those days, a private got eight dollars a month. But it was sometimes four or five months between paydays. A private drew an additional twenty-five cents a day for building roads, digging ditches or doing other non-military grunt work.

The Mexican War (1846-48) had provided not only officers but uniforms. A young lieutenant described them:

"The uniform coats hitherto supplied have been fashioned with such a notable disregard for the proportions of the human body that it has been a matter of impossibility to wear them as issued. The finest-looking soldiers in the world, thus outfitted, would offer a ridiculous appearance.

"The coats are much too short-waisted. The jackets are cut large, if not larger, around the waist, than about the chest: too tight for comfort in one place, they are absurdly loose in the other. The trousers shaped upon equally distorted models, were so tight-legged that a large foot, sometimes, could only with great difficulty be forced through them, whilst their volume of seat was immense."

The fort was a key station for the Butterfield Overland Mail from 1858 to 1861. Big changes came in 1861. Texas seceded. Joe Johnston and Robert E. Lee went east to trade their blue uniforms for gray ones with stars.

The Butterfield line shut down. And Fort Chadbourne was occupied by Confederate troops, whose commander was promptly killed by Indians. Later, Confederate troops from Fort Chadbourne fought in one of the frontier's most inglorious Indian combats, the Battle of Dove Creek.

On January 8, 1865, at the confluence of Spring and Dove creeks, sixteen miles south of San Angelo, Captain Henry Fossett's 370 state border guards unwisely attacked about 1400 Kickapoos, who were peacefully crossing Texas en route to Mexico from Indian Territory.

The Texans probably mistook the Kickapoos, who were minding their own business, for Comanches or Kiowas, who'd been raiding settlements. Numbers are unreliable. Clearly, however, the Kickapoos kicked the Confederates' cans. The Texans lost thirty-six, with sixty more wounded. The Kickapoos, led by Chief No-Ko-Wat, lost eleven with thirty-one wounded. The Confederates retreated to the settlements on the Colorado River. The Kickapoos continued to Mexico.

After the Civil War, federal troops marched into Fort Chadbourne. They repaired some of the buildings that had been burned and damaged by rebel tenants. But in 1867, Oak Creek, the fort's water source, got dusty. The army abandoned the fort as an impossible permanent garrison. Fifty miles to the southwest, Fort Concho, on a more reliable river, was coming into its glory.

Incidentally, Fort Concho in San Angelo remains a gloriously well-preserved and restored frontier fort. Meanwhile, Fort Chadbourne crumbled. In the late 1860s, Fort Chadbourne was a way station for the El Paso Stage Line. In the 1870s, the Army's most effective Indian fighter in Texas, Colonel Ranald Mackenzie, on sorties against the Plains Indians, bivouacked his troopers at the fort.

Troops from Fort Concho used Fort Chadbourne as a picket or outer post and camped at Chadbourne while on scouting patrols. The Goodnight-Loving Trail passed through the ruined fort. Cowboys tried to dodge Indian bands while herding Texas cattle to northern markets, which had been spurred by demand for government beef to feed, yes, to Indians on reservations. Like an old soldier, Fort Chadbourne faded away.

Military historian Bill Fisher of San Angelo inspired me to tour the ruins. A former photo analyst for the CIA, Fisher had researched Fort Chadbourne for the West Texas State Historical Association.

Speaking of a battle at the fort, he called it "a massacre." He said half a dozen Indian women were shot down by troops when a fight broke out at the fort. One warrior was killed.

Speaking of women, the soldiers weren't without them, he told me. And they weren't all colonels' ladies:

"They were laundresses. They are specifically mentioned in army regulations, which state that each company was allowed four women to act as washerwomen, and that they would receive rations each day.

"They were allowed to collect their fees at the pay table on paydays. There's always been much speculation. Some say they were legalized prostitutes that the army allowed for the entertainment of the troops.

"Whatever their condition, married or not, these unfortunate women lived in outrageous circumstances. The maps of Fort Chadbourne show the laundresses' quarters directly behind the enlisted men's quarters. Maps of forts often show they were near privies and stables. Inspection reports stated that the women's quarters were tents, shacks, log huts or dugouts. It's difficult to understand how any woman would want to live the life of an army laundress. However, these were hard times. In spite of pitiful conditions, a woman could get a ration a day, a place to live and medical assistance. Additional benefits might be obtained, such as goods the men traded for sexual favors. In any case, five will get you ten that prostitutes were on duty at 'the Dutchman's Hog Ranch'—a drinking and gambling hall that lay across Oak Creek from the fort."

Historian Harold Johnston of San Angelo found the following in General David S. Stanley's memoirs:

"One very beautiful, bright moonlit night in September (1855), we were awakened by some strange noise like someone groaning and calling, and going out we found a soldier by the name of Mattock, who was being helped to the hospital by a soldier who lived with his wife near the [Oak] creek. Mattock had been over the creek to the hut of a Dutchman who sold liquor. Having filled up, he was on his way home, very happy no doubt, and at the crossing of the creek, which was in deep banks, five or six Comanches waylaid him, and as he passed commenced shooting at his back with bows and arrows.

"Now comes the incredible part of the story. Mattock had fourteen arrows in him. He bristled with them like a porcupine. Three of these arrows had gone so far through him that the surgeon extracted them by pulling them through the man's body. In two weeks time, Mattock was walking around and his only disability was finally from a superficial wound which lacerated a nerve."

Folks here in Coke County still wonder what that Dutchman was selling and where you can buy it nowadays.

Between Abilene and San Angelo, the Fort Chadbourne ruins are on the 24,000-acre Chadbourne Ranch, whose resident expert is Bob Huckabee. Bob gave me a tour of the ruins and a first-rate history lecture. A former Dallas resident, Bob pilots the Chadbourne Ranch Air Force—a Mooney aircraft and a Bell helicopter.

Fond of the ruins—which are prime or pristine or whatever you call unspoiled ruins—Bob spends his idle hours studying the old stone piles. They lie just outside the view of cars passing on U.S. 277.

✳✳✳

A Frontier Soldier's Lot Was Not a Happy One

A thicket of rock chimneys still stands to remind the prairie dogs that this place was once an Army post. Misbegotten in 1851, Fort Phantom Hill was stuck out here on the Clear Fork of the Brazos as one of a line of forts that supposedly divided Texas between the unscalped and the Comanches.

You had your choice of two kinds of drinking water at Phantom Hill—brackish or absent. Timbers had to be hauled forty miles for the officers' quarters. Enlisted men lived in huts that only a mud dauber could love. Probably because vitamins don't have thorns, vegetables refused to grow on Phantom Hill. An innovative Army surgeon urged that the men's rations of bacon, bread and coffee be rounded out with pickles.

Ghostly legends cloak the naming of Phantom Hill. A favorite one is that the hill, when approached from a certain angle, seems to disappear. Maybe. But numerous men surely disappeared. Phantomlike, they went over the hill.

Desertion was a serious offense in those days. Everything was a serious offense under the Army's old Articles of War. They listed a charge or two for every offense under the sun—and there was a lot of sun in West Texas. Anything the first ninety-eight charges missed was covered by the ninety-ninth—"conduct prejudicial to good order and discipline."

I came to these ruins in Jones County to review my notes on B. J. Fisher's lecture on military justice. He had spoken to the West Texas State Historical Association meeting in the Taylor County seat of Abilene in November 1990.

After the meeting, I drove to the ruins. No one was home except a prairie dog family whose members idly watched me. Although abandoned as a garrison in 1854, hours before somebody mysteriously torched it, Phantom Hill remained a landmark. It was a camping place for soldiers and travelers. In 1858, it became way station number fifty-four for stagecoaches on the Butterfield Trail.

Now private property, the isolated ruins were opened to the public in the 1970s by owner James M. Alexander. The result is a history lesson that is free, photogenic, and worth the fourteen-mile drive on FM 600 from Abilene. Besides, Phantom Hill is a good spot to ponder military justice, if those terms aren't mutually exclusive.

Historian Fisher is a retired photographic interpreter for the CIA. His work dates back to JFK's figurative eyeball-to-eyeball confrontation with Nikita Khrushchev during the Cuban missile crisis. Remember? Khrushchev blinked.

While based in Washington, D.C., Fisher, in off hours, prowled the National Archives to study records of the Army on the Texas frontier. Fisher said: "The Articles of War permitted a sentence of death for desertion. Actually, punishment on the frontier stopped short of this final solution. The case of Private Michael Hays of Company I, First Infantry Regiment, is typical."

On 20 November 1852, Private Hays was assigned to guard duty at Fort Terrett (on the North Llano River). He failed to appear at the guard mounting. When Lieutenant F. J. Denman ordered a sergeant to take Hays to the guardhouse, Hays struck the sergeant in the face and called him an SOB.

Hays was still confined in the guardhouse on Christmas Day, 1852. Apparently wishing to spend Christmas elsewhere, Hays escaped and headed toward Fredericksburg (Gillespie County). He was caught the next day by a party sent to apprehend him. Hayes was charged with desertion, neglect of duty and conduct prejudicial to good order and discipline.

He was found guilty on all three charges and received the following sentence: "forfeiture of all pay and allowances except what might be owed to the camp laundresses; to have his head shaved; to be indelibly marked with the letter D, one and a half inches in length on his left hip; to receive fifty lashes on his back, well laid on, in the presence of the paraded battalion; and to be dishonorably drummed out of the service."

Following tradition, after the flogging, the prisoner's guards poured brine on his whipped back. With shaved head, he was paraded around the post with the drums and fife playing the rogues march. The lyrics went: "Poor old soldier, Poor old soldier, Tarred and feathered and sent to hell, Because he wouldn't soldier well."

The prisoner was then escorted out of the garrison and ordered to stay out. The tattooed hip prevented his re-enlisting. He was gone again—but this time on the Army's terms.

Fisher said, "What was perhaps the most serious case of the 1850s was tried at a general court-martial convened at Fort Mason [in what is now Mason County]. Private Archibald McDonald of Company D, Second Cavalry, was charged with violation of the fifty-second Article of War—cowardice in the face of the enemy."

The specification read: "That the said Private Archibald McDonald, being one of a scouting party, under the command of First Sergeant Walter McDonald of Company D, Second Cavalry, and being engaged in a fight with the Indians, did shamefully misbehave in such a cowardly manner that it was necessary for the sergeant, in command of the party, to threaten to shoot him if he did not do his duty. All this near the Concho River, Texas, on or about the 12th day of February 1857."

The court found Private McDonald guilty. He was sentenced to be "hanged by the neck until dead, at such time as the president of the United States desired." But President James Buchanan didn't desire it. McDonald got off with a dishonorable discharge.

In his research, Fisher found that some officers devoted more time to courts-martial than to fighting Indians. Take Lieutenant Colonel Robert E. Lee's Texas tour before the Civil War. On September 2, 1856, Lee departed his command at Camp Cooper, another post on the Clear Fork, for Fort Ringgold on the Rio Grande to serve on a general court-martial trying Major Giles Porter for repeated acts of drunkenness.

Lee arrived at Ringgold after traveling twenty-seven days. On September 30, the court moved from Ringgold to Fort Brown, at the mouth of the Rio Grande. Lee arrived there November 4. On February 6, 1857, Lee was relieved from the Porter case and assigned to another court convening at Indianola on the Gulf Coast. Lee didn't return to his command at Camp Cooper, in what is now Throckmorton County, until April 19, 1857—an absence of seven months.

Incidentally, Major Porter was eventually convicted of conduct prejudicial to good order and discipline. He was sentenced to be dismissed from the Army. Later, President Buchanan mitigated the sentence to suspension from rank and pay for one year.

You will recall that Private Michael Hays ran away from Fort Terrett on Christmas Day, 1852. There's more to that story. The sentinel ordered to guard him was Private Alexander Benko of Company I, First Infantry. Private Benko, apparently feeling warm and large in the yule afterglow, allowed Hays to escape without firing a shot.

Benko was arrested and tried for neglect of duty. Found guilty, he was fined twelve dollars and sentenced to wear a ball and chain under guard for three months. That Christmas of 1852 at Fort Terrett must have been a merry one.

Fisher said, "It was during this most joyous of all seasons that Private John Ward also met his downfall. Ward's general court-

martial charges stated that he had been repeatedly drunk between June 1, 1852, and January 27, 1853.

"Private Ward deserted on December 23, 1852, and was
hauled back, still drunk, two days later. On January 3, 1853, Ward
was, not surprisingly, in the post hospital. Deciding to chuck the
whole thing, he left a note on his pillow stating that he had
decided not to soldier any more.

"He then took himself off to a groggery about a mile distant
and stayed until brought back, dead drunk, on January 27. He
was found guilty and was summarily whipped, shaved, and
drummed out of the Army."

Fisher's briefcase bulges with military melodramas. He said,
"Flogging was abolished in 1862; branding and tattooing in 1872.
In 1887 it became illegal to force prisoners to carry heavy logs and
in 1893 the wearing of balls and chains was forbidden. The Army
stopped cruel and unusual punishment in its own good time. But
even today many a first sergeant carries around in his head a
blacklist of sadsacks in his outfit. Their names come to mind
every time there is an unpleasant duty to perform." Some of us
knew that.

✳✳✳

Old "Buffalo Soldiers" Recall Horseback Days

Although many of the old soldiers had known combat, they
mostly swapped peacetime stories. They were Buffalo Soldiers.
And they talked about the Old Army. For them, the Old Army
ended with World War II.

Buffalo Soldiers—a name harking back to the Indian wars—
were troops of Negro units of the U.S. Army. In early years, they
were assigned to police the hostile tribes on the frontier. The black
soldiers, often former slaves, provided a buffer to Texas between
white settlers and raiding Indians.

The name lingers. When members of the 9th and 10th Cavalry
Association gathered at the Houston Grand Hotel in 1985 for

what they counted their 119th reunion, they proudly called themselves Buffalo Soldiers.

The 120 men at the meeting were the remaining troopers of the army's last horse cavalry regiments.

Trained for both fighting and spectacular parade, the horsemen of the 9th and 10th were dismounted before reaching combat in World War II. Disbanded, the Buffalo Soldiers were promptly reassigned, many to combat outfits.

Later, in time to win new regimental battle streamers in Vietnam, the 9th and 10th were reorganized. They were mechanized and racially mixed. In the Old Army, only the black cavalry's officers were white. (One was John J. Pershing, the army commander of World War I. The general's nickname, "Black Jack," came from his early years with the black cavalrymen.)

Houstonian Bill Prince, seventy-one, recruited the Buffalo Soldiers for the reunion. Two, now in their nineties, had chased Pancho Villa. And Prince goes way back, too. He lied about his age to join the 10th at age fourteen in 1928. He patrolled the restless Mexican border: "Seemed like every time the Mexicans had an election, they would also have a revolution."

Back then, cavalrymen trained their horses to gunfire in mounted target practice, firing 45-caliber automatics just over the horses' ears. The drills required a steady hand and a steady seat. Prince reminisced with David Allen, sixty-eight, of Wichita, Kansas, who joined the 10th in 1936.

"I always loved horses," Prince said. "My family owns six. I still ride for pleasure."

Both the horse soldiers agreed that cavalrymen generally liked their mounts and cussed them no more than was necessary. For example, a horse named Sugar was fondly recalled by Allen, despite all the housekeeping and upkeeping that Sugar required. "A cavalryman took care of his horse before he took care of himself," said Prince, now a master sergeant.

Both men, combat soldiers in World War II, remembered when a private drew twenty-one bucks a month, minus $1.75 for laundry. But Allen remembered, too, what a Depression buck would buy.

"A pint of good whiskey was seventy-five cents. A jukebox song was a nickel. A bowl of chili downtown cost you a dime. Why, you could rent a five-room house for $7 a month."

Allen is the secretary and historian of the group. In his computer at home, he has stored the massive, medal-bedecked official history of the two regiments. A couple of years ago, he had a hand in reprinting a book, the *Roster* of the 10th. First published in 1867, 30th anniversary of the regiment, the book includes memoirs of the Indian fighters.

D Troop's Sergeant Peter Clayborne was one. He was hunting ripe plums and not Indians when he wandered away from his outfit in 1867:

"He was about to reach up and gather the fruit which hung temptingly on thorny boughs when sprang up five Indians who had been sleeping in the sand. The Indians had apparently never seen a colored man and supposing him to be some rare specimen of humanity from an unknown country, possibly an agent of the Evil Spirit of the Plains, they halted long enough to make sure they were not mistaken and ran a distance as fast as their feet could carry them.

"Clayborne was frozen with terror. He could not move. He saw the Indians stop and begin to retrace their steps toward him. The warriors came nearer and at last boldly began to inspect the color and quality of his scalp. His . . . hair excited their curiosity. Their intimate contact finally broke the spell which bound him and Clayborne turned from the savages and fled toward safety at the top of his speed. He was thoroughly winded on reaching camp. By degrees he stammered out his story and was promptly greeted by an arrest for leaving the camp without permission and without arms."

The black skin and hair of the troopers suggested to the Indians the nickname "Buffalo Soldiers." The Indians also called them "black white men."

The 1985 reunion was the 108th anniversary of a tour of hell by men of the 10th's Troop A. In the *Roster*, Trooper Thomas Allsup recalled the sun-blasted August long ago:

"The troop left Fort Concho (in what is now San Angelo) in pursuit of hostiles. A fresh trail was struck leading westward. This was followed until night overtook the column and a dry camp was made.

"Next morning the march was resumed without a drop of water. The canteens were empty. Three men were abandoned on the trail.

"The first sergeant and three men deserted the command. Men were nearly naked. The heat was so intense that the men had cast their clothing away.

"Sixteen men and the two officers resumed the march on the morning of the third day. By 10 A.M., the column had dwindled to seven men and two officers. No water to be found. A slight storm of rain descended which lasted about three minutes. Those who were able spread out their rubber blankets and caught a few precious drops. Tongues were hanging out of the mouths and eyeballs were starting from their sockets. By licking the wet surface of the blankets some were able to reduce the swelling of their tongues sufficiently to partially close their mouths. All but about a dozen horses died or strayed.

"A glimpse was caught of the retreating Indians. The savages carried water in skins and thus were able to pass over these great wastes.

"Every conceivable experiment was resorted to to supply drink to the dying men. Blood and other moisture from living and dead animals was tried with agonizing failure.

"The manner of some men dying of thirst is very peculiar. Clutching at vacancy they fall with a cry to the ground and become rigid. They even bit their own flesh with such fierceness as to take a piece out."

Troop A was rescued when comrades from Troop G, out on a scout, chanced upon the scene. By that time, the men of Troop A had been without water for eighty-six hours.

Two of the abandoned men perished. Four deserters were booted from the army into prison for a year. People at Fort Concho said it was a horror. Even the commander of Troop A, Captain Nicholas Nolan, quietly admitted that he made a mistake in trying to chase Indians across the Staked Plains in August without prospects of water.

✳✳✳

COURAGE EARNED BLACK SEMINOLES A PLACE IN HISTORY

In a sprawling building beneath San Antonio's Tower of the Americas, James Patrick McGuire spoke of the tools, toys and weapons on display at the Institute of Texan Cultures. "We borrow everything."

He was talking about the institute, but he could have been describing the cumulative culture of Texas. Collections and recollections of the various folks who people this state—Alsatian to Welsh, Jewish to Japanese—were arranged on a deck the size of a football field.

The institute, owned by the University of Texas, is nothing but thorough. Program manager McGuire didn't blink when I asked whether he had any information on the state's smallest ethnic minority, the black Seminoles. He guided me to the institute's library.

In about two minutes, I was holding a file covering virtually everything that has been published (and a few unpublished manuscripts) concerning these fascinating but little-known Indians.

Their range is the brush country just north of the Mexican border near Bracketville, a town of 1600 that is the Kinney County seat. (The only other Kinney County settlement, by the way, is Spofford, with seventy-seven mortals.) About sixty of the black Indians reside in the Brackettville area near old Fort Clark.

I closed the file and headed west on U.S. Highway 90 to cross the Hondo, the Sabinal, the Frio and the bone-dry Nueces rivers. I was pondering the unlucky hand that fate had dealt the black Indians. When I visited them about fifteen years ago, I found several who spoke only Spanish and a hybrid Indian tongue.

Others drawled English. Many followed a religion that was called Baptist but included some unexpected twists: They ritualized fasting and honored a taboo against pork at praise-house feasts.

These black Seminoles are descended from the men of the U. S. Army called the Seminole Negro-Indian Scouts.

The Scouts never numbered more than fifty, but the unit cut a proud swath through Texas history. In the Army's battles against hostile Indians in the 1870s and early 1880s, the Scouts were covered with decorations for valor.

Their story began in Florida, where runaway slaves took refuge among the Seminoles. The upshot was complete assimilation. Although white explorers at first assumed they were slaves of the Indians, the black Seminoles, more accurately, were allies of the red Seminoles.

The black Indians fought against U.S. troops when Florida was annexed. But eventually they were transported to Indian Territory (now part of Oklahoma). Their black skin made them profitable kidnap victims for Creek Indians and other slavers. Most Seminoles—black and red—became angered by their domineering Creek neighbors. Many lit out for Mexico. They were welcomed by the Mexican government and ended up battling Indian raiders and gringo adventurers along the Texas border.

Most of the red Seminoles returned to the U.S. after a few years. Because of U.S. slavery, however, the black Seminoles remained in Mexico. Then, after abolition, they split up.

One band was living at Nacimiento, in the Mexican state of Coahuila not far from Eagle Pass, when a black Army recruiter showed up to invite them to return to the United States and to join the campaign against the savage Indians who were preying on Texans. The inducements to enlist are unrecorded, but the black Seminoles speak of a "treaty" or a "treatment" as if a signed document once existed. Whatever the terms of the agreement, they appealed to the black Seminole braves. By 1870, a few had begun scouting. Others followed.

It was bloody work. What the new troopers lacked in military polish (some wore buffalo-horn war bonnets), they made up in tracking and fighting talents.

On April 25, 1875, 1st Lieutenant John Lapham Bullis, accompanied by three Scouts—Sergeant John Ward, trumpeter Isaac Payne and trooper Pompey Factor—picked up the tracks of more than seventy stolen horses. Pursuit led to the Eagle' Nest Crossing on the Pecos. There, they found twenty-five or thirty Comanches trying to cross with the stolen horses.

Three Comanches were killed and a fourth was wounded before the warriors, most of them armed with Winchesters, realized that they heavily outnumbered the soldiers.

Escaping the swarming Comanches, the Scouts looked back and saw Bullis—who was black but not a Seminole or a Scout—in trouble. His nervous young horse had been spooked. He'd been left afoot among the Comanches. They were closing in for the kill. "We can't leave the lieutenant, boys," Ward yelled. Wheeling, the Scouts charged.

The Comanches laid down a hot stream of fire on the Scouts. Ward's carbine sling was sliced by a bullet. Then, as he helped the lieutenant mount up behind him, Ward felt his carbine's stock smashed by another bullet. Firing at Comanches on all sides, the Scouts, with their rescued lieutenant, were able to ride through the angry savages.

"They saved my hair," wrote Bullis, who lived to become a brigadier general. The fight earned each of the three Scouts the Congressional Medal of Honor.

When I returned to Brackettville, I stopped in a store for a soda pop. Two little girls were buying bubble gum. They were black, classic black. But Indian features are often subdued or nonexistent among the black Seminoles. Roger Brown, 18, had told me that when he leaves Brackettville, people sometimes don't believe he is an Indian.

I said hello to the little girls.

They were eleven-year-old Dorothy Ward and her three-year-old sister, Latoya Ward. Dorothy said their mother, Beverly, is a deputy county clerk at the Kinney County courthouse on Fritter Street.

"We're Seminoles," Dorothy Ward said.

Ward. Of course. Dorothy and Latoya, I learned, are the great-great-granddaughters of Sergeant John Ward, who led Isaac

Payne and Pompey Factor through the Comanches 109 years ago
to save Lt. John Lapham Bullis at Eagle's Nest Crossing on the
Pecos.

Occasionally, history will hit you like the beam of a headlight
on a dark night.

✳✳✳

How the Vote Was Won

Suffering suffragists.

A few women living in Texas may recall the prejudices they
overcame in winning the right to vote. Some of the arguments
sound quaint today. Others may still be heard:

1. Texas women have never voted and, therefore, never
should.

2. Suffrage goes against the Bible.

3. Men are doing a good job of running government.

4. Politics is dirty and unfit for ladies.

5. Suffrage will break up homes because it will make women
independent and lead them to insanity, immorality and divorce.

6. Women are too emotional.

7. States' rights will be undermined and lead to Negro rule.

8. Female suffrage is a plot by the Bolsheviks and Socialists to
take over America.

At the Texas State Historical Association meeting in Galveston
in 1987, Ruthe Winegarten of Austin counted old woes and talked
about the women's suffrage struggle in Texas from 1868 to 1920.

She said Texas women began agitating for the vote right after
the Civil War when ex-slaves were pushing for political rights. A
Reconstruction convention voted down a women's suffrage resolution (52-13) in 1868. Six of the nine black delegates supported
votes for women.

At the Constitutional Convention of 1875, delegates, ignoring
a petition from suffragists, adopted a new constitution that

defined who could vote. Women were excluded, being lumped with idiots, lunatics, paupers and felons. Texas women weren't amused.

But women made inroads. By 1873, some had joined the Grange, a farm movement. And in 1879, a black woman, called Madam Walker, toured Texas speaking on "The Political Destiny of the Colored Race."

The first white woman to call publicly for women's suffrage in Texas was Mariana Folsom, a Unitarian minister who had moved to Texas from Iowa. In 1881, she said, "We cannot rise in rebellion as men do, but we will stand and demand the right to be heard and have our votes counted."

That same year, Jenny Beauchamp of Denton, wife of a Baptist preacher, was pointing out that black men had gotten the vote in 1870 (15th Amendment). She warned: "No other country has degraded women as America has. I do not intend to say woman will ever avenge her own wrongs. . . . But there is a God in heaven that fights the battles of the weak."

In 1893, Rebecca Henry Hayes of Galveston, vice president of Susan B. Anthony's National American Woman Suffrage Association, organized a statewide meeting. Photographer Hayes and eight other influential women called the convention. Among them were two physicians, two journalists and a representative from the farmers' movement. Others were members of the Women's Christian Temperance Union, which in 1888 had become the first state organization to endorse suffrage.

In May 1893, at the fancy Windsor Hotel in Dallas, thirty-nine women and nine men gathered to form the Texas Equal Rights Association (TERA). One of the founders, Dr. Grace Danforth, asked a *Dallas Morning News* reporter: "Is not the queen of Great Britain a woman?"

The following year, the TERA-ists met in Fort Worth, where Margaret Watson of Beaumont warned that ridicule was the movement's greatest enemy. She told delegates to ignore remarks about "short-haired women and long-haired men."

One of the activists at that meeting was Pauline Periwinkle, who had organized the first suffrage club in Dallas. She was president of the Dallas Federation of Women's Clubs and a writer for *The Morning News*. For a generation, she wrote hard-hitting columns in support of suffrage.

In November 1894, *The Morning News* reported that the local suffrage club would "appear before the next Legislature with a petition a mile long asking for the franchisement of women, who are tired of having no higher mission than making dumplings."

But things fell apart. TERA foundered on a seemingly harm-less question—whether to invite Susan B. Anthony to speak in Texas. Rebecca Hayes felt the South wasn't ready for a suffragist speaker from the North. Most TERA-ists disagreed. Unity was fractured.

Even so, dumplings were neglected. Tracts circulated. In 1905, a provocative book describing the legal status of women in Texas concludes: "Women may hold any judicial or legislative office in our state. As a member of the legislature she may assist in framing our laws; as judge, she may assist in construing them; and as governor, she may see that they are properly executed. She may not vote."

In 1912, an Austin woman shockingly ran for county super-intendent of schools. Editorial writers whistled: "Heigh ho, here comes a woman candidate. She may be a suffragist, but never a suffragette. Suffragettes are apt to be forty or more, belligerent and homely, and this Travis county lady is a long way from answering to any of these descriptions." She won.

That same year a rich San Antonio woman, Eleanor Brackenridge, hosted a statewide suffrage convention. She was one of the first American women to serve on the board of a bank. She was a member of the Texas Woman's University board of regents and was a founder of the Texas PTA, although she never married and had no children. She and wealthy Annette Finnigan of Houston reclaimed the old TERA thrust.

In 1915, Minnie Fisher Cunningham of Galveston, the first woman in Texas to get a pharmacy degree, rose to leadership in the movement. Able, she was soon called to Washington to serve the national drive for enfranchisement. Within a year, nationally, she quadrupled suffragist forces. Her right arm in Texas was Jane Y. McCallum of Austin.

Mrs. McCallum had a degree in journalism from the University of Texas, five children, and a husband. She patrolled Capitol corridors, lobbying legislators.

A senator told her: "You ought to get married."

"But I am married."

"Then you ought to be having children."

"I have five. How many do you suggest I have?"

"Then you should be home taking care of them."

"They are in school and their grandmother is there."

"Then you should be home darning stockings."

The *Houston Chronicle* fell into line, editorializing: "Where is the pedestal that millions of women and girls now earning their pitiful livelihood by nerve-racking toil are enthroned upon? It doesn't exist for more than half the women and girls. . . . In countless instances they are working under outrageous conditions and at less than a living wage. If this army of women must depend upon the chivalry and the pedestal, God Almighty help them. They need the ballot to achieve economic and social justice."

As other big city papers assumed a similar stance, the suffragists sensed they were on the home stretch.

Historian Winegarten, a lecturer for the Texas Foundation for Women's Resources, is author of *Texas Women: A Pictorial History* (Eakin Press) and *I Am Annie Mae* (Rosegarden Press). She said the history of the women's suffrage campaign in Texas is told in a book, *Citizens at Last*, published by Ellen Temple Publishing of Lufkin and based on the research of Dr. A. Elizabeth Taylor.

The struggle wasn't a straight line to a happy ending. Rapidly, during and after World War I, thousands of Texas women united. Aware of the movement's ties to the temperance union, the liquor lobby, accurately fearing prohibition, opposed female suffrage. Powerful wets like Governor Jim Ferguson (whose impeachment the suffragists supported) and South Texas political boss Jim Wells snipped at petticoat politics. The wife of Wells headed the Texas Association Opposed to Woman Suffrage.

Mrs. Wells' group warned: "Women in suffrage states are serving on juries in murder cases, commercialized vice cases, and whiskey cases. It must be a grand and glorious feeling for a woman to be drawn as juror on a murder case, likely to last two months, when the children of the family have contracted the measles."

Determined, suffragists were deaf to such arguments.

After Ferguson's ouster, Governor William P. Hobby, impressed by the women's collective clout, blessed a bill that passed both houses giving women the vote. He signed it March 26, 1918.

The women had seventeen days to register voters for July primaries. Remarkably, they signed up 386,000 women. Beneficiaries included Hobby and Annie Webb Blanton, the first statewide female candidate, who was running for state school superintendent. They won by immense majorities.

Then victorious Hobby handed the suffragists an odd reversal. He chose to submit the female-vote question to the Texas male electorate as a proposed amendment to the state constitution. It had two provisions. One would allow women to vote. The other would disenfranchise resident aliens. Because it was a special election, women couldn't vote on May 24, 1919. But the aliens could. The amendment failed by 25,000 votes.

Suffragists promptly aimed their total effort to the proposed federal amendment that could enfranchise all U.S. women. Heavily lobbied, both Texas senators and ten of the eighteen Texas congressmen favored the measure.

And so, in June 1919, a month after Texas voters had defeated the state amendment, the Texas Legislature became the first in the south to ratify the federal suffrage amendment. On August 25, 1920, Hobby signed the ratification proclamation.

The following day the 19th Amendment to the U.S. Constitution took effect. It read: "The rights of citizens of the United States to vote shall not be denied or abridged by the United States or by any state on account of sex."

Minnie Fisher Cunningham said, "We went up against and helped to break the most ruthless and powerful machine that had ever fastened its tentacles on Texas."

Jane Y. McCallum said, "We were citizens at last."

✳✳✳

✳ PART II ✳

✳ Texas Outlaws ✳

✻✻✻

Old Texas Laws Gave Death More Often Than Liberty

Slammer jam, that persisting twentieth-century problem of no room at the pen, was eliminated by early Texas lawmakers, who favored a short drop to a long sentence.

They hanged burglars, for example. They even hanged burglars' helpers.

They went after the whole mob:

"Every person who shall be accessory before the fact to any murder, arson, rape, robbery or burglary, on conviction thereof, shall suffer death."

In 1836, Sam Houston, president of the Republic of Texas, signed into law "An Act Punishing Crimes and Misdemeanors."

As a penal code, it was tougher than a cheap fajita—but plenty cheap.

Floggings and brandings did not cost much. And a quick hanging offered a lot of behavioral modification for the few tax bucks expended.

Avoided were tax tabs for roomy cells, meals, clothes and whatever was the nineteenth-century equivalent of TV sets. Indeed, prisoners were often allowed to study nature while chained to trees.

Attorney David B. Brooks, a legal scholar, explained all this to me at the University of Texas Law School library in 1987. Brooks had just written two volumes on *Texas County Government, Special Districts, and Authorities* for the West Publishing Company.

In his research, he came across old Texas laws that would keep the lights burning late at the American Civil Liberties Union.

Speaking of burning, early Texans apparently did not object to convicts walking the streets if they were properly branded. Those convicted of manslaughter, for example, were marked with an *M*. Thieves got a *T*. The judge put the brand wherever it would do the most good.

89

Under the code of the Republic, repeat offenders were assessed doubled fines, penalties and prison terms.

Perjurers got fifty lashes on their bare backs. People who encouraged perjurers got fifty lashes on their bare backs, too.

Counterfeiters were hanged—along with their helpers.

"Living together" was frowned on:

"Every man and woman who shall live together in adultery or fornication shall be deemed guilty of a high misdemeanor and on conviction thereof, shall be fined in any sum not less than one hundred nor more than one thousand dollars, and may be imprisoned for any term not exceeding one year."

So much for trial marriage.

Butchers, bakers, brewers, distillers and others who sold "unwholesome food or drink" were fined any sum that suited the judges' moods. On second conviction, they were similarly fined and then given thirty-nine lashes on their bare backs.

Any jailer who freely allowed a prisoner to escape would "suffer the same punishment and penalties as the prisoner so escaping should have suffered, had he been convicted of the crime."

The statute of limitations for any felony was one year, but that did not apply to anyone "fleeing from justice." The code, in most cases, required a guilty party to repay the Republic for the cost of his trial and to restore the losses of his victim.

A dueling death was deemed a murder by the 1836 act. And any bearer of a challenge to another party could be fined and imprisoned at the discretion of the judge. The Texans had lost too many men to Indians and Mexicans to indulge in the luxury of killing one another.

In 1839, Republic President Mirabeau B. Lamar signed into law an act that not only provided the death penalty for horse thieves but death also for "every person who shall aid or assist in the stealing." Even looking like a horse thief was dangerous.

Texas laws were sometimes tough on horses, too. Dallas County, created in 1846, secured special legislation in 1862 to relieve a local crisis: "It shall be unlawful for any citizen of Dallas County to allow any stallion or jack, over the age of two years to run at large."

Any citizen "who may be annoyed by any such animal shall have the right to take up and in the presence of two or more respectable witnesses, castrate the same"—the animal, presumably, not the respectable witnesses.

Liquor laws were already becoming complicated by 1863, when Dallas won from the legislature a ban on the "sale of intoxicating liquors in the vicinity of the town of Dallas." The law stipulated: "It shall not be lawful to sell any intoxicating liquors, whether alcoholic, malt, distilled, or brewed, within five miles of the town." Offenders could be fined up to $500.

Nobody was fined, however, until the lawmakers passed a supplementary act, pinning down the prohibition of booze sales. "Within five miles of the town of Dallas," the supplementary act states, "shall be so construed as to have effect and force *within the limits* of said town." There will always be a sharp lawyer.

In 1895, Dallas got an act passed that, if enforced, might have long ago solved the problems of homicidal Central Expressway. The act authorized county commissioners to require road labor not only from county convicts, but from private citizens as well. A man was required to work on the roads five days each year, or buy an exemption from the county treasurer for $3.

Some of the old laws sound quaint. From a 1987 perspective, the 1866 law that provided a $10 fine for vagrancy may seem downright dangerous in its definition:

"A vagrant is hereby declared to be an idle person."

Don't let the boss see that one.

✳✳✳

PICTURING THE BAD GUYS

Listen to this description of Ike Cravey, who was accused of murder in San Saba County nearly a century ago. You'd know him anywhere.

"Age thirty-seven years; height six feet two inches; weight 180 pounds; color white; complexion dark or sallow; eyes blue; hair brown; occupation farmer and stockman, $300 reward by

Governor. Large hawk-bill nose, upper front teeth out, short chin, catfish mouth, very bearded, light mustache, wears No. 10 shoe."

Whether Cravey was ever caught I can't say. He may have hightailed it for the Indian Territory or Mexico. But Cravey was surely captured on paper—and in few words.

The sketching of a desperate character in a paragraph with quick pen strokes is an art form that flourished in the days before mug shots and fingerprints became common.

An 1891 example from Denton County:

"Gidcumb, J. T.—Murder and arson. Age thirty years: height five feet seven inches; weight 135 or 140 pounds; color white, hair sandy. Thin lips; has sore eyes; wears goggles all the time; freckled face; red mustache; slender built."

And from Bexar County that year:

"Fitts or Fritts, Joe—Assault to kill and murder. Height five feet ten inches; weight 170 pounds; color white; complexion light or red face; hair light brown; occupation scalper in railroad tickets; wore light sandy mustache but blacked it; round and heavy through the shoulders; when walking leans head well forward; has folks living in Montague County; was in company with a variety woman; was in trouble with some woman at Fort Worth in 1889; he formerly kept hotel at Bonham, Texas."

Without a photo or fingerprints and on the strength of these descriptions alone, I'll bet you I could have spotted sore-eyed J. T. or headlong, womanizing Joe if either had showed up on our turf.

During the last quarter of the last century, a Texas Ranger carried in his saddlebags a seldom-mentioned weapon against rampant outlawry—a book.

Variously called *The Crime Book* or *The Book of Knaves*, the volume was officially titled *A List of Fugitives From Justice*. It was irreverently nicknamed the *Rangers' Bible*. The book was compiled from sheriffs' reports sent to the office of the state adjutant general, who commanded the Rangers back then.

Surprisingly, given that some rural sheriffs were only semi-literate, like many of the voters who elected them, the best word sketches are almost artistically vivid. But the *List* had other aims.

When Rangers could get away with it, they used the *List* in lieu of an arrest warrant. Commonly, a name's appearance in the book was sufficient to land its owner in jail or worse. Any good lawyer, of course, could defeat shenanigans like this.

The *List,* published in Austin, probably appeared as early as 1875 or 1876, but the oldest copy I've seen is an 1878 edition at the University of Texas at Austin's Barker History Center. The Barker has several later editions of the sometimes annual publication.

Colorful characters populate the books. Consider this 1900 entry from Bosque County:

"Conway, T. J.—Embezzlement. Age thirty-five, height five feet eleven inches, weight 170 pounds, color white, complexion light, eyes blue, hair dark, occupation Baptist preacher. Reward $50 by sheriff. He has brother in Navarro County and one in Stephens. This preacher is large boned, little stooped shouldered; generally wears a light mustache; wears long preacher coat. If he is not preaching now, he is more than liable to take part in singing in Baptist churches. He goes backward and forward from Territory to Texas."

Or, from Castro County:

"Evans, Walter, alias Big Foot Bill or Wild Bill—Theft of cattle. Age twenty-one or twenty-two years, height five feet eleven inches, weight 165 pounds, complexion dark, eyes dark. Very plain cowlick on forehead; very long hands, and large, long feet; sometimes hair very long; no beard; herded sheep on Handy ranch in Gaines County on Sulphur Draw; is not a cowboy, but works on cow ranches at times. Reward $100 by sheriff."

Or, from Galveston County:

"Johnson, Harry, alias Texas Harry—Theft. Age twenty-seven years, height five feet six or seven inches, weight 140 pounds, color white, complexion fair, eyes blue, hair light. Eats glass; sticks pins in his person; found around dives and variety shows."

The 1900 edition is the final *List of Fugitives* published, I'm pretty sure. Earlier this year, a Texas rare book dealer offered one for $400. They're scarce. Anyhow, by 1900, sketch-writing was in full flower.

In contrast, sheriffs in the earliest edition of the *List* didn't try to round out fully a subject's persona. Entries in the 1878 *List*, for example, are often merely a name with a criminal charge logged beside it. Occasionally, the entry is embellished with a personality quirk—"likes to stay drunk" or "fond of lewd women" or "has a whiny voice."

Sketch-writing ambitiously improved with each new edition. Here's an 1887 entry from Angelina County, an oddity, a murderous medico:

"Windham, John D.—Murder in two cases. Age about seventy-two years; height about five feet one inch; blue eyes; gray hair; small features; very much accomplished; is an M.D. When last heard of was in Callahan County, Texas, practicing medicine."

Speaking of doctors, nearly everyone seemed to have anatomical glitches in those days. The number of subjects with bullet holes in them, growths, wens, smallpox scars, running sores, or missing fingers and "extra fingers" is alarming. Who would need a mug shot or fingerprints to identify a character like this one from Tarrant County?

"Pierce, Frank—Murder. Age thirty-two years, height five feet eight inches, weight 150 pounds, color white, complexion light, eyes blue, hair light, occupation carpenter and machinist. Cross-eyed, left arm off above the elbow; talks fast. Reward $200 by state."

Many years ago, former Ranger George Durham spoke of using a *Book of Knaves* in the middle 1870s that contained the names of 5100 outlaws. That sounds like a bunch in a state with fewer than a million people, but not all these folks were desperadoes.

One could enter the *List* by stealing a hog or committing adultery. "Seduction" was a common complaint. A sheriff writing for the *List* could be selective or arbitrary in marginal cases. And, depending on his mood, he might note that a subject was "very ugly" or "thinks he's tough" or "a Democrat."

In the parlance of the pollsters, one's negatives in the community must have had a lot to do with it. Still, 5100 is an army of fugitives.

Ranger Durham was the last survivor of Captain L. H. McNelly's so-called "death squad," a special force of Rangers with a reputation for killing outlaws. (Footnote: Tubercular McNelly, who had fought bravely for the state of Texas, was apparently dropped from the Rangers because of his medical bills. A cost-conscious adjutant general may have saved a few bucks. Durham reported that when McNelly died in 1877 he weighed less than 60 pounds. The ex-Ranger captain was thirty-three.)

An ex-Ranger gone bad and several ex-sheriffs are memorialized in the *List*. Sheriffs liked to run off with their county's tax receipts.

Few women are present—an occasional murderess or bigamist. Mexican-Americans with a fondness for other people's beef made the books. Black characters owned memorable monikers like "Stingaree" or "Banjo Bill."

Rewards for wanted men ranged all over the cowlot. A murderer might not be worth a penny. Or he might be worth $1000, a year's earnings for many a poor boy. Five bucks was offered for a young boy who had voted illegally in Somervell County. Whether he voted against the sheriff isn't mentioned.

In 1878, Dallas County was offering $200 for a murder suspect named Dudley Buchanan. But a citizen named A. W. Perry, perhaps a well-heeled relative of the victim, was sweetening the offer with an additional $500.

That same year, Hood County was offering $500 each for William Mitchell and Milt Graves, accused of several killings in a family feud. They got away.

But in the 1900 *List*, William Mitchell shows up again, wanted for a murder in Shelby County also. Mitchell eventually rated a book all his own. Historian C. L. Sonnichsen's *Outlaw: Bill Mitchell, Alias Baldy Russell*. (See article on page 105)

Mitchell was caught but escaped from prison forever, and Milt Graves was never caught.

By 1900, the end of the art form was near. In that edition of *A List of Fugitives From Justice* is this entry from Tarrant County:

"Ellis, Charles, alias W. L. Burres—Murder and train robbery, seven cases. Age 26 years, height five feet eight or nine inches, weight 160 pounds, color white, complexion light, eyes light blue, hair light brown. Reward $575 by State, Santa Fe and Wells Fargo Express Co.; hair is inclined to be curly and is worn tolerably long; he is quick spoken and in actions; nervous temperament, carriage erect."

The sheriff added:

"Photograph on application."

***

ON THE TRAIL OF THE TRUE TALE OF A GUNFIGHTER

One of Texas' most colorful and mysterious gunfighters, King Fisher, was shot to death 100 years ago. A riddled puzzle, he is buried with a lot of unanswered questions in Uvalde's Pioneer Cemetery.

Much of what little is known about Fisher is erroneous. Even the birth date on his tombstone is incorrect. The stone itself also seems wrong. Its newly polished surface is obviously not a century old. Wrong too is the grave, moved to the present site in the 1950s.

The usually reliable *Handbook of Texas History*, published by the Texas State Historical Association, is all wet about Fisher. He was born in Collin County in 1854. The handbook gives his location of birth as Kentucky.

On a plaque placed at the Uvalde cemetery in 1973, the Texas Historical Commission attempted a fair precis:

"Celebrated outlaw who became a peace officer. Once undisputed ruler of a 5000-square-mile area of Southwest Texas, centered in Eagle Pass and known as *King Fisher's Territory*. . . .

"A complex and forceful individual, he imposed order in a lawless border area. His henchmen rustled cattle and terrorized resisting settlers but also protected them from outside intruders. Near his ranch was a sign reading: 'This is King Fisher's Road. Take the other.' Many prominent men, including Porfirio Diaz, president of Mexico, counted him a friend. . . .

"Devoted to his wife and daughters, he reformed after being arrested in 1876 by Ranger Captain L. H. McNelly. He was acting Uvalde County sheriff when, on March 11, 1884, he and the notorious Ben Thompson were killed from ambush at a vaudeville theater in San Antonio."

Retired U.S. Representative O. C. Fisher of Junction is a second cousin of King Fisher. The sixteen-term congressman wrote a book: *King Fisher: His Life and Times* (University of Oklahoma Press). Speaking of his relative's arrest, O. C. Fisher said, "King wore two of the fanciest pistols the Texas Rangers had ever seen. Gold streaks showed on the grips, and the hammers and barrels shined like glass."

In the congressman's book is a description of the gunman by Ranger George Durham:

"Fisher was . . . the most perfect specimen of a frontier dandy and desperado I ever met. He was tall, beautifully handsome. He wore the finest clothing procurable, but all of the picturesque, border, dime-novel kind. His broad-brimmed white Mexican sombrero was profusely ornamented with gold and silver lace and had a golden snake for a band. His fine buckskin Mexican short jacket was heavily embroidered with gold. His shirt was of the finest and thinnest linen and open at the throat, with a silk handkerchief knotted loosely about the wide collar. A brilliant crimson sash was wound about his waist, and his legs were hidden by a wonderful pair of chaparejos, or chaps as cowboys called them. . . ."

Fisher, the lawmaker, said of Fisher, the lawbreaker: "He lived on the border at a time when people more or less made their own laws."

King Fisher's biographer further believes that the gunfighter had a religious experience that changed his life. The reformed Fisher won the respect of the citizens of Uvalde County in his last years.

"Had he lived a few more months, King, who was acting sheriff, certainly would have been elected sheriff of Uvalde County," O. C. Fisher said. "Personally, I think the man was sincere."

King Fisher's road to crime had an early start. As a teenager, he was convicted of a burglary in Goliad and sentenced to the state prison in Huntsville. He was pardoned after four months.

O. C. Fisher found the records of King's arrival at the prison: "Age sixteen; height, five nine; weight, 135; complexion, fair; hair, brown; education, not given; occupation, laborer."

A sort of apologist for his second cousin, O. C. Fisher admits, "King may have taken some liberties with livestock."

But the former congressman is probably correct in theorizing that King died because he happened to be in the company of Ben Thompson.

Gambler Thompson, a former Austin marshal, was, by all accounts, drinking heavily when he ran into Deputy Sheriff Fisher, who was in Austin on Uvalde County business. When King prepared to return home, Thompson decided to accompany him as far as San Antonio. After the train ride from Austin, the hell-raising Thompson made a fatal blunder. With Fisher in tow, Thompson headed for the Vaudeville Theater and Gambling Hall, whose proprietor Thompson had shot to death two years earlier. The dead man's friends were waiting for Thompson. They blasted Thompson. The hail of bullets got Fisher, too.

Uvalde writer Eva Sanderlin said a crowd of thousands quickly gathered outside the gambling hall. The killings made headlines across the nation.

O. C. Fisher said, "They said it was the biggest funeral Uvalde ever saw."

✳✳✳

WHO WERE THE REDHEADED WARRIORS?

A puzzling figure in Texas frontier chronicles is the red-headed stranger who fought on the side of Comanches and Kiowas against the settlers.

In various decades of the nineteenth century, he was often sighted in battles. Ample evidence exists that more than one redhead sided with the tribesmen.

The mystery of the elusive red-haired warriors is more than a century old, but Doyle Marshall, a silver-haired writer, is tracking them down.

For more than a dozen years, Mr. Marshall researched hair-raising frontier stories for his new book, *A Cry Unheard*, focusing on troubles in Parker and Palo Pinto counties.

"Historians have been perplexed by the red-haired men," he said. "Settlers wondered whether they'd encountered a captive white who'd grown up with a tribe or a renegade after plunder."

He can cite examples of both. But no sympathetic *Dances With Wolves* scenario finds its way into his speculations. Talk turned to the mysterious redheads when I stopped by his farm near Aledo in Parker County in 1992. He writes there when he's not at his desk in the Fort Worth office of the U. S. General Services Administration.

"Plains Indians sometimes communicated with Anglo criminals who advised them on lucrative opportunities, troop positions and risks," he said. "Many frontiersmen believed that outlaw whites were inciting raids. They could plunder and shift the blame to Indians.

"In June 1859, the Texas governor's peace commission reported that Indians were aided by a band of white men operating from Kansas to the Rio Grande."

For example, in 1857 a small band of Indians, in company with a red-haired man, raided a cabin in Erath County, killing a man but sparing his wife and daughter.

Citing a notorious case of the era, Mr. Marshall described how in 1858, under the direction of a red-haired man, Indians and three or four other white men pillaged the homes of the Mason and Cambern families in Jack County's Lost Valley. They killed four adults and three children. Young Thomas Cambern was forced on a horse behind the English-speaking red-haired man. Travelers on the Marcy-California Trail observed the raiders and chased them. To lighten his load, the red-haired man shoved the captive from the horse. The travelers rescued the boy.

Details are sketchy, but in 1905, half a century after the Mason-Cambern massacre, a Texan named H. G. Bedford identified the red-haired marauder as "Bill Willis," who was lynched near Austin a few years after the murders when vigilantes concluded that he'd been driving stolen cattle into Mexico.

But the red-haired raider may have been "John Garner," who was lynched in McLennan County by Texas Ranger Buck Barry and a vigilance committee. The man was hanged after he was implicated in the killing of two Jack County families. Yet another suspect was named by rancher Charles Goodnight, who met in New Mexico a "Dutchman" called "Tecalot" (Owl) who fit the description of the red-haired man in the Jack County attack. The Owl's fate is unrecorded.

In his later years, W. K. Baylor, son of an Indian agent, recalled a red-haired man and associates who caused trouble about 1859 on the old Comanche reservation in Shackelford-Throckmorton counties. He blamed them for the murders of a couple of settlers.

Riders with Indian agent R. S. Neighbors were attacked in 1859 near the Red River by an Indian war party. After fighting off the attackers, a member of the Neighbors party noticed that the Indian he'd killed had short hair. When the dead man's war paint was washed off, he proved to be a red-haired white man.

Another red-haired raider was still at large. During the last four painful days of her life in 1860, Martha Sherman, who'd been assaulted and scalped, spoke repeatedly of her attacker as "that big old redheaded Indian."

In 1864, a red-haired adviser was spotted among the several hundred Kiowas and Comanches in the bloody Elm Creek raid in Young County near old Fort Belknap. And, in the spring of 1866, three captive white children found a red-haired man named "George" living with the Comanches. Mr. Marshall conjectures that "George" led a lethal Comanche raid on the Warlene Valley School in Hamilton County in July 1867. A boy taken captive there said later that the red-haired leader had given him food.

Cavalry Captain R. G. Carter believed that a white man killed by troopers in an 1872 Indian fight was Thomas F. M. McLean, a U. S. Military Academy reject.

Because of his unruly shock of red hair and ungainly manner, Cadet McLean, appointed to West Point in 1844, was nicknamed "Bison" or "Bise," Captain Carter reported.

Dismissed from the academy for undesirable conduct, he drifted west and into trouble with the law.

Mr. Marshall said: "Perhaps he reasoned that life as a desperado in a civilized society was too hazardous. He fell in with and became a leader in a band of Comanches."

Captain Carter learned of Bise McLean from General John P. Hatch, who had known him at the academy. The general recalled spotting Bise at Fredericksburg in Gillespie County after a raid on the town by a war party in 1867. But Bise vanished at the approach of his former classmate.

The story of Bise McLean was pieced together after Colonel Ranald Mackenzie's Fourth Cavalry troops fought a band of Kotsoteka Comanches led by Mow-wi (Mow-way or Shaking Hand) on September 29, 1872, on the North Fork of the Red River. The body of a white man with bushy red hair, a dead ringer for Bise McLean, was found on the battlefield.

One night in 1870, Texas Ranger Captain J. B. Earhart shot one of several Indian horse-raiders at his ranch sixteen miles east of Jacksboro on the Butterfield Stage Line. Dawn revealed a red-haired, blue-eyed Anglo of middle age, who in all other respects appeared to be an Indian.

Mr. Marshall's list of red-haired warriors goes on. And he's hoping to find more, although his book's in print and already scarce. He said, "It seems odd that so many red-haired whites were seen with the Plains Indians during the period 1858 to 1875. Perhaps the Indians had an affinity for red hair. Red-haired girl captives seem to have been favored. And red-haired boy captives Herman Lehmann, Rudolph Fischer and Tehan ('Texan,' a white kid who chose life as a Kiowa) were greatly loved by their captors."

LET THE RECORD SHOW JANE WAS HANGED FIRST

Generations of Texans have grown up believing that Chipita Rodriguez, a convicted killer who was launched into legend from a South Texas tree limb on November 13, 1863, was the only woman legally hanged in Texas. No way, Jose.

A decade before Chipita was executed in San Patricio County, a woman was legally hanged in Dallas County. The murderer convicted by Dallas County jurors was a slave named Jane, sometimes called Jane Elkins. Today she is a dim, distant figure. But that she hanged is a fact.

Texas history books often give Chipita a solitary distinction she didn't want or deserve. For example, in 1970, Vernon Smylie of Corpus Christi wrote *A Noose for Chipita*. The book's cover proclaims: "The strange case of the only woman ever legally hanged in Texas." An entry on Chipita in the *Handbook of Texas*, compiled by the Texas State Historical Association, begins: "Chipita Rodriguez was the only woman ever legally hanged in Texas. Chipita (possibly a misspelling of Chepita, a diminutive of Chepa, nickname for Josefa) lived in a hut at a way station for travelers on the Welder ranch lands on the Aransas River on a trail that led from adjoining Refugio County down to the Rio Grande and Mexico. San Patricio County records show that in August, 1863, she along with Juan Silvera (Juan 'Chiquito') was accused of the murder of an unknown man whose body was found in the Aransas River near Chipita's cabin. Later accounts call the man John Savage, a horse trader on his way to Mexico carrying gold. . . . "

The *Handbook*, a reference bible for Texas historians, is now being revised and enlarged for the 1990s by historical association researchers and editors under the direction of Ron Tyler, an able historian. Tyler, in the new edition, should accord Dallas County its long overdue recognition as a community of woman hangers. Incidentally, Texas hasn't claimed a woman's life since the state began performing all executions at Huntsville in 1924. Unofficially, some may count Bonnie Parker, executed in Louisiana.

Through the years, Jane has been ignored while Chipita has captured much attention in newspapers, magazines and books. Chipita's hanging inspired a piece in *Old West* magazine head-lined "The Curse That Killed San Patricio Town." Something cursed that town. Once an important commercial center and county seat, it's a dot on today's map. Sinton is now the county seat.

Chipita's ghost haunts the Nueces River banks where the hanging tree stood. Or so wrote Marylyn Underwood in a popu-lar 1981 book, *Legendary Ladies of Texas*. One cannot blame Chipita—who denied the murder charge—for being restless. If she didn't get a bum rap, she got a bum trial. The whole case was circumstantial. Moreover, the sheriff who arrested her served as foreman of the grand jury that indicted her. Apparently, three of the grand jurors served on the trial jury. Four members of the grand jury and trial jury had faced felony indictments shortly before dealing with Chipita. Apparently, six of the grand jurors were employed by the county or had lawsuits pending before the trial judge. And the prosecutor had been under two indictments that were dropped before Chipita's trial.

At least it was swift. Two days after the fall term of court began in 1863, Chipita was indicted. Two days after that, she was convicted. The following day she was sentenced to die thirty-four days later, a Friday the 13th. Chipita's attorney withdrew a motion for a new trial. And the judge ignored the jury's recom-mendation of mercy. The recommendation stemmed from her advanced years. Her exact age isn't known. Juan Silvera, who was fifty, was convicted of second-degree murder and sentenced to five years in prison.

Although universally forgotten outside Dallas, Jane's case is familiar to some local history buffs and courthouse staffers. For example, Sheriff's Detective June Gunn, Deputy Nancy Stout, retired Deputy O'Byrne Cox and Donald Payton of the Dallas County Historical Society told me what they knew about Jane's case.

The staff at the Texas/Dallas History and Archives Division of Dallas' J. Erik Jonsson Library informed me further that librarian Gary Jennings had produced a volume of district court records which preserves the tragic case of the "State of Texas vs Jane, a Slave."

Dated May 16, 1853 is this report: "We the jury find the defendant guilty of murder in the first degree. We further find that the defendant is a slave of the value of seven hundred dollars and that the owner of the defendant has done nothing to evade or defeat the execution of the law upon said defendant. (signed) D. R. Cameron, foreman."

And on May 17 the entry reads: " . . . And it being demanded of said Jane if she had anything to say why judgment and sentence of death should not there be passed upon her and the said Jane saying nothing thereto: It is therefore ordered adjudged and decreed by the court that the sheriff of Dallas County keep the said Jane in close confinement in the common jail of Dallas County until Friday the 27th of the present month of May, and that . . . between the hours of eleven o'clock A.M. and three o'clock P.M. the sheriff . . . take said Jane from the common jail of said county and convey her to a gallows erected for that purpose and there . . . hang the said Jane by the neck until she is dead. . . . "

Furthermore, in the 1992 publication, *WPA Dallas Guide and History*—written by the Texas Writers' Project of the Works Projects Administration—is this paragraph:

"It was in 1853 that the first legal execution took place in the county. This was the hanging of Jane Elkins, a slave who had murdered a man named Wisdom at Farmers Branch. After a trial before Judge John H. Reagan, most notable jurist of his time, the woman was hanged May 27, 1853."

And in an 1892 publication, *Memorial and Biographical History of Dallas County, Texas*, W. P. Overton, seventy-one, who'd come to Dallas County in 1844, was quoted:

"The first legal hanging was in 1853 or 1854. A negress was executed for knocking a man in the head with an ax at Cedar Springs. He had hired her and she murdered him while he was asleep. I can't recall their names."

Overton's fuzzy memory can be forgiven. Nearly everyone forgets Jane.

✳✳✳

WRITER TURNED DETECTIVE TO TRACE BLOODY FEUD

People on all sides of the nuclear energy quarrel may suspect that a curse hangs over Comanche Peak, the Hood County landmark that gave its name to a sometimes luckless nuclear power plant across the line in Somervell County. Cooney Mitchell's ghost would never dispute that notion.

Old Cooney and his son Bill were hunting cows near Comanche Peak 120 years ago when they stumbled upon the migrating family of Perminter Truitt. Tradition says the Truitts were hungry and that Cooney and Bill took them home to Mitchell's Bend on the Brazos. The meeting of the two families set the stage for a bloody feud, an enduring fight that within months would put the elder Mitchell's neck in a hangman's noose and would put the lifelong brand of outlaw on his son.

On a visit to Texas Christian University, late historian C. L. Sonnichsen talked of the Mitchell-Truitt conflict. A specialist on Texas feuds, Sonnichsen wrote about the Mitchells and Truitts in his book *Ten Texas Feuds*. He told how the neighbors fell out over a strip of land claimed by both. The matter landed in court in Granbury, the seat of Hood County. The Truitts won.

Hood County historian T. T. Ewell wrote before the turn of the century: "The lawless spirit of these times finally culminated in the killing of Sam and Ike Truitt and serious wounding of James Truitt in March 1874." The brothers were shot about seven miles south of Granbury as the Truitts rode home from the trial. The Mitchells were quickly blamed. Nelson "Cooney" Mitchell was convicted and sentenced to death. Bill Mitchell got away.

While Cooney Mitchell awaited execution, his guards shot and killed Cooney's youngest son, Jeff, as the boy was creeping in darkness toward the Hood County Jail. Sonnichsen revealed that Jeff was carrying a vial of laudanum that would have given the elder Mitchell an option to the indignity of the noose.

In a gallows speech, Cooney Mitchell called on Bill Mitchell—wherever he was—"to hunt down his father's murderers." A crowd of about 5,000 gathered for what would be Hood County's first and last legal hanging. The old man spotted Jim Truitt, who'd been a key witness against him. Truitt had recovered from his wounds to become a Methodist minister. Cooney Mitchell called out to the Reverend Truitt: "When you wanted to go to preaching, didn't I buy you the first suit of clothes you ever had? Didn't I buy you a Bible—a good Bible—to start you out?"

Bill Mitchell remained at large. Nearly a dozen years passed. Jim Truitt, who'd preached in several pulpits, had settled in Shelby County, where he began publishing the *Timpson Times*. On the evening of July 20, 1886, the pastor sat at home with his Bible in his lap. His wife was across the room, reading a new copy of the *Times*. Their little daughter played with her dolls. Suddenly, without knocking, a stranger walked into the room. "Is this Reverend James Truitt?"

"Yes, sir," answered Mrs. Truitt. "What is your business with him?"

The stranger quickly revealed his business. He drew a sixgun and shot the preacher in the head. Just as cool as a julep, he walked outside, mounted a claybank horse and rode unhurriedly out of town. The widow Truitt was screaming like a panther.

To find the killer, Shelby County officials called on Sheriff A. J. Spradley, a keen manhunter from neighboring Nacogdoches County. Spradley scored. From a witness who'd seen the stranger, Spradley learned that the killer carried dangling on a string from his saddle a small coffee pot. That not only suggested to Spradley that the gunman had traveled a distance, but it was as useful as a license tag on the claybank horse. The lawman trailed the killer across Texas, ever westward.

To make a long and fascinating hunt short and dull, Spradley's detective work identified the murderer. Eventually—in 1907—Spradley's work led to the arrest in New Mexico of Bill Mitchell, who hardly ever used that name except on formal occasions when he was on trial. He was indicted in Hood County for killing the Truitt boys and then taken to East Texas to answer for the murder in Timpson. For the next five years, he was a familiar figure in Texas courtrooms. He beat the Hood County case. But after hung juries and changes of venue, he finally was convicted in Cherokee County of killing the preacher in Shelby County. On March 16, 1912, the Texas Court of Criminal Appeals upheld his life sentence. So, almost forty years after the first blood was shed, Bill Mitchell went to prison. He was sixty-four. After serving a little more than two years, he escaped.

Sonnichsen left things at that point in *Ten Texas Feuds*. When the book appeared, relatives from both sides of the feud sought out Sonnichsen to expand on the story. Once again, Sonnichsen was smitten by the tale. He did some detective work that Sheriff Spradley might have envied, and the result was another book.

In *Outlaw*, Sonnichsen traced Bill Mitchell through nearly half a century outside the law—all because of five minutes of red hatred in 1874. The author trailed the outlaw to his death from a heart attack in 1928—something no lawman had been able to do. Sonnichsen said, "A romantic may be distressed to learn that Baldy Russell (or whatever name Bill Mitchell happened to be using) was an illiterate, egg-bald outlaw who took a wife and three children with him on the dodge—a cranky old man of sixty-one years when he was sent to prison; sixty-three when he escaped and went back into the shadows."

An elderly outlaw is hard to imagine. But an elderly outlaw is just what Baldy Russell turned into.

✳✳✳

BESSIE'S DEATH IN 1877 STILL CAUSES DEBATE

Gems flashing as she sashayed out of the Brooks Hotel on Vale Street 111 winters ago, Diamond Bessie was dressed fit to kill.

And that's exactly what happened.

When they found her in the woods south of town on February 5, 1877, she was wearing kid shoes, silk stockings with a blue flower design, one white and one blue garter, a chemise of linen, a plain white underskirt, a flannel petticoat, a black silk shirt, a gray skirt of waterproof material, a woolen basque and polonaise, a heavy black cloak and lap-over braid for the buttons, a collar, a purple necktie and a black velvet hat cunningly tilted over the bullet hole in the side of her head.

Stripping the corpse for the coroner, women were puzzled by a personal article they found on Bessie. "I do not know what it is and can't name it," swore one. Neither could others. Officially, it was recorded as a "nondescript." Bessie's garters have been missing ever since that inventory. Moreover, her unforgettable diamonds were gone.

But the most urgent mystery—then and now—is: Who killed her?

The facts are as murky as Big Cypress Bayou. Tradition assigns guilt to Abe Rothschild—Bessie's companion or husband or pimp. Abe is consistently convicted by popular opinion in Marion County.

"A bum rap," says James W. Byrd, who claims Abe didn't kill her. A professor of English at East Texas State University, Dr. Byrd was drawn to the case decades ago through his passion for folklore. Diamond Bessie is enthroned by folklorists as the tragic queen of the swamps.

Tourists can see Bessie's grave in Oakwood Cemetery, where Dr. Byrd leaves red roses. "I know she appreciates a gentleman caller," as Tennessee Williams would say.

Dr. Byrd gives a bare-bones account of the killing:

"Abe and his designated bride registered at the hotel as 'A. Monroe and wife' on January 18, 1877. At the end of three days, the couple supposedly went on an unusual midwinter picnic in the woods. And two weeks later, a woman gathering firewood found the body, shot through the head.

"Murder wasn't rare in Jefferson, a wide-open town with gambling, saloons, cockfights and racetracks, but this one shocked the city and rocked the state. Abe was tracked down and tried for murder—three times."

The first trial in Jefferson resulted in a hung jury. When venue was changed to Harrison County, Rothschild was not only sentenced to death but—get this—he was ordered to pay the cost of his prosecution.

Reversed on appeal, the case played a return engagement in Jefferson where Abe's third murder jury walked him. Or ran him, as it were. Jurors delayed their verdict, legend holds, until a northbound train approaching Jefferson blew its whistle. Call it swift justice. Abe leaped into a waiting carriage and hurried to the depot.

The stratagem supposedly let Abe escape an angry mob with a whole skin. Still, he'd had seven years of confinement in various jails, an impressive amount of hard time by today's standards.

Citing legend, Dr. Byrd says, "Jefferson people affirm that $1000 bills were handed down through a trap door in the ceiling of the jury room and that a grand piano was shortly seen at the residence of each juror."

Jim Byrd feels obliged to defend maligned Abe.

"The only seemingly guilty thing Abe Rothschild did was flee to his hometown, Cincinnati, and drunkenly shoot out his own eye."

Complaining of misconceptions that persist, Dr. Byrd says, "Abe was no more a member of the family of banker Rothschilds than I'm a rich Virginia Byrd. That the final Jefferson jury was bribed is the most flimsy folklore. Jurors knew he was innocent of murder—even though he was a Yankee Jew, a gambling dude and a cocky whoremonger.

"In the folk play presented annually as part of a historical pilgrimage to Jefferson's antebellum homes, a maid tells of a night of drunken 'wife' abuse on the eve of Abe and Bessie's winter picnic. But for the picnic they wore smiles and diamonds. The maid also said that Abe wore two of Bessie's diamond rings when he returned from the picnic alone. That would have been stupid of him. But his photo shows fingers too big for women's rings.

"Besides, he could have taken those diamonds from this drunken whore anytime he wished, wife or not. The Italian bartender agrees with the maid about the diamond rings. But how many bars do you suppose there were in Jefferson? And what are the chances that Abe would go back and show the rings to the same bartender?

"A prostitute in the play testifies—as one actually did (Isabella Gouldy)—that she saw Bessie with another man 'the next Thursday' after Abe left. Logically, the witness had been checking out the competition. She saw Bessie pin her garter on that afternoon at 5 o'clock and she saw the pinned garter on the dead body at the funeral home that night. The calm prostitute is more convincing than the hysterical maid.

"The testimony of the coroner, refuting expert testimony, saved Abe's neck. The coroner, a justice of the peace who functioned as coroner, testified that the body could not have lain in the woods well-preserved for two weeks. He mentioned the strange fact that not even the scraps of the picnic lunch had been disturbed by animals.

"*The Texas Bar Journal*, no less, reveals that Bessie had become a man's mistress at fifteen, and later a prostitute. It reveals that Abe put her on the street and he took her money in Cincinnati—even during the Republican convention. Abe is recorded as treating Bessie as pimps do on *Miami Vice* each week and in Dallas every night.

"Two newspaper accounts mention the marriage of Abe and Bessie, but no proof has been found. It is doubtful that a marriage took place, but it doesn't matter. Married pimps who put their wives on the street are as numerous as cheating evangelists. Alas, my longtime and distinguished upperclass friend, the late lawyer and author Traylor Russell (*The Diamond Bessie Murder and the Rothschild Trials*, Texian Press, 1971), who knew the court record, couldn't conceive of that contemporary and age-old fact. Russell thought Abe guilty.

"But Abe was considered guilty mainly because of prejudice. He was a Yankee Jew and had money for expensive lawyers. He gladly left Bessie behind in Jefferson. She had a way of making a living in a town where sporting men found saloons, gambling halls and, just across a bridge, beautiful woods available for an inexpensive poke. After Abe was gone a week, any one of two dozen Johns [customers] could have killed her and left by boat or train."

Don't expect Dr. Byrd's defense of Abe Rothschild to change things. Even a fellow ETSU English professor, Fred Tarpley—author of *Jefferson: Riverport to the Southwest*—disputes Dr. Byrd's verdict.

"There's no question about it. Abe murdered Bessie," Dr. Tarpley says, proving that English professors are exactly like psychiatrists. You can find one to testify on either side of a murder case.

✳✳✳

OUTLAW'S CAPTURE WAS AN INSIDE JOB

Among the hair-triggered characters who lived or sojourned in Dallas and Fort Worth in frontier days were Belle Starr (née Myra Maybelle Shirley), the Younger brothers, Long-hair Jim Courtright, Luke Short, Doc Holliday and Frank James, Jesse's brother. And Jack Duncan.

Jack Who? That was my reaction until Killeen lawyer Rick Miller gave me a history lesson.

John Riley "Jack" Duncan was the bounty hunter who tracked down the deadliest gunfighter of them all, John Wesley Hardin. Famous in his day, Duncan is now forgotten. He occupies an unmarked grave in Dallas' Greenwood Cemetery.

Better remembered is Jack's older brother, Simeon Duncan, facetiously known as "the Commodore" for his grandiose plan a century ago to convert the snag-studded Trinity River into a canal for barge and boat traffic between Dallas and Galveston Bay.

Bounty Hunter, Rick Miller's biography of Jack Duncan, may rescue the old-time sleuth from obscurity.

Duncan at various times worked as a Dallas policeman and as a private detective. Motivated by rewards offered for outlaws, he acquired a reputation as a relentless manhunter.

In 1877, Texas Ranger Captain Lee Hall quietly called on Duncan in Dallas. The upshot was Duncan's resignation from the Dallas Police Department and enlistment as a Ranger private. Hall needed a fearless, perhaps bullet-proof, undercover agent to track down Hardin, the notorious gunman who had fled the state to parts unknown.

Among dozens of killings, Hardin was accused of slaying Brown County Deputy Sheriff Charles Webb in Comanche. When Jack Duncan finished his assignment, the Comanche shooting would eventually cost Hardin a twenty-five-year prison sentence. But that's getting ahead of the story. Hall had no problem recruiting Duncan, who was then earning about $600 a year. Duncan found irresistible the reward offered for Hardin—$4000.

Gonzales County was a likely place to strike Hardin's trail, the lawmen reckoned. Hardin's role in behalf of the Taylor faction in the bloody Sutton-Taylor feud in Gonzales and DeWitt counties in 1873-74 had figuratively put several notches on his six-gun. And the outlaw had in-laws there.

"It was planned that Duncan, in disguise, would approach and become friendly with relatives of Hardin and his wife. The officers reasoned that someone in Gonzales County was bound to be in contact with the fugitive killer," said Miller. He quoted an adjutant general's report describing a "strong band of thieves and murderers, headed by John Hardin," that had terrorized Gonzales County.

Veteran Ranger John B. Armstrong had volunteered to help bring in Hardin, but Armstrong was well known as a Ranger. Duncan's mission was kept secret. Armstrong and Hall knew any slip would alert Hardin's friends and forfeit the life of their man in Gonzales County.

Miller relates how Duncan, adopting the name of "Williams," entered Gonzales County, where he won acceptance as a laborer on several farm jobs. "He began cultivating the friendship of a number of people in the area, including Neal Bowen, Hardin's father-in-law. Duncan passed himself off as sympathetic to the Taylor faction and as having experienced some trouble with the law himself. Bowen operated a small grocery, and Duncan patiently built a relationship with the older man, visiting him on a regular basis. Within a very short time, Neal Bowen took him into his house as a boarder."

Possibly, suggested Miller, "Williams" cinched his position among Hardin supporters with such statements as: "I wish he (Hardin) would kill all of Comanche and I'd help him do it."

At this point, the game centered on the question of who would make the first mistake. Luckily for Duncan, it was Neal Bowen. During a round of drinking in Cuero in neighboring DeWitt County, Duncan tricked Bowen into writing a letter to his son-in-law, Hardin. With the help of a trusting postmaster, Duncan later examined the letter. It was addressed to "Mr. J. H. Swain, Pollard, Alabama." Scanning the contents, Duncan knew he'd found Wes Hardin.

Duncan wired a cryptic message to Ranger Lt. Armstrong: "Come get your horse." Several Rangers soon rode into Gonzales County, making a great show of slapping manacles on "Williams," and boasting that they'd captured "one of Hardin's gang."

Armstrong asked State Adjutant General William Steele to send warrants for the arrest of Hardin and "Swain" to Montgomery, Alabama. Duncan and Armstrong got off the train in Montgomery on August 20, 1877. Duncan went to Pollard, just north of the Alabama-Florida line, where he learned that "Swain" lived in Whiting, a tiny community south of Pollard. He walked to Whiting, where a merchant told him that "Swain" was on a gambling trip to Pensacola, Florida. Duncan wired Armstrong in Montgomery, asking the Ranger lieutenant to meet him in Whiting. Unknown to "J. H. Swain," who was sporting in Pensacola, the jaws of a trap were finally closing on John Wesley Hardin.

Hardin was captured aboard a train at Pensacola on August 23, 1877, but only after wrestling with the Rangers and local lawmen. Unable to draw a small revolver concealed in his clothing, the cursing, struggling Hardin was finally pistol-whipped senseless by Armstrong. A companion of Hardin on the train was killed in peripheral gun-play by deputies stationed around the depot.

Duncan and Armstrong then stunned the local lawmen by telling them they'd actually captured Wes Hardin. The local sheriff was paid $500 for his help. On their return, the Texans split the balance of the $4000 reward. The Pensacola lawmen burned.

Hardin spent the next seventeen years in prison. After winning a governor's pardon in 1894, he settled in El Paso, hoping to build a career on his new law license that he had studied for in prison. But the lawyer mostly drank, gambled and got into fights. One August night in 1895, El Paso Constable John Selman got the drop on Hardin in a saloon. Selman gave Hardin no chance to draw. He fatally gunned him down.

Meanwhile, back in Dallas, Jack Duncan's habits weren't much better than Hardin's. He was often in trouble with the law, fighting off prosecution for charges that ranged from misdemeanors to murder. He was a regular at the bordello of Mollie Cross. There, on the night of February 9, 1878, he was shot with his own six-gun by one of his favorites, Hattie Washburn.

Sweet on Duncan, Hattie was never able to make up her mind whether she plugged him on purpose. Whatever, Duncan recuperated from a lung wound but spent the remainder of his life with a silver tube in his throat. He was able to speak intelligibly only by fingering the tube's opening in his throat.

Duncan continued as an able bounty hunter. His biographer tallied at least 16 rewards—other than the one for Hardin—that came Duncan's way, rewards amounting to more than $8000. Duncan's rewards were supplements to his fees as a private detective. Like many investigators who work undercover, Duncan was camera-shy. Miller, who illustrated his book with pictures of virtually everyone else mentioned in the story, was never able to track down a photo of Duncan, if indeed one exists. Photos of many early Dallas policemen are seen in *Bounty Hunter*, along with glimpses of developing Dallas.

Perhaps symbolic of the passing of the Old West was the death of Duncan in a car wreck in 1911.

✳✳✳

No Kidding, Billy May Have Died in Texas in 1950

Billy the Kid. You betcha. Died right there on the sidewalk, he did. Happened in front of Fred Jaggars' real estate office. Well, it's Fred's place now. Back then it was the *Hico News Review*. Let's see, that was in 1950, two days after Christmas.

If he could have lived three more days, he would have been ninety-one—not bad for a desperado. Man, he had knife scars and old bullet holes all over him. But it was a heart attack that finally got him. Some say he truly died of a broken heart because a governor of New Mexico wouldn't pardon him. Billy the Kid never did have much luck with governors of New Mexico.

On it goes. Pieces of the story still enliven lazy conversations in Hico, a town of 1375 people, a declining population that is swollen each year by July's Old Settlers Reunion.

In 1986, several refugees from a hot July afternoon sat in the cool of Judge Bob Hefner's courtroom, idly jawing away a lull in the dockets. They spoke of Billy the Kid and how Hamilton County and Hico should put up markers that tell tourists the tale of the Kid's lost years.

Bob Hefner is the Texaco dealer who presides over the combination Hico municipal court and justice of the peace court. He is a true believer who rallies other true believers. They claim Billy the Kid—or Billy the Nonagenerian—gasped his last in Hico. The Kid folded up on the sidewalk, threw one arm across a parked car's bumper and expired with his boots on.

A surprising number of believers can be found in Texas, not to mention New Mexico and Arizona. Skeptics may see the problem of a recurring Billy the Kid in a sort of cosmic light. See, to rank as a big-time folk hero or folk villain you've got to outgrow your first grave. Look at Jesse James, John Wilkes Booth, Oscar Wilde, Marshal Ney, Lee Harvey Oswald, Adolf Hitler, Glenn Miller and Bobby Ewing.

And Emiliano Zapata will be back if we ever need him again.

Billy the Kid was a natural—or a supernatural—for this kind of stuff. And on another level, putting a legalistic gavel to it, the Kid never died the purported first time.

Sure, Pat Garrett, sheriff of Lincoln County, New Mexico Territory, supposedly canceled the Kid's ticket with a six-gun blast in Pete Maxwell's place at Fort Sumner, New Mexico Territory, on a July night in 1881 when the Kid was twenty-one. So, try to find legal proof of that, an authentic death certificate. Historians can't. When Garrett applied to collect a $500 reward for the Kid once offered by New Mexico Territorial Governor

Lew Wallace (the army general, incidentally, who wrote *Ben Hur*), the sheriff produced a paper he claimed to be a copy of a verdict by a coroner's jury. This was admittedly a copy of the finding of a second coroner's jury to study the case. The report of an earlier coroner's jury was supposedly lost. Both original documents went thataway or somewhere.

Garrett's application for the reward was flatly rejected. Acting Governor W. G. Ritch had assumed office. Among other things, Ritch stated that the territory wouldn't pay rewards offered personally by Wallace.

Eventually, after much politicking, an act of the legislature rewarded Garrett $500. Billy the Kid was born to drive biographers crazy. If he was born. There's no record.

A wonderful legend says Billy the Kid was born in New York City. But the office staff of the clerk of Manhattan, where the birth was supposed to have happened, has never found a record of it. Going beyond the dust cloud stirred up by early dime novels and later $20 novels, a serious 1956 book by Frazier Hunt, *The Tragic Days of Billy the Kid* states:

"Many people in Silver City (N.M.T.) learned that his real name was Henry McCarty and they called him that. At times he was also known as Henry Antrim, which was a combination of his own given name and the surname of his stepfather, William H. Antrim. It wasn't long, however, until he was generally referred to as Billy Antrim, and Kid Antrim, then as the Kid— later as Billy Kid, and in the end as Billy the Kid.

"It was a full two years after he had left Silver City and when he was in grave trouble over the killing of the blacksmith (F. P. Cahill on August 17, 1877) that he began to use the formal name of William H. Bonney; obviously the William H. was borrowed from the given name of his stepfather. No one knows from whence came the surname Bonney. It was an accepted formula of the frontier for a man on the dodge to use an alias, and when he felt he needed one the boy very probably simply hand-picked and adopted William H. Bonney."

Billy the Kid scholars today, in tallying his homicides, usually begin with the blacksmith, deleting the popular fable that the Kid killed his first man at age twelve while defending his mother's honor. The number of figurative notches allowed on the Kid's six-gun has been drastically whittled down by modern historians. Billy the Folk Figure killed twenty-one men (a racist count that excluded Indians and Mexicans) in his twenty-one years.

Texan Bill O'Neal in his 1979 *Encyclopedia of Western Gunfighters* gives the Kid only four sure kills and five possibles in sixteen gunfights. The Kid, in fact, barely earns a spot in O'Neal's top ten western gunfighters.

The Kid's reputation was created during the aptly designated Lincoln County War, a cattle conflict that turned thousands of New Mexicans into partisans. Kills are hard to confirm when numerous people are shooting at one another.

Through the years, partisanship generated by the cattle war has clouded research on the Kid. Witnesses emotionally interpreted events. The upshot is that the biography of Billy the Kid, a deadly rustler but never a bandit, is filled with holes and question marks.

Bob Hefner and the true believers think that they can fill all the gaps in the story of Billy the Kid by directing researchers to Ollie L. "Brushy Bill" Roberts, the old man who died on a Hico street in 1950.

Brushy Bill, in the closing years of his life in Hamilton and Hico, claimed he was the gunman once known as Billy the Kid. Indeed, Brushy Bill persuasively impressed many old-timers and researchers with his knowledge of the Lincoln County War and incidents in the life of Billy the Kid.

Brushy Bill so impressed a Texas lawyer named William V. Morrison that Morrison devoted the closing years of his life to trying to establish Brushy Bill's identity. Ultimately, Morrison arranged for New Mexico Governor Thomas Mabry to interview Brushy Bill on November 29, 1950. Brushy Bill, alias Billy the Kid, was applying for a pardon. His application was supported by many documents, including sworn statements by a number of aged witnesses that he was indeed Billy the Kid.

Pathetically, Brushy Bill was flustered by the presence of a crowd of reporters and state police in the governor's office. He became ill and had to lie down. In the end, in his old age, Brushy Bill was denied formal recognition as Billy the Kid—an identification that Brushy Bill had supposedly spent most of his life trying to dodge. Legally, a noose still awaited Billy the Kid.

In an attempt to rejuvenate what he thinks were the justifiable claims of Ollie Roberts, Bob Hefner asked his brother Bill Hefner, a Hico contractor, to mount an investigation. They are fourth-generation Hamiltonians who fled Hico as young men only to return after tiring of big-city rat cages. Ollie Roberts had told people he was born on a cattle drive in Taylor County, near Abilene. There's no record of his birth or early life, presumably because he bounced around so much. Even information on his death certificate, supplied by his third wife, may be erroneous. It makes him about a decade younger than he claimed.

Ollie Roberts' claims could be easily tossed out the window except for the vast amount of specific information he knew about Billy the Kid and his times. Where did he learn all that stuff? He sometimes stunned experts and filled historical holes with reasonable information.

The way Ollie Roberts told it, he escaped from that misunderstanding at Pete Maxwell's with three bullet wounds. His pal—Billy Barlow—was killed in the scrape and later buried in the ballyhooed grave of Billy the Kid that draws tourists to Fort Sumner. No Billy Barlow turns up in records of the period. But the frontier always attracted unknown men.

True believers are bolstered by William Tunstill of the Western History Research Center in Roswell, New Mexico. Tunstill insists, after years of research, that Ollie Roberts was Billy the Kid.

Bob Hefner says, "I believe that Ollie Roberts was Billy the Kid because so many people tried to disprove him and couldn't do it."

A fine mess, Ollie.

THE HANGING OF WILD BILL LONGLEY

In his Lee County jail cell on October 10, 1878, the eve of his hanging for one of many murders, Texas desperado Wild Bill Longley wrote to his kinfolks:

"I don't dread this thing. Tomorrow at this time I'll be in a better place . . . ."

Did he mean Louisiana?

A lot of people suspect that Wild Bill pulled a fast one and escaped to Louisiana or some place to live out a long, tame life. The suspicion is that Bill or his kin bribed the hangman. A harness was hidden beneath Bill's clothes. Hooked to the hangman's noose, the apparatus absorbed the neck-snapping shock of the drop from the gibbet. Or so goes the tale.

Giddings junk dealer Woodrow Wilson had faith in that story. In 1987, he stuck his neck way out to prove to doubters that anyone who wears mountain climbing rigging for underwear can survive a hanging. On a $1500 scaffold built from pine planks near the shoulder of U.S. Highway 290, just outside Giddings, the seat of Lee County, Woodrow Wilson starred in a re-enactment of the hanging of Bill Longley.

Woodrow survived just as he believes Bill did. "I put my neck on the line," said Woodrow, whose ears were bloodied by the seven-foot drop. He reported that his yanked ears were healing up OK. "What hurts is that I've got four kids and not a damn one showed up for the hanging."

Woodrow's wife, Bernice, who knew Woodrow had no insurance, and his sister, Frances Graeter of Giddings, who was praying, hid in the concession stand during the hanging.

Woodrow said, "Bill Longley was my great uncle. He's a part of Giddings' history, whether Giddings people like it or not."

And Giddings people stayed away in multitudes. Most of the 100 witnesses who showed up were out-of-town news people or descendants of the old outlaw.

Massaging his ears after the hanging, Woodrow made a speech: "I'm trying to put Giddings on the map. We got no help from nobody with this thing. We got no cooperation from nobody from the Chamber of Commerce on down, and it didn't cost none of them a damn thing." The animated martyr was alive and kicking. "Some of these people may want to run me out of town. But Giddings is one of the best little towns in Texas, and I want people to know about it.

"Now you take Round Rock, where Sam Bass got shot. Round Rock is a progressive town. When they have a Sam Bass celebration, they get 10,000 people out in hot July weather."

Mellowing, he said, "I want to thank my wife. She's a wonderful woman. She didn't try to talk me outta this because she knows I got too much Bill Longley stubbornness. I wouldn't trade my wife for 15 or 20 others just like her."

Woodrow hired a band—the Country Cousins—to play for his hanging. A karate academy did chops and kicks. Souvenirs, soda pop and sandwiches brought in $400 or so against Woodrow's avowed investment of about $3000 in the day's events. Signs around his flea market read "Watch for fire ants" and "Watch your children. Lock your car. If you cannot accept these terms then please leave." A big sign facing the highway read, "Bill Longley Hang Out."

Wild Bill Longley was one of those touchy Southerners, like gunman John Wesley Hardin of Texas, who never hesitated at gunplay. One of Wild Bill's complaints when he was sentenced to hang was that fast-gun Hardin, finally convicted of murder, had gotten off with a prison sentence. The prison term gave Hardin time to write a self-serving autobiography before he was paroled and gunned down in El Paso.

Although Bill Longley was a prolific writer of biographical letters during the long imprisonment before his hanging, his recorded story is far from complete. He became a murderer as a teen-ager. The number of men he killed ranges from fewer than a dozen to more than 30, depending on the teller of the tale. Some were shot in the back. Some were unarmed.

In a letter, Bill wrote that he regretted only one of his killings, a cowboy shot down for acting suspiciously. The cowboy was acting suspiciously, it turned out, because he was on the dodge from the law, just like Bill.

Legends obscured facts of Bill's wide-ranging adventures. He had many close scrapes. He broke out of jails, he bribed guards, he outrode posses. It's told that once, suspected of stealing horses, he was strung up to a tree by a mob, but as the vigilantes rode away, one fired a parting shot at Bill's dangling body. Bill's life was saved when the shot cut strands of rope, lowering his feet to the earth. That incident was recalled after Bill's hanging in Giddings, where in the first attempt to hang him, the rope stretched, permitting his long legs to dangle to the ground. He was hoisted again. Folks told one another, "Bill Longley hanged three times."

Whether the third time was charmed is the subject of speculation. Woodrow says Longley didn't die at age twenty-eight, as the official record dictates, but rode like the wind to Louisiana, where he changed his name, became a respectable family man and died of complications after prostate surgery at age seventy-one.

Bill supposedly has a stone in a Giddings cemetery, but Woodrow said Bill isn't beneath it. Showing me photos of another gravestone, Woodrow said it was Bill's grave in Louisiana.

"My cousin researched all this and wrote a book about it. He's not here today and I won't mention his name. A lawyer told him that if the word gets out, the family in Louisiana may sue him for putting out that they're akin to Bill Longley."

Others are proud to be kin to Wild Bill. For example, Neill Longley, a Houston radiologist, and John Longley, a La Porte accountant, had driven to Giddings to join other descendants in exercising bragging rights to their granddaddy's older brother, Bill Longley.

Neill told me that his granddaddy, James Longley, was present when Wild Bill murdered Wilson Anderson in Lee County. One of Bill's reasons, Neill said, was that he suspected Anderson of killing a Longley cousin. His other reason was drunkenness.

After shooting Anderson in a field he'd been plowing, Wild Bill fled what is now Lee County (in those days it was still part of Washington County) and continued his wild career, eventually alighting in Louisiana's De Soto Parish.

In June 1877, Sheriff Milton Mast of Nacogdoches County and his deputy, Bill Burrows, invaded Louisiana, captured the Texas bad man, and escorted him back to Texas. During appeals of his death sentence, Wild Bill was jailed in Galveston County, away from the inflamed atmosphere of Giddings. Bill's executioner was Sheriff Jim Brown. Woodrow said Sheriff Brown was crooked as a dog's back leg and was bribed to let Bill survive the hanging.

A lot of people believe the hanging ended Bill Longley. Neill Longley is one. "They showed the crowd that he was dead by twisting his neck 180 degrees in either direction," said Neill.

Historian A. C. Greene is another who doubts that Bill got out of Giddings alive after the hanging. Greene's great-grandmother married Bill Longley's father. Greene cited newspaper stories that described the neck-twisting demonstration.

In an old account I saw, Bill's neck was described by a witness as having been stretched to twice its normal length by the hanging. The stories will go on forever. He went to South America. He moved to Bell County. He ended up in Louisiana.

One thing's sure, Wild Bill Longley deserved a lot more hanging than he ever got.

✳✳✳

DARING TRAIN ROBBER GOT THE GOODS, NOT THE GLORY

At midmorning on December 11, 1886, Rube and his gang hijacked a Fort Worth & Denver passenger train that had stopped for water in the little tank town of Bellevue in Clay County. The train was an hour out of Wichita Falls and bound for Fort Worth.

Maybe the gunmen had been up late celebrating December 11, Rube's birthday. How else is one to explain their ignoring an express car with a fat, unlocked safe? Beyond that, the amateurs wasted expensive minutes jawing while relieving the train crew of about twenty dollars and three pocket watches. Meanwhile, passengers were busily hiding valuables.

By the time the gunmen reached the coaches, the passengers had stuffed most of their money and jewelry into their boots, into their bosoms, under their seats, and into their bloomers. In the bandits' best stumbling move of the day, they discovered a mysterious $740 in a brass spittoon. The press reckoned that the robbers got only about $1000 and a few rings and watches of the $12,000 in cash and maybe $5000 worth of jewelry aboard the train. Look, it was Rube's first train robbery.

The initial robbery gave no inkling of Rube's promise. Only later, with each new robbery, was his virtuosity revealed. Rube perfected techniques that bordered on brilliance. He learned all the tricks of the crossties and he developed new ones. For example, a favorite stratagem of Rube's was to force engineers to halt their trains on trestles, the loftier the better. That confined troublesome passengers to their coaches.

Rube blossomed. His eighth and final train robbery would be a technical masterpiece. He would perform solo. Single-handedly, he would rob a train. All the bells and whistles should have been Rube's. So will someone please explain why the songs, poems, and movies are all about Jesse James, Sam Bass, and Butch Cassidy?

I mean, why not Rube Burrow?

"He needed a good press agent," said Texas historian C. Richard King. We were talking about Rube in King's literary hideout, a converted barn in the Erath County courthouse town of Stephenville.

"Seriously," said King, "the dime novelists who promoted the careers of some of the other outlaws never got around to the Rube Burrow story."

It's a story King knows because Rube ranched in Erath County until he went down the owl hoot trail. King described Burrow as a respectable citizen during his years in Erath County. "I recall early newspaper references to him as a fine fellow. One editor mentioned that he was glad to see that Rube Burrow was back in town."

Charitably, King theorized that Rube was a hard-working stiff who fell victim to a devastating drought that scorched West Texas worse than usual about the time that Rube went bad.

In the fall of 1873, Rube had left his native Alabama and drifted to the farm of his uncle, Joel Burrow, an Erath County homesteader. Rube was joined by Jim, a younger brother by four years. Rube showed no fear of hard work. He helped his uncle and he labored for wages on the Mexican Central Railroad, a line he never robbed.

In 1876, he married Virginia Alverson, an Alabama belle, and they had two children. Virginia died in 1880 and Rube asked Jim, who was homesick for Alabama anyway, to deliver his mother-less children to the old folks at home in Lamar County, Alabama. Rube married Adeline Hoover of Erath County in 1884, the year that Jim returned to Texas with a bride. The brothers bought some land and farmed it. They prospered for a time. But Rube kept hearing stories about Sam Bass and train robberies.

Then came Bellevue. Then came Gordon in Palo Pinto County, where Rube and his boys at 1:00 A.M. on January 23, 1887, tapped the Texas & Pacific for a couple of thousand dollars from the express car and several thousand more from a mail car. Rube made the engineer stop the passenger cars on a trestle, but the gang this time spared the passengers' belongings. Many of the passengers were armed. Four U.S. soldiers had rifles but little enthusiasm for battle. Aching for a fight, however, was a passenger named Henry Lewis, the sheriff of Dallas County.

With his coach parked on the trestle in the pitch-black night, Sheriff Lewis could do little more than empty his six-gun into the darkness. The lawman's bullets did no physical damage to the five bandits. But one of Rube's new recruits, Harrison Askew, abandoning his brief life of crime, ran off into the night shouting: "For God's sake, let me out of this. I can't stand it." Since it was a new year, the *Fort Worth Gazette* tagged it, "A new era in brigandage."

On January 30, *The Dallas Morning News*, detecting an increase in train attacks, editorialized against passengers' carrying large sums of money: "Since the adoption of bank drafts and postal money orders, the carrying of money except in small sums can be entirely avoided."

On June 4, 1887, Rube and company robbed a Texas & Pacific train straddling a trestle at Benbrook in Tarrant County. Estimates of the loot ranged up to $10,000. Again, passengers were spared. They gave the bandits a cheer as they rode away. U.S. Marshal Ben Cabell of Dallas offered $500 reward for any of the robbers and pledged that he would "soon corral the banditti."

On September 20, 1887, same song, same verse, same line: Texas & Pacific—except this time the train was headed the other way, toward Fort Worth. Engineer John Baker said two masked men climbed into the cab and one said, "The same place as before." Baker parked her again on the trestle at Mary's Creek.

The express and postal people clammed up about the loss. But *The Morning News* reported, "There is hardly any doubt but that the haul was a big one." Passengers weren't molested, but the express messenger said, "The robbers took everything valuable in the car. They even looked in the stove and tore out the grate. Oh, they had their business down pat."

Texas was getting too hot for the Burrows. They went across the border into Arkansas before pulling another train robbery. This time it was a St. Louis, Arkansas & Texas passenger train at Genoa, just east of Texarkana. The passengers got off free, but the express and mail cars yielded about $10,000, much of it Louisiana lottery money.

January 1888 found the brothers hiding in Alabama, in their home county of Lamar. Although they'd been identified by captured members of the gang, they felt safest among their kin and friends. But things were warm all over.

Rube and Jim ventured to Montgomery, where they were jumped by lawmen. In a shoot-out, Rube wounded a printer for the *Montgomery Advertiser*, who'd tried to assist officers. Jim was nabbed and returned to Arkansas, where he rotted in a cell and died before he could be brought to trial for the Genoa job.

Meanwhile, Rube hid out in the woods and swamps. He posed as a cotton picker for a while and was good at it. On December 15, 1888, he and a pal he called Joe Jackson robbed an Illinois Central train of more than $2000 at Duck Hill, Mississippi. An armed conductor and one passenger battled the bandits. In the gunfight, the passenger was killed—probably by Rube, who was a much better shot than Jackson. In July, Rube further bloodied his reputation. He murdered an Alabama postmaster who had refused to deliver a wig and fake beard that Rube had ordered under an assumed name.

On September 25, 1889, Rube and two companions robbed a Mobile & Ohio train at Buckatunna, Mississippi. They got $2000 or $3000. Rube was on the lam for the rest of his desperate life. Pursued by lawmen, Pinkertons and citizens seeking thousands of dollars in reward money, Rube lived like an animal in the swamps of Florida.

Alone, incredibly, he robbed a Louisville & Nashville train at Flomaton, Alabama, on September 1, 1890. He got less than $300 for this one, his masterpiece. Detectives hounded him. At last, he was arrested after a wrestling match with his captors near Myrtlewood, Alabama, on October 7, 1890. He was jailed in nearby Linden. Within hours, Rube had armed himself, busted out and gone looking for lawmen to shoot. He found Deputy Sheriff Jefferson Davis Carter. In a duel, Rube shot Carter in the shoulder with a .45. Carter shot Rube with a .32. Carter lived. Rube died.

Rube is buried in Lamar County, Alabama, under a persistently vandalized marker that says "Rube Burrows." The misspelling of Rube's name on his tombstone merely underscores his eternal need for a good press agent.

✳✳✳

Bill Dalton Shot Straight in Bank Note

One day in early 1894, a prominent citizen of Longview was jolted when he opened an envelope in the day's mail. A scrawled note fell out:

We take this method of informing you that on or about the twenty-third day of May, A.D. 1894, we will rob the First National Bank of Longview. So take notice accordingly and withdraw your deposit as this is a straight tip. For further information see Charles Specklemeyer or the under-signed.

Yours for business,

B. & F.

When the note was shown to bank officials, they judged it a hoax. But the tip was straight. Charles Specklemeyer was headed for Longview.

Bill Dalton had authored the note. (B. & F.—Bill & Friends?) Dalton was a twenty-nine-year-old bandit whose outlaw brothers' gang had been shot to pieces on October 5, 1892, while robbing two banks in Coffeyville, Kansas. In that gun battle, three citizens and four bandits were killed. Brothers Bob and Grat Dalton died. Emmett Dalton was dangerously wounded.

The Daltons were from Missouri. But far-flung Bill had led a reputable life in California until the Coffeyville slaughter. He hurried to Emmett's bedside. Bill O'Neal, author of the *Encyclopedia of Western Gunfighters*, told me what came next:

"Bill Dalton resentfully criticized the people of Coffeyville, claiming they had looted and abused his fallen brothers. Bitterly he contemplated that three of his brothers had died violently, (Frank Dalton, a deputy U.S. marshal, had been killed in 1887 by whiskey runners), and Emmett now faced prison for life. He felt compelled to strike back at society. When outlaw Bill Doolin offered him a chance, Dalton took up a criminal's life. Doolin, a key member of the Dalton gang, had escaped the Coffeyville massacre only because his horse had gone lame on the road into town. Subsequently Doolin formed a band of robbers known to the press as the "Okla-hombres." Dalton became his second in command, in company with Bitter Creek Newcomb, Red Buck George Weightman, Little Bill Raidler, Tulsa Jack Blake, Dynamite Dick (Dan Clifton), Arkansas Tom Jones (Roy Daugherty), Little Dick West, Charley Pierce, Bob Grounds, Alf Sohn and Ol Yantis.

"In September 1893, the gang was cornered by a posse in Ingalls, Oklahoma Territory, but Dalton blasted his way out of town, killing a lawman in the process. Reward of $500, dead or alive, was posted for each Okla-hombre."

O'Neal, who teaches history at Panola College in Carthage, further said: "On April 1, 1894, Dalton and Bitter Creek Newcomb entered a store in Sacred Heart, Oklahoma Territory. The owner, a former peace officer, recognized Dalton and went for a gun.

Once again, Dalton shot his way to safety. But his survival instincts told him it was time to break away from the Okla-hombres.

"Dalton hid on Houston Wallace's farm, twenty-five miles northwest of Ardmore, Indian Territory. Wallace's brother Jim was there. Jim Wallace had married the daughter of a Longview-area farmer. Jim had deserted his bride within a month, but he talked to Bill Dalton about the enticingly prosperous Longview bank. Dalton liked the idea. He mailed his prankish note to Longview."

After researching the Longview robbery, O'Neal returned to the scene of the crime to present his findings to a meeting of the East Texas Historical Association in Longview. In mid-April 1894, Dalton and Jim Wallace had ridden into Gregg County and camped near Longview on the banks of the Sabine. They fished, plotted the robbery and recruited two accomplices—the Nite brothers, Jim and Big Asa.

On a drizzly May 23—right on schedule—Wallace strapped on a brace of revolvers and crammed 300 cartridges into his saddle-bags. Dalton put on a long, gray duster. The gang, lethally armed and well mounted, rode into town at mid-afternoon. While Big Asa and Wallace led get-away horses into the alley behind the bank, Dalton and Jim Nite entered the front door. Dalton handed a note to bank president Joe Clemmons:

May 23d, 1894.

This will introduce you to Chas. Specklemeyer, who wants some money and will have it.

B. & F.

Remarkably, Dalton's note, with other robbery relics, is preserved at the Gregg County Historical Museum, an East Texas show place. Director Ellie Caston, like O'Neal, is well acquainted with the young town's deadliest day. In 1894, Longview, with about 3000 residents, was just twenty-four years old.

Banker Clemmons at first assumed Specklemeyer's note was a charity request, O'Neal told me. But Dalton clarified things by hauling out a revolver and telling everyone to reach. With a burlap bag, Jim Nite ravaged the vault. He bagged coins, bills and—significantly—unsigned twenty-dollar bank notes.

Cashier Tom Clemmons, the president's brother, impulsively grabbed Dalton's six-gun. Repeatedly Dalton vainly pulled the trigger. Each time the hammer fell on the flesh of Tom Clemmons' hand. Witnesses bolted. Merchant John Welborne and Josh Cooke, a bank employee, rushed into the street, yelling: "They're robbing the bank." Bartender George Buckingham barreled out of Jerry Munden's Saloon, firing at Wallace until the outlaw dropped him with a mortal wound.

"Wallace was filled with battle lust," O'Neal said. "He began to roar out war whoops, blasting any man he saw. City Marshal Matt Muckleroy challenged Wallace, but the outlaw knocked him down with a shot in the chest. The lawman was in luck. Wallace's slug slammed into a silver dollar in Muckleroy's shirt pocket. He was out of action, but later recuperated."

Millworker Charles Learn was fatally wounded. J. W. McQueen, however, recovered from the gunshot souvenir he received from Wallace. Wallace fired at a black man sitting on a box in front of a saloon. Grazing the man's head, the slug drilled into the saloon, where it ripped the finger-tip of a startled boozer, who hadn't asked for another shot.

Lawyer Charles Lacy, armed with a rifle, ran into a feed store next to the bank. At a rear window, he took aim at Wallace's back. He killed Wallace with one shot. Big Asa fired a couple of wild bullets at Lacy.

The surviving outlaws swung into their saddles. The Clemmons brothers were made hostages and forced to ride along on the getaway. Dalton led them west on Tyler Street, then wheeled north on a logging trail. A mile out of town, the banker brothers were released. And Dalton reined in long enough to hand a message with two Winchester cartridges to a passer-by:

You'll get plenty of these if you follow too close.

Charles Specklemeyer.

Gregg County Sheriff Jack Howard's posse soon lost the bandits' trail. In Longview, angry citizens lynched Wallace's corpse. Bankers calculated that about $2000 was missing from the vault. Wallace's hat-band was marked "W. O. Dunston's Big Cash Store, Ardmore." Territorial lawmen were notified.

Early in June, some of the unsigned bank notes from Longview were passed in Ardmore. Then Houston Wallace and two women were arrested for illegal possession of a case of whiskey in Indian Territory. Lawmen smelled an outlaw nest.

A nine-man posse rode out to search the Houston Wallace farm. At dawn on June 8, while Bill Dalton impatiently awaited the return of Houston Wallace and the women, he stepped outside and spotted U.S. Marshal Seldon Lindsey. Dalton ducked back into the house, grabbed a revolver and clambered out a back window. As he sprinted for a ravine, Deputy U.S. Marshal Loss Hart shouted for him to halt. Dalton pointed his six-gun at Hart. But Hart fired first. The bullet tore through Dalton's chest, and he dropped, dying.

William Marion Dalton's death not only brought down the curtain on the last of the outlaw Dalton brothers, but presaged the violent eradication of the Nite brothers, Bill Doolin and most of his Okla-hombres.

A happy exception was Emmett Dalton, who recovered from his Coffeyville wounds in a Kansas prison. He was pardoned from his life sentence in 1907 and wed the sweetheart of his youth. He moved to Los Angeles, where he became a building contractor. Ultimately, he wrote movies and acted in bit parts. In Los Angeles, at the age of sixty-six, he died in 1937 with his boots off.

Bill Dalton's embalmed corpse was displayed in Ardmore for five days. Hundreds of people, many of them from Longview, traveled to Ardmore to look at the dead outlaw. He had given Longview a day to remember.

Scores of shots were fired on May 23, 1894. Four victims were wounded, seven if you count the slight injuries at the saloon and Tom Clemmons' hammered hand. Two courageous citizens, George Buckingham and Charles Learn, died from gunshots. Bandit Jim Wallace was killed.

And Charles Specklemeyer got the business, sure enough.

*** ***

PINK FLOWERS MARK A BADMAN'S GRAVE

Who brings flowers to the grave of John Wesley Hardin? Leaning against a biting norther in 1988, Leon Claire Metz and I blinked at the pink plastic nosegay planted in the windswept hardpan that has covered the gunfighter for ninety-two years.

"Flowers are always here. They change. Sometimes they're real ones," said Leon. "People carry them off or the wind blows them away. I haven't the vaguest idea who brings them. Hardin's descendants don't live anywhere near El Paso. It's odd."

We stood in a neglected corner of old Concordia Cemetery, a square-mile enclave of thousands upon thousands of El Paso's most permanent residents. I'd rousted Leon from a warm bed to guide me to the murdered gunman's plot in this desolate graveyard. Such are the perks of Leon's position as El Paso's leading expert on Hardin and his times.

With publication of his *John Selman: Texas Gunfighter* twenty-two years ago, Metz became the biographer of Hardin's killer. And the definitive biography of Hardin will be written only when Metz writes it. Soon, he promises.

Hardin's legend is secure. A preacher's son and a touchy Southerner, he was the greatest six-gun duelist of them all. Forty men fell before his guns and not many got up. He read the law while doing fifteen hard years in prison for killing a lawman, won a governor's pardon, and hung out his shingle in El Paso. Leon told me all the sleazy details of Hardin's final drunken, adulterous, gambling and bloody days in El Paso.

To tell it briefly, Hardin, forty-two, got crossways with Old John Selman, a shot-up, beat-up, stove-up gunman, who'd been "Old John" for as long as anyone could remember. Selman was winding down long careers on all sides of the law as a hobbling El Paso constable when Hardin swaggered into town.

Selman got the drop on unsuspecting Hardin at the Acme Saloon one drunken night in 1895. He drilled the ace gunman of the Western World with three .45 slugs, one through the brain. Hardin was rolling cupped dice at the bar one moment, dead the next. "Four sixes to beat," were Hardin's last words. He didn't draw either of his Colts. "Hardin didn't have a chance," said Leon. "He must have gone to the floor thinking that he was coming down with another monumental hangover."

A plaque on a downtown dress shop marks the Acme's old site. The plaque's easy to find. Hardin's grave, unless you know someone, is more difficult. Before 1965, it was impossible to find. It was unmarked.

The late C. L. Sonnichsen, who spent many years illuminating El Paso history before moving to Tucson, was instrumental in getting the grave marked for Hardin's descendants. "It was the end of twenty years of frustration," Sonnichsen recalled. "Marking a grave ought not to be a major undertaking, but this one resisted all efforts. John Wesley Hardin, dead and buried, made almost as much trouble for his friends and relatives who wanted that marker placed as he had for carpetbaggers, gamblers and assorted gunmen during his life."

When Sonnichsen, as agent for the family, approached William R. Walker, Concordia's caretaker, about putting a stone over JWH, Walker was aggressively hostile. "He seemed to have a real obsession about the Hardin grave," Sonnichsen observed. The caretaker, whose files concealed the grave's location, suggested that Sonnichsen stay to hell out of the graveyard. Frankly, after seeing Hardin's part of the burial ground, I find it hard to believe that it ever had a caretaker.

Sonnichsen persevered, but so did Walker, who feared that if the grave were marked vandals would tear up his cemetery, a process that had already begun. While he lived, Walker vowed, the location of Hardin's grave wouldn't be revealed. It wasn't.

Walker's successor, the late Tom Dooley, similarly refused to cooperate. He didn't wish to encourage the perpetuation of the memory of a blot on Texas history like John Wesley Hardin. Sonnichsen describes Dooley as "a short, dark, worried-looking fellow in khakis with a red face, a hook nose, and a watery eye, the result of seeking relief from his burdens at Tony's bar a few steps away."

Only after many months and threats of a lawsuit did Dooley bend to family wishes and delve into his yellowed records to locate the grave.

In an essay, "The Grave of John Wesley Hardin," Sonnichsen told how Dooley was miffed by a pest who was researching a book on John Selman. The pest's name, of course, was Leon Claire Metz. The caretaker referred to Leon as "that policeman." It's true, Leon was an El Paso policeman for a short time.

Leon had brought one of Selman's granddaughters to Concordia to find Old John's grave. Dooley had complained to Sonnichsen: "He threatened to put me in jail if I didn't dig up the records on Selman. I went over every record we had here, and there was nothing on him."

For Leon, that's been a lasting frustration. Old John Selman is out there somewhere among the thousands of others, including several misplaced figures in the Selman-Hardin saga.

Some parts of Concordia, dating back to the 1840s, are exclusive and well-tended: Masonic, Catholic, Jesuit, Chinese, Jewish, black and military. But Hardin lies in a dismally low rent portion. Concordia speaks of the history of the border country, grist for Leon's mill. His history of the Mexican border—entitled *Border*—was published by Mangan Books in El Paso.

Leon pointed to a stone twenty feet from Hardin's. "I recall that Dooley walked me right past Hardin's grave to that stone over there. There he instructed me to write about heroes, like the man buried there, instead of murderers."

The stone was inscribed: "Hiram Reed—July 17, 1819—Feb. 6, 1895. Pioneer Baptist preacher, chaplain and statesman." Dooley lectured Leon: "This man changed the world for the better. Those SOBs you write about, those gunfighters, were the scum of the earth."

Despite Dooleys, Walkers and others, the gunfighter's grave finally was memorialized with $102 worth of granite that, without sentiment, states: "John Wesley Hardin. May 26, 1853—Aug. 19, 1895." Many battered stones in Concordia have been shoved over by fun-loving vandals. Reverend Reed's is one of them. Hardin's twenty-two-year-old horizontal stone is in place, looking shiny new. But the little pink flowers are puzzling.

✳✳✳

Old-Style Bandits Had Panache

In Texas, the 1920s and 1930s must have been a sort of belle epoque for bank robbers. Fast getaway cars had hit the mass market before police radios. More banks are robbed now than then, I'm told. But so few bandits get away with it now that today's bank robbers are diagnosed as a little weak north of the ears.

In the 1920s and 1930s, Texans were fascinated by the dash and style of bank robbers. Moreover, a big score could permanently shut down a small uninsured bank, leaving depositors sitting on the curb with their tongues hanging out. Today, deposits are insured, and big scores are generally reserved for self-dealing bankers and their friends.

In 1931, the *Sherman Daily Democrat* routinely ran a front page box, usually a paragraph or two, under the standing headline: "Today's Bank Robberies." For example, on Sunday, April 5, the box read: "Philadelphia, Pa.—Two men held up the Mercantile Bank here Saturday and escaped with about $6000."

Closer to home in Grayson County, lesser larcenies made news. The period's hard times were reflected in a raid on the hen house of P. A. Smith of Sherman. The chicken thief took four setting hens and—get this—the eggs they were hatching. But on Tuesday afternoon, April 7, 1931, distant heists and hen house raids were forgotten. *Democrat* readers were jolted by screaming headlines: "LOCAL BANK ROBBED OF $40,000." Just as slick as fashionably oiled hair, neatly dressed bandits had strolled into the Central State Bank at 2:30 P.M. and herded about fifteen customers and bank workers into a vault. The bandits drove off five minutes later in a new Buick with $10,000 in liberty bonds and $30,000 cash, all insured against just this sort of thing. The bandits got clean away.

Bank president Barlow Roberts had walked in on the robbery. He was politely greeted at the door and ushered into the vault by ace bank bandit Harvey Bailey, who headed the gang. Bailey anonymously robbed dozens of banks of hundreds of thousands of bucks before he was ever caught. In his later years, Bailey talked about his career, mentioning the Sherman job, with Texas historian J. Evetts Haley of Midland. I talked with Haley, who liked Bailey so well that he wrote a book about him, *Robbing Banks Was My Business.*

"Harvey was smart," said Haley. "He told me that any fool can rob a bank. But getting away with it is the hard part." As with nearly all his heists, Bailey was never convicted of the Sherman robbery. In his gang that afternoon were several underworld luminaries. Verne Miller and Frank Nash were killers fated for violent deaths.

Nash would die spectacularly along with four lawmen on June 17, 1933, in the Kansas City Union Station Massacre. Lawmen were transferring Nash, who'd been nabbed in Hot Springs, from a train to a car when they became targets of gunmen, two firing submachine guns. Miller was one of the machine-gunners. Mysteriously, Miller's bullet-scarred, nude body would be found on the outskirts of Detroit five months later. No one is sure whether Nash was killed in an attempt to free him or to shut him up. And no one today is sure who murdered Miller.

But on the day of the Central State robbery, another public enemy waited for the fleeing bandits with a second getaway car nearly 200 miles away. George "Machine Gun" Kelly sat in a new Cadillac on the shores of Caddo Lake. Kelly would ultimately die in prison, but not before figuring in the ruin of Harvey Bailey.

That was all in the future, of course. On that April afternoon in Sherman in 1931, everyone stayed as cool as an ice-house watermelon. *The Democrat* reported that victims cooperated with the bandits: "Mrs. Tom Smith, an elderly woman, said she held up her hands when she saw others doing so, but did not understand the significance of the gestures until one of the robbers told her obligingly, 'We're holding up this bank.'

Not a shot was fired.

Haley told me that Harvey Bailey was a gentleman, despite his hard calling. He never killed anyone, although, considering the crowd in which he moved, he must have been tempted at times.

Missouri-born Bailey began his illicit career as a bootlegger, but found robbing banks more profitable. Haley said, "He was never stopped, never hurt and never apprehended in the robbery of any bank he set out to rob. But after years of fantastic success he was finally taken by the law on the Old Mission Hills Golf Links at Kansas City while playing a round with three other gentlemen."

That was 1932. Bailey got ten to fifty years for robbery of a Fort Scott, Kansas, bank. Within a few months, during a Memorial Day convict baseball game at the Kansas State Penitentiary, he led a group of desperate prisoners in a bold, bullet-sprayed, daylight escape. Bailey was wounded but got away.

Haley described what followed: "While still walking with a cane he took two profitable Oklahoma banks, and then drove to the Shannon Farm, near Paradise, in Wise County, Texas, to return Machine Gun Kelly's weapon that he had borrowed for his last robbery. Dead on his feet after two days and nights of driving, he went to sleep on a cot in Boss Shannon's (Shannon was married to Kelly's mother-in-law) back yard on the very night that a squad of G-Men and Texas officers were quietly moving in on that hideout of the Charles Urschel kidnappers."

Bailey wasn't one of the Urschel kidnappers as was Kelly, but Bailey was at the right place at the wrong time. He was scooped up with other suspects in the kidnapping of Urschel, an Oklahoma oilionaire, who had been ransomed for $200,000.

Haley said Bailey "was carried in chains to Dallas and was lodged on the ninth floor, in the death row, of Dallas County's brand new escape-proof jail. On Labor Day 1933, he disarmed his guard, locked him and a half dozen others in various cells and made his way through the last barred door, abducted an officer and his car.

"He was boxed in by cordons of officers, retaken at Ardmore, Oklahoma, and relayed to Oklahoma City to be tried for conspiracy and kidnapping in the Urschel case."

That Bailey had no part in the kidnapping had little effect on the outcome of his trial. Although he might have been legally locked up for centuries for his crimes, he actually got a life sentence for a crime he didn't commit. He did time at Leavenworth and Alcatraz, and finished his federal time at Seagoville, near Dallas. He was returned to Kansas to do two more years at

Lansing, the prison he'd departed so abruptly on Memorial Day 1932.

On March 30, 1964, Bailey was paroled, a white-haired man of seventy-six. He settled in Joplin, Missouri, married for the second time, and went to work in a furniture factory. Octogenarian Haley said Bailey continued making furniture until well into his eighties. "Harvey had a lot of character," said the prize-winning historian. If it mattered, Harvey Bailey had the last laugh. He died in 1979. At age ninety-one, he had outlived his generation of cops and robbers.

✳✳✳

Riches Were Easy Come, Easy Go for Train Robber

"I feel pretty good," reckoned the last of the great train robbers, grinning and offering me a firm hand. "I just took my arthritis pill."

Genial, ivory-haired Joe Newton poised on his parlor sofa, more closely resembled somebody's grandpa—which he isn't—than a bandit who robbed five trains and nearly eighty banks—which he is.

Joe was the youngest member and is the only survivor of the Newton brothers, a gang of Roaring '20s outlaws that plagued bankers, cops, postal inspectors and, with a vengeance, insurance companies. The Newtons were quicksilver slick and painstakingly anonymous until they became overnight sensations after the $3 million robbery of a Chicago, Milwaukee & St. Paul mail train outside Roundout, Illinois, on June 12, 1924.

For his part, Joe would as soon have remained an unknown thief.

Joe grew up with his brothers Jess, Doc and Willis in Uvalde County. As his brothers did, Joe expects one day to die from natural causes.

"If you're going to write about this, you better put in there that I don't think it was something very smart that I done. I was a damn fool for doing it.

"I could have owned a big piece of Texas if I hadn't got into it. I was a cowboy. I was working and saving my money to go to the Big Bend. Hell, you could buy land out there for a dollar an acre back then. About that time, I got a letter with two $20 bills in it from my brother Willis. He told me to come to Tulsa because he had a good job for me."

Willis, who'd had small scrapes with the law, was twelve years older than Joe, who was cleaner than his coonhound's teeth.

Joe put his saddle and rigging in a burlap bag and caught a train to Tulsa.

"What's that?" demanded Willis.

"My saddle," said Joe.

"What the hell you doing with a saddle?"

"You said you had a good job for me. The only thing I know is cowboying."

"Throw that damn thing away. We're going to rob some banks."

"That don't sit well with me, Willis. They shoot people for robbing banks."

"We ain't going to get shot."

(Fact is, Joe never did get shot until his friend Peewee Van Pelt stung him with thirteen birdshot while they were dove hunting a couple of years ago.)

Anyhow, Willis gave Joe a handful of $100 bills and said stealing from banks wouldn't be like taking money that actually belonged to somebody. It would all be insured. Nobody would get hurt. Moreover, Willis reminded Joe that their great-granddaddy back in Tennessee had been rooked bad by an insurance company. There was a score to settle.

"That story was passed down from one generation to the next," Joe says. "It was either my great-grandpa or great-great-grandpa. I never met them. Them $100 bills did more than anything to sway me over. I went out and bought me a suit or two and, although I'm a Baptist, I decided to go with him. Willis was always popping off about me being 'a damn good Baptist.'

"The bank robbing business isn't much fun. But after a while, you learn what to do. You don't worry about being scared or excited. But when Willis invited me to Tulsa, I don't think he had robbed very damn many banks. He was still learning."

In 1921, the Newtons hooked up with a pretty good bank burglar. He taught them how to blast safes after trimming their doors with carefully poured nitroglycerin and shaped soap. "He didn't like to do it himself because the nitro fumes made him real sick. . . .Anyhow, everything is simple after you learn how to do it."

Favoring Studebakers because "there weren't many roads and they could go about anywhere a wagon could," the Newtons zipped across America's middle and as far west as California, making withdrawals from banks. In Texas, the Newtons hit banks in Winters, Boerne, San Marcos and no one knows how many et ceteras.

In 1922, while the Medina County town of Hondo slept, they busted into both of Hondo's banks and drove away with about $40,000. Their operandi's modus was usually to case a small town bank, return in darkness months later, get the drop on the local night watchman, then take the money and run.

At times they shifted their style. In Comal County, Joe recalls, "We walked into a New Braunfels bank in broad daylight and helped ourselves to I forget how much."

They kept moving. In Toronto, for example, they ambitiously tried to rob more than a dozen bank messengers who were leaving a state clearing house with satchels filled with cash. The Newtons got away with $82,000 Canadian but, in the resulting shoot-out, had to wing a couple of the well-armed victims.

"You don't kill anybody. That's the main thing," Joe says. "But you've got to hurt somebody once in a while or somebody's going to shoot you."

Trains were tricky. In Texarkana, Arkansas, they accidentally burned up a mail car—with the loot—while trying to smoke out an armed clerk. They robbed five trains, none in Texas. (Willis, however, did rob one near Uvalde.) The staggering score in Roundout, Illinois, didn't come cheap.

Aboard the train, two Newtons pulled guns on the engineer and fireman, ordering them to stop at a prearranged spot where

Joe and the others, including two non-Newtons recruited for the big job, climbed aboard. They escaped with more than fifty sacks of money and securities, but not before one of the confused non-Newtons had wounded Doc Newton several times. The brothers, who buried the loot, were seeking medical help for Doc when they were arrested.

They languished in jail for six months before agreeing to produce the $3 million in exchange for short prison terms. The brothers got three years each. Joe was released after one hard year in Leavenworth.

He was dogged by the notoriety of the $3 million heist, however. In 1936, he was behind bars again, convicted with Willis of robbing a bank in Medford, Oklahoma. Joe, who had been running a filling station in Tulsa, denied that charge. He said witnesses could place him in San Antonio at the time of that robbery. Nevertheless, he got twenty years. Willis did eight years.

All four Newtons drifted back to Uvalde, where Joe ran a filling station until he retired. In time, the others died peacefully.

Uvalde people talked, of course. Uvalde native Margaret Rambie remembers that when she was growing up, the kids ascribed vast fortunes in silver dollars to the Newton brothers.

Joe laughed. "You spend it. You run through a lot. And every once in a while somebody gets arrested and then the lawyer gets most of it. We had to give back every damn penny from Roundout. They had everything listed on a piece of paper. Then I had to pay a lawyer $6000."

Does Joe ever sense that Uvalde people are whispering about buried loot?

"Whisper, hell. They come and talk to me about it for a long time and then offer to help me dig it up."

Laughing, he slapped his knee. "I've got a lot of partners. Yeah."

✻✻✻

THE DAY SANTA BROUGHT A LITTLE CHRISTMAS FEAR

Main Street in Cisco glittered with Christmas festoonery as Freda Weiser and I stood casing the old bank in 1984.

Well, people *call* it Main Street, although that's never been the real name. Today it's Conrad Hilton Avenue, so designated because it runs by Conrad Hilton's first hotel, the Mobley, a boomtown money mill, a red-brick two-story flophouse Hilton acquired in 1919.

Freda and I talked, however, of 1927 and that year's Christmas season, a time when Hilton's hotel empire reached no farther than Dallas and Cisco's Main Street was formally Avenue D.

"It was a bright, mild day, sort of like today," said Freda, her eighty-one-year-old blue eyes studying shoppers on the sidewalks. She was speaking of a day made infamous in Texas history, a day when a bank robber disguised himself as Santa Claus.

The old bank building is deserted. The First National Bank of Cisco moved in 1982 to upscale quarters a couple of blocks away. Beside the old bank, we turned into the alley that connected Avenue E, on the west, with what was Avenue D, on the east. Freda said the abandoned bulletproof drive-in window in the alley had once been a door.

She had reason to recall that exit. Santa and his helpers used that door to reach their getaway car after robbing the bank.

The building's 1967 State Historical Survey Committee plaque abbreviates the long, ghastly tale:

Scene of daring Santa Claus bank robbery, Dec. 23, 1927.

During Christmas festivities, costumed Santa and three fellow bandits looted bank of $12,200 in cash and $150,000 in securities. They escaped through gun battle with two little girls as hostages. A three day manhunt followed.

The children and money were recovered; the robbers captured. Six persons were killed, eight injured. Later a mob lynched 'Santa' when he broke out of jail.

Freda was a twenty-four-year-old bookkeeper with light brown hair. Then Freda Stroebel, she was fresh off the farm and delighted to be earning fifty bucks a month. She'd been working at the bank for about six months. With a pleasant smile, she blamed Santa and his gunmen for putting gray in her hair. Today the retired widow's hair is all white, and she is the bank's only surviving employee from 1927.

On that eve before Christmas Eve so long ago, she and co-worker Vance Littleton were in the bookkeeping room at the rear of the bank. The two little girls mentioned in the plaque were Laverne Comer, twelve, and Emma May Robinson, ten. They'd asked Freda how much savings they had remaining for Christmas shopping.

From the counting room, the view of the front of the bank was obstructed by a partition. Those in the room had missed Santa's entrance at the front. They were startled when Mrs. B. P. Blasengame pushed her six-year-old daughter, Frances, into the room.

"The bank's being robbed," gasped Mrs. Blasengame, shoving her daughter toward the door into the alley.

"Stop," shouted Henry Helms, entering the room. Waving two handguns, Helms, thirty-two, was a dangerous man. He'd been sentenced to five years for robbery in Wichita County only the year before. He'd been paroled by Governor Miriam Ferguson.

That Mrs. Blasengame didn't stop but struck out straight for the nearby Cisco police headquarters could have been an omen of things to come for Helms and his three younger companions who had tackled the prosperous but vulnerable bank.

Quickly the Cisco folks armed themselves. Merchants dragged out weapons long hidden beneath their counters. Hardware dealers began passing out arms to every able-bodied man. Adding to the citizens' zest for the battle was a $5000 reward for dead bank robbers that had been posted by the Texas Bankers Association. The reward was paid only for *dead* bank robbers. Adding to the bandits' desperation was a Texas statute that made bank robbery an offense punishable by death.

Within minutes, Patrolman George Carmichael was at the Avenue E opening of the alley, and Police Chief Bit Bedford was at the Avenue D end. They were joined by armed volunteers. The getaway car, a big Buick stolen in Wichita Falls, was parked near the alley door to the bank.

The bank became a shooting gallery. At Littleton's suggestion, he and Freda crawled beneath a table. They were soon ordered out, however, by the man dressed as Santa Claus. He was a bandit who shared Helms' taste for easy money. He was Marshall Ratliff, who had been convicted for robbing a bank at nearby Valera a year earlier. He, too, had been pardoned by Governor Ferguson.

For weeks, the four bandits had been lying around Wichita Falls plotting the Cisco job. Ratliff required a disguise because he was known in Cisco, where his mother had run a cafe. He was the "brains" of the outfit insofar as any brains were involved. He selected the Santa Claus suit as a perfect disguise.

A third bandit was Robert Hill, twenty-two, who'd done two concurrent two-year prison terms for burglary. His story was a sad one. An orphan, Hill had once been sent to the reformatory in Gatesville just because nobody could think of anywhere else to place him. The fourth bandit, Louis Davis, had no criminal record. He was described as a hard-working family man who badly needed money. Davis would be the first to die, cut down in the gunbattle.

And the battle was raging when Helms noticed Freda staring at him. He snarled, "Don't look at me like that." She told me: "I guess he didn't want me to identify him later."

The bandits herded their hostages into the deadly crossfire that traversed the alley.

"Bank Cashier Alex Spears went out the door. He was hit in the jaw," recalled Freda. "Oscar Cliett [a wholesale grocer who had chanced to be in the bank], was beside me. He was hit in the toe. 'Santa' was using me for a shield," she said.

The bandits forced the little girls into the car and tossed in their burlap bag of loot. Bullets were flying everywhere, Freda said. Marion Olson, a Harvard student home for the holidays, had crawled into the car and then tumbled out, bleeding from a thigh wound.

"Santa Claus told me to get into the car," remembered Freda. "I didn't say anything but I refused to go with them. One reason is that our own people were shooting at the car. They were going crazy, shooting everywhere. Everybody had come out with a gun."

Freda wasn't sure whether she was more afraid of the bandits or the ad hoc committee of citizen gunmen. She and E. J. Poe, a teller, were standing paralyzed as bullets whizzed by.

"A dentist yelled out of his upstairs window at us. He told us to go into the little alley," said Freda.

The commercial district was a labyrinth of alleyways. Luckily, an extremely narrow one handily intersected the larger alley. It was a dead end, but it was out of the direct line of fire. Freda said she and Poe dashed into it. As she ran the few steps to the mouth of the narrow alley, she passed the crumpled, bloody form of Patrolman Carmichael, who'd been shot down as he moved along the alley toward the getaway car. He wasn't moving. He was dying.

In the narrow alley, Poe and Freda lay flat on the ground and listened to the shooting. "I would have been more scared but I guess I was just dumb. I was calmer than Mr. Poe. He was scared. He was nervous. He nearly died."

The battle, which had begun just after noon, was over in about fifteen minutes. The car finally roared out onto Avenue D and headed south, passing the fallen, mortally wounded Police Chief Bedford.

A posse of tin lizzies formed to pursue the fugitives. Meanwhile, Helms was tossing tacks into the road to puncture tires. The bandits' Buick was almost out of gas. There's a question about whether the gas tank had been pierced.

Approaching them was a car driven by a Rising Star school boy, Woodrow Wilson Harris, fourteen. The bandits drew down on the boy, forcing him and his family from the car. Quickly, the robbers transferred loot, weapons, ammo and their dying companion, Davis, from the getaway car to the Harris auto. Only when they tried to depart did they realize that young Harris had made off with the ignition keys. The posse was coming. They piled out and began throwing stuff back into their disabled Buick. They left behind the dying Davis and, unwittingly, their bag of loot.

The Buick made it a few miles into the wilds south of Cisco where the bloodied bandits left the little girls unharmed and struck out on foot. The resulting manhunt was the biggest ever undertaken in West Texas. Texas Ranger Tom Hickman moved in to coordinate posses and lawmen from seven or eight counties.

After a long chase that involved kidnapping, car thefts, gunbattles and exposure to freezing weather, the three wounded fugitives were nabbed.

Then began rounds of prosecution that demanded much testimony from Freda and other witnesses. Helms eventually was electrocuted at Huntsville. Hill got off with a life sentence and ultimately was paroled. With a new name, he is said to be a respectable citizen today in West Texas. A spectacular death was reserved for Ratliff.

Feigning insanity, Ratliff, fighting a death sentence, was returned to the Eastland County Jail, a legal ploy of prosecutors. There, in an escape attempt on November 18, 1929, he seized a six-shooter and fatally wounded a popular jailer called Uncle Tom Jones.

A mob dragged Ratliff from the jail, tossed a rope over a cable between two electrical poles and swung him up by the neck. When the first rope snapped and Ratliff fell, a merchant quickly provided a new rope. The vigilantes swung up Ratliff again. He choked to death. A naked corpse dangled in the chill wind.

Speaking of the tragic story that began at the bank, Freda told me: "If you go through something like that, you're inclined to think that the bandits got what they deserved. They didn't show anyone any mercy. But I always kind of felt sorry for Robert Hill."

The sun was fading. It was time to drive back to Freda's house on 23rd Street. She wanted to address some Christmas cards.

✳✳✳

Bonnie-Clyde Team Eclipsed Bonnie's Roy

Romantics and screenwriters always forget Roy Thornton. But you can bet Clyde Barrow never did.

Tattooed on Bonnie Parker's right thigh was the indelible reminder: "Bonnie and Roy." See, Bonnie and Roy were man and wife. And when Bonnie and Clyde, those notorious star-crossed lovers, were gunned down by lawmen in 1934, Bonnie was still Mrs. Roy Thornton.

In the 1920s, Bonnie and Roy were schoolmates in Cement City, a West Dallas neighborhood as tough as its name. Roy was a couple of years older than Bonnie. He dropped out after seven years. Bonnie dated several boys, but by the time the petite, taffy-haired high school girl was sixteen in 1926, she was married to Roy. He was a clean-cut guy with dark brown hair and light brown eyes. Ruddy and slender, he stood five feet seven. Comparing photos of Clyde and Roy, women invariably say Roy was better-looking.

Bonnie and Roy set up housekeeping in West Dallas. He was a welder—OK, an apprentice burglar. From the start, the marriage was rocky. Roy had a habit of leaving. He'd disappear for weeks at a time. During his absences, teary-eyed Bonnie would try to locate him, appealing to his friends and kinfolks. She could never run him down, her folks recalled. Apparently, Bonnie wanted the on-and-off marriage to work—until she met Clyde in 1930. After that, Roy was nothing but a tattoo.

Rumors once hinted that Bonnie had a child by Roy. Or had an abortion. Another rumor had her pregnant when she was killed. Ted Hinton of Dallas, one of the lawmen who ambushed Bonnie and Clyde in Louisiana, was quoted:

"Bonnie had had some trouble trying to have a child with Roy Thornton when she was young. After the doctor performed his surgery, Bonnie lost any hope of having a child of her own." The late Hinton was gallantly circumspect. But Blanche Barrow, widow of Buck Barrow, Clyde's brother, doesn't believe the rumors. She informed me, "Bonnie told me she had never been pregnant." Whatever, Bonnie and Clyde clicked. They made music. (Clyde could play a tolerable "Melancholy Baby" on his sax.) But mostly, they made headlines, big ones.

Anonymously, Roy seethed. One of his acquaintances said that Roy wanted to kill Clyde. But you had to stand in line to do that. In love or other pursuits, Roy was rarely lucky.

A single paragraph under a modest headline in *The Dallas Morning News* on May 23, 1933—exactly a year before Clyde and Bonnie were shot to pieces—spelled Roy's fate:

"Sentences of fifty years each were assessed Monday against Oscar Lafferty and Roy Thornton when they pleaded guilty before Judge Noland G. Williams in Criminal District Court No. Two to the robbery of W. L. Bogie, 1818 Park Row, of a watch and automobile March 27." Mrs. Thornton wasn't mentioned.

By the time Bonnie left him in 1930, Roy was pointed toward prison. For example, in Austin that year, he was booked "for investigation." In July, the following year he was picked up by Dallas police "for investigation." These "investigations" meant he was arousing the suspicion of cops. No real charges resulted. But on January 15, 1932, Roy was arrested in Waxahachie and charged with a Red Oak burglary. Indictment ultimately earned him a five-year prison sentence.

He appealed and made bail. Then he was collared by police in New Orleans in April 1933 for carrying a concealed weapon. Tagged a fugitive from Dallas County, he was escorted back to Texas. Again, he made bail.

One night late the following month, W. L. Bogie, a railroad worker, was leaving the Oak Cliff Masonic Lodge, when two gunmen took his watch and his only dollar. In his car, they drove him out on Eagle Ford Road and tied him to a fence. He spent three lonely hours trying to get rescued.

The fifty-year armed-robbery jolt, with the concurrent five-year Red Oak burglary term, gave Roy time to reflect on his wife's wild fling with Clyde. Roy was behind bars when he read about their fatal ambush. His reaction is unrecorded. But we know that Roy was a troublesome prisoner.

In a 1984 book, *The Meanest Man in Texas*, Don Umphrey, a Southern Methodist University professor, told the story of another Clyde, an old hardcase named Clyde Thompson, who killed four men before he got religion. Clyde Thompson recalled Roy's tour at Retrieve Prison Farm in Brazoria County:

"Roy was not good at farm work. He was often behind and ended up standing on barrels. In frustration, he swung at a guard. Instead of being sent to the hole, he was made to stand on a barrel for seven consecutive days and nights. As the week passed, his legs swelled to twice their normal size, and then they turned black. But there was no relenting on the part of the guards. Finally, his legs burst open. He was taken to a hospital where he spent two months."

When Texas prison officials set up a "Little Alcatraz" unit at Eastham Prison Farm in Houston County to deal with the state's most intractable creme de la crime, both Clyde Thompson and Roy made the cut.

And on October 3, 1937, Roy finally became famous for fifteen minutes. Twenty-seven of Texas' toughest cons tried to crash out of Little Alcatraz. Overpowering a couple of guards, they moved upstairs in a wing of Eastham's main building, headed for the prison armory. Their plan was to distribute weapons to a mob of prisoners. A mass escape would follow, they supposed. The escape plan was dumb, but Clyde Thompson always maintained that somebody squealed. Whatever, leaders didn't fully consider that to reach the armory they'd have to pass through the guards' sleeping quarters. Guard J. M. Thomas, relieved from picket duty, had just entered the dormitory to wash up for supper. Alone, he heard the convicts outside his door shushing one another as they crept up the stairs.

"I grabbed my rifle, leveled it at the screen-door opening into the hallway. In a second, Thornton appeared at the door with a [hostage] guard in front of him. They were about twelve feet from me. I saw the convict's arm reach for the door. I fired. The bullet struck him in the neck. He fell." Thomas began levering shots from his Winchester so rapidly that witnesses later said it "sounded like a machine gun."

Alarmed, other guards came running. The cons, armed with their hostages' sidearms, engaged the guards in a brief gun battle.

Cons ran for their cells. A guard suffered a slight stab wound in the fight. The escape leaders were mowed down.

Clyde Thompson was shot through the right shoulder. Forrest Gibson, a one-eyed murderer who'd killed a guard in an escape from Retrieve earlier that year, was gravely wounded.

Killed alongside Thornton was Austin Avers, who was serving life sentences from three counties and had escaped a dozen times from Texas and Oklahoma jails and prisons. Avers was the man convicted for smuggling guns into the Walls prison at Huntsville in July 1934 to enable Raymond Hamilton, Joe Palmer and others to make their spectacular escape from the prison death house. Hamilton and Palmer were executed in 1935.

When the prison medic looked over Roy's stripped body, he noted the neck wound and a second bullet wound in his right side. And he noted tattoos: three hearts in a wreath on Roy's right forearm and a pistol on the center of his stomach. No "Bonnie and Roy" was recorded.

Prison officials telegraphed Roy's family. When no one claimed the body, they buried him at Eastham. The prison farm Roy hated became his permanent address.

✳✳✳

In Olden Days, the Outlaws Outdrew 'em All

What did Dallas folks do half a century ago on a Super Sunday before they were wired to watch football teams play in the Super Bowl?

Dig deep in some old trunk for a copy of *The Dallas Morning News* for Sunday, January 20, 1935. There lies a surprising answer.

The impression leaps at you. People relieved the moneyless monotony of the Great Depression by closely following the adventures of criminals. Yes.

Scanning old headlines, you can imagine thousands of otherwise bored readers tracking with pencil marks on homemade charts the activities of public enemies. Newspapers should have published criminal charts the way hurricane tracking charts are sometimes published nowadays.

Take Raymond Hamilton, a flashy young bandit from West Dallas. He had been blamed for two bank robberies that week.

Identified as one of two gunmen who took $500 from the First National Bank of Handley (in Tarrant County) at 9:30 A.M. Saturday, Hamilton was described as "leader of the death house escape at Huntsville several months ago." Earlier in the week, he'd been hunted in Leon County after four gunmen took $7,011.50 from the Citizens State Bank of Buffalo.

The report was stranger than fact. Different witnesses described two different Raymond Hamiltons among the four Buffalo bandits. For all we know, three or maybe all four were Raymond Hamilton.

Raymond Hamilton was sensational. He had escaped from the death house at Huntsville on July 22, 1934. He'd been condemned for killing a prison guard in an earlier breakout. And listen, just a little over two months down the road, on March 27, 1935, after taking nearly a grand from a bank in Prentiss, Mississippi, he and a buddy would disarm a whole posse—more than a dozen, maybe two dozen guys. A whole posse.

And he loved to taunt cops by writing letters to them. After two prison escapes, he wrote to Texas prison officials to tell them how to run the penitentiary.

Concerned about his press, Hamilton once amiably kidnapped Harry McCormick, a Houston newspaper man, to dictate the Raymond Hamilton story as told by Raymond Hamilton. McCormick, who later worked as a police reported for *The Dallas Morning News*, became a legend.

Hamilton had been a running mate of Clyde Barrow and Bonnie Parker. Of course, by January 20, 1935, Bonnie and Clyde had been put out to pasture, or more correctly, put under the pasture. They had gone the way of John Dillinger, Pretty Boy Floyd, Baby Face Nelson and a dozen others who, for a time, captured the public's attention.

To be sure, there's plenty of scary crime news around today. But it's not the same. In the old days, the underworld provided three-dimensional characters. And, moreover, they had a much longer run than contemporary thugs. The faceless felons of today pull one or two desperate jobs and are knocked off or locked up.

There are exceptions. But who really wants to hear Henry Lee Lucas drone his hundreds of murder confessions?

In the eternal game of cops and robbers, there may be more robbers nowadays, but there are also more cops. And they are better trained and better equipped. No one can successfully bet against today's cops.

January 20, 1935. What a week it had been. On Wednesday in Oklawaha, Florida, Ma Barker and her son Freddie had been killed by lawmen's submachine guns in a furious five-hour battle. Ma, fifty-five, died with her submachine gun in her arms, the same arms that once had cradled her outlaw sons. Doc, one of them, had been arrested just the week before in Chicago.

On that Saturday, Dallas radio listeners learned, Alvin Karpis, "Old Creepy" of the Barker-Karpis gang, had just machine-gunned his way out of a police trap in Atlantic City, New Jersey.

That Sunday, readers of *The News* were provided the latest word from the trial of doomed Bruno Hauptmann in the Lindbergh kidnapping case and treated to an Associated Press photo of Dutch Schultz being arrested in New York for income tax evasion, the same sin that had landed Al Capone in Alcatraz a year earlier. Schultz couldn't wait to be convicted. Mobsters killed him. Anyone who's seen the all-dancing, all-singing, all-shooting film *The Cotton Club* knows the fate of Schultz.

In a way, 1935 might have been a watershed for public fascination with hoodlumdom. The most colorful criminal characters were departing the state. Raymond Hamilton, before the year was out, would be arrested in Fort Worth and electrocuted. Karpis would be arrested in New Orleans the following year by J. Edgar Hoover, in person.

Our fascination with old-time outlaws always will linger. But by January 20, 1935, the public's romance with real-live public enemies was headed for the rocks.

Telling it Straight

Taking the shade, the big veranda open to Avenue A was tranquil and cool at midday in April of 1984. Out in the sunshine, a dozen birds were singing. Al Slaton spoke: "You know, about the worst place in the world to kill a person is a drive-in movie."

A mirthless smile crossed his Cherokee features as Slaton recalled June 7, 1972, the night he shot Robert Hugh Barber.

Slaton had killed another man years before. But that was in a prison knife fight in Oklahoma. No one got upset. Violent deaths of convicts didn't wrinkle many brows. A shooting in a drive-in theater, however, can upset the entire movie-going public.

Slaton had been a wild kid, and he grew into a wild man. He was a thief who was arrested almost 100 times. He did more than twenty years in assorted prisons. For a couple of reasons, Slaton is a real oddity.

Number one, he is alive. Number two, he works for the federal government. He's got a GS-4 civil service rating and stands a good chance for promotion. But that's getting ahead of his story.

Slaton was telling how he shot his old friend five times in the head during that movie at Austin's Chief Drive-In. The killing, in plan and execution, wasn't what you'd mistake for the perfect crime.

"There was an off-duty highway patrolman and his family in a car on one side. Over the other way was an off-duty police officer. The place was crowded. Witnesses everywhere.

"But I had to do it. I knew damn well that I was in danger and some other people, too, as long as Barber lived."

Barber had been a pal of Slaton's for about twenty years, in and out of prison. Slaton said Barber had murdered more than a dozen people, among them a Fort Worth policeman. He had become "a mad dog," Slaton said, too dangerous to live.

Slaton sensed that he would be living on borrowed time until he stopped Barber's clock. A few days before, Barber had driven from Houston to Austin, where Slaton was living, to show off the bullet riddled body of a new victim, a mutual friend, a Houston bandit named Paul E. Myre.

"In Houston, Barber and Christina, his wife, had taken Paul out on the town, wined him and dined him. They were bar-hopping in a car when Barber reached across Christina and shot Paul in the head. Blood and brains went all over Christina. She was scared to death of her husband. My girlfriend knew all about it. We all feared Barber."

Slaton was trying to get straight, working in the rehabilitation section of the Austin State Hospital. Then Barber showed up with the mess in his car.

Leaving Slaton and his girlfriend stunned, Barber drove off toward Houston with his grisly cargo. Slaton was certain that Barber would return soon to eliminate the witnesses he had crazily created. So Slaton had bought a snub-nosed .38-caliber pistol by the time Barber returned to Austin.

"He was drinking vodka. He wanted to kill a policeman, any policeman. He ran red lights and stop signs trying to attract one. Finally, he drove into that movie."

About fifteen or twenty minutes into the film, *The Hot Rock*, an adventure yarn about jewel thieves, Slaton made his move. "I could tell Barber was getting mad. He was drinking that vodka, cussing and threatening. I thought, 'If I'm going to do it, I better do it now.' I reached for the purse and slipped the gun from it. When he turned in the seat toward me, I shot him in the eye. I was just in time. Barber had a .38 in his hand."

Because his door was open a crack, Barber tumbled out of the car. Slaton crawled out, shot Barber four more times in the head, and shoved him back into the car.

"I got behind the wheel. The car didn't want to start. People were all over the place. Those off-duty officers must have been unarmed or didn't want a gunfight in that crowd. But everybody was looking at us. Cars were moving around. I finally got Barber's car going, but with people and cars every which way, it was a miracle that I got out of there."

Slaton hauled the body out in the sticks and dumped it. The next day, after some soul-searching, he consulted with two ministers. Prayerfully, Slaton phoned an acquaintance, an Austin municipal court judge named Ronnie Earle (later district attorney of Travis County). Then Slaton guided law enforcement officers to Barber's corpse. He was indicted for murder with malice.

A good record in Austin had earned Slaton the sympathy of influential friends, including several ministers. With their help and, moreover, a powerful court room defense by attorney Warren Burnett, Slaton beat the rap. Testimony by law enforcement officers helped. Barber was a cop killer. Some officers took the view that instead of a trial, Slaton should have been given a medal.

Slaton wasn't freed, however. He was tripped up by a federal handgun-possession charge. He served a couple of years in Leavenworth, a federal prison in Kansas where he found standards "humanely advanced from those of Texas or Oklahoma state prisons." Because of his work in Austin, Slaton was assigned to the prison hospital. There, he worked and studied hard.

"Leavenworth wasn't degrading. They made me feel responsible. The experience changed my attitude," he said.

A change in Slaton was past due. He'd spent most of his life in trouble. Besides, Jess Hay, a Dallas financier who tried for years to reform Slaton, had issued an ultimatum after the Austin killing. "This is it," he told Slaton. "If you mess up again, you're on your own." Hay and Slaton go way back. They had met at a Methodist church in Dallas.

Slaton got out of Leavenworth in December 1974 and moved to Temple because he had worn out his welcome in Texas' largest cities. Soon Temple police were questioning his landlady and neighbors about his activities. Looking over Slaton's record, Leonard Hancock, the Temple police chief, wondered why an Alvin D. Slaton had to land in his town. "He was about as bad as they come," Hancock reckoned.

Well, Slaton stood the world on its ear. He went straight.

He got a job as a nursing assistant at Temple's Santa Fe Hospital. Off duty, he worked with paraplegics and quadriplegics. He worked with kids, warning them to stay out of trouble.

After laying a cornerstone on a new reputation, Slaton discovered he might qualify for a federal job. He applied for work with the Veterans Administration. Slaton believes the feds quizzed everyone he'd ever known. Finally, in 1978, he was cleared for a job as a nursing assistant in the psychiatric section of the VA Medical Center in Waco.

Within two weeks, he was having problems. Personal problems. Conscience. Patients were being beaten up, locked up and continually abused.

He was painfully aware of the traditional fate of whistle-blowers.

"But something had to be done. What was happening was terrible," he said. Slaton began writing anonymous letters to newspapers about brutality in the psychiatric section.

Several dailies, including *The Dallas Morning News*, began digging up stories about the conditions. Ultimately, an official investigation was launched. Slaton identified himself as the anonymous tipster and in a nine-page, single-spaced affidavit described the abuses he had seen. In the last paragraph, he noted:

"I am proud to be a VA employee and as a result of speaking out I am concerned about my job since I need it. . . . "

Slaton not only retained his job but also was promoted and transferred to Temple's Olin E. Teague Veterans Center, an institution that he calls "first class."

Hay reappeared to help the reformed con open Al Slaton's Rose Garden, which provides housing for elderly and indigent people.

On the Rose Garden's veranda the day I talked to him, Slaton sat chain smoking Kools and talking about the late Robert Hugh Barber.

"You may have trouble accepting this," Slaton said. "But I loved him. Hell, I bought the stone for his grave."

※※※

Last Meals: Inmate Orders Rarely Exotic

Before reviewing the last meals of the 27 men executed by the state of Texas since 1982, let me pose a question.

What would you order?

Seven courses and seven wines? Or is the event too somber for festive flavors, too sober for drinks that daze?

Understandably, you or I might opt for a favorite comfort food, lots of it, and heavy on the butter. Sentimentally, you might crave some long-ago dish that your mom used to make—or maybe one that your sweetie used to burn.

Philosophically, we might decide to just fast.

Officials of the Texas Department of Corrections cater to condemned men—within reason. But there's no wine cellar, so don't even think about a jeroboam of Mad-Dog 20-20.

And forget flights of fancy like nasturtium soup. A yen for watermelon in midwinter, for example, was judged unreasonable. The melancholy menu is limited to what's in the prison pantry.

It's a big pantry, luckily. Back in the days of the electric chair, a 300-pound killer once wished for and got: a dozen fried eggs, a two-pound T-bone steak, an inch-thick center-cut slice of ham, a few unrecorded side dishes, a gallon of lemonade and a quart of ice cream.

In those days, the diner traditionally shared his last meal with other guys on Death Row. But the jumbo prisoner personally polished off everything but one bite of ham.

The late Don Reid of the *Huntsville Item* recalled how Assistant Warden (and executioner) Joe Byrd would appear at the cell of a man whose time had run out. Byrd would read the prisoner's death warrant and then ask what he'd like for dinner. (Readers who've seen the death warrant will never forget it. Although it resembles any other legal document, it is dramatically and unforgettably laced with a black ribbon.)

Reid noted that by the time the warrant is read the condemned man will have already been thinking about his last meal. "This is an important part of the ritual," observed Reid.

"Silently he hands Byrd a slip of paper through the bars. Byrd studies it and smiles. Hot rolls. A large bowl of strawberries, and ice cream—five orders. Byrd knows the man will manage to send four of the bowls to the others along death row."

As designated witness to Texas executions for the Associated Press, Reid, who saw 189 men die in the electric chair, would sometimes join a friendly inmate for his last meal. Reid recalled one cook's questioning an order for five slices of chocolate cake until he remembered there were five men on death row. The cook sent an entire cake. While some men fasted, others ate heartily.

From 1924 to 1964, when courts decided to give executioners a rest, a total of 361 men were electrocuted by the state. The favorite entree during the period was T-bone steak, sometimes rivaled by shark-sized orders of fried shrimp.

Before 1924, condemned prisoners were hanged by sheriffs of the counties where they were convicted. Last meals were dictated by the mood of the sheriff. But in a section on enforcing judgment in capital cases, the Code of Criminal Procedure of those days states: "The sheriff shall comply with any reasonable request of the convict."

Executions were reinstated in 1982 with lethal injection as the prescribed method of execution. Death row was moved from its old address at the Walls unit in Huntsville to the Ellis Unit, sixteen miles northeast of Huntsville.

Hours before a prisoner's date with death, he's moved from Ellis back to the Walls and into a cell adjoining the execution chamber. If he's to die right after midnight, his last meal is served about 6:30 or 7 P.M. Following is a list of the last meals of doomed diners, all convicted murderers, from 1982 to the spring of 1992. I'm grateful to assistant director Charles L. Brown of TDCJ's institutional division for pulling records. Each man's name is followed by his age, execution date, race, county where he was convicted, and the dinner he was served before his final exit:

Charles Brooks, 40, (12-7-82), black, Tarrant: T-bone steak, french fries, catsup, worchestershire sauce, rolls, peach cobbler, iced tea. (I'm told Mr. Brooks complained that he couldn't get shrimp.)

James David Autry, 29, (3-14-84), white, Jefferson: hamburger, french fries, Dr Pepper.

Ronald D. O'Bryan, 39, (3-31-84), white, Harris: T-bone steak (medium well to well done), french fries, catsup, corn, sweet peas, rolls, lettuce and tomato salad, french dressing, iced tea with artificial sweetener, saltines, ice cream, Boston cream pie.

Thomas A. Barefoot, 39, (10-30-84), white, Bell: chef soup with crackers, chili with beans, steamed rice, seasoned pinto beans, corn O'Brien, seasoned mustard greens, hot spiced beets, iced tea.

Doyle Skillern, 49, (1-16-85), white, Lubbock: T-bone steak, baked potato, butter, sweet peas, rolls, banana pudding, coffee.

Stephen P. Morin, 34, (3-13-85), white, Jefferson: unleavened bread.

Jesse de la Rosa, 24, (5-15-85), hispanic, Bexar: spanish rice, refried beans, flour tortillas, jalapeño peppers, T-bone steak, tea, chocolate cake.

Charles Milton, 34, (6-25-85), black, Tarrant: T-bone steak, french fries, tossed green salad, french dressing, catsup, hot rolls, chocolate cake.

Henry Martinez Porter, 43, (7-9-85), hispanic, Tarrant: flour tortillas, T-bone steak, refried beans, tossed salad, jalapeño peppers, ice cream, chocolate cake.

Charles Rumbaugh, 28, (9-11-85), white, Potter: one flour tortilla, water.

Charles Bass, 30, (3-12-86), white, Harris: plain cheese sandwich.

Jeffery A. Barney, 28, (4-16-86), white, Harris: two boxes of frosted flakes and one pint of milk.

Jay K. Pinkerton, 24, (5-15-86), white, Nueces-Potter: fish sandwich, french fries, milk.

Rudy Ramos Esquivel, 50, (6-09-86), hispanic, Harris: fried chicken breast, corn on the cob, french fries, jalapeño pepper, pecan pie.

Kenneth Brock, 37, (6-19-86), white, Harris: large double-meat cheeseburger with mustard, french fries, Dr Pepper.

Randy Woolls, 36, (8-20-86), white, Tom Green: cheeseburger, french fries, chocolate cake, iced tea.

Larry Smith, 30, (8-22-86), black, Dallas: smothered steak and gravy, french fries, lemon pie, Coca-Cola.

Chester Wicker, 37, (8-26-86), white, Galveston: lettuce and tomatoes.

Michael Wayne Evans, 30, (12-4-86), black, Dallas: no last meal requested.

Richard Andrade, 25, (12-18-86), hispanic, Nueces: pizza, pinto beans, spanish rice, cake.

Raymond Hernandez, 44, (1-30-87), hispanic, El Paso: beef tacos, beef enchiladas, jalapeño peppers, salad, onion rings, chopped onion, hot sauce, shredded cheese, coffee.

Eliseo H. Moreno, 27, (3-4-87), hispanic, Fort Bend: four cheese enchiladas, two fish patties, french fries, milk, catsup, lemon pie.

Anthony C. Williams, 27, (5-28-87), black, Harris: fish, tartar sauce, french fries, catsup, light bread, milk.

Elliott R. Johnson, 28, (6-24-87), black, Jefferson: cheeseburger, french fries.

John R. Thompson, 32, (7-8-87), white, Bexar: freshly squeezed orange juice.

Joseph Starvaggi, 34, (9-10-87), white, Montgomery: no last meal requested.

Robert Streetman, 27, (1-7-88), white, Hardin: half dozen scrambled eggs, flour tortillas, french fries, catsup, iced tea.

Donald Franklin, 37, (11-3-88), black, Nueces: hamburger, french fries, catsup.

Raymond Landry, 39, (12-13-88), black, Harris: no last meal requested.

Leon R. King, 44, (3-22-89), black, Harris: no last meal requested.

Stephen McCoy, 40, (5-24-89), white, Harris: cheeseburger, french fries, strawberry milkshake.

James Paster, 44, (9-20-89), white, Harris: no last meal requested.

Carlos Deluna, 27, (12-7-89), hispanic, Nueces: no last meal requested.

Jerome Butler, 54, (4-21-90), black, Harris: T-bone steak, four pieces chicken (two breasts, two legs), fresh corn, iced tea.

Johnny Anderson, 30, (5-17-90), white, Jefferson: three hamburgers, french fries, chocolate ice cream with nuts, iced tea.

James Smith, 37, (6-26-90), black, Harris: yogurt.

Mikel Derrick, 33, (7-18-90), white, Harris: rib eye steak, tossed green salad with blue cheese dressing, baked potato with sour cream. (But refused meal.)

Lawrence Buxton, 38, (2-26-91), black, Harris: filet mignon, pineapple upside down cake, chocolate milkshake.

Ignacio Cuevas, 59, (5-23-91), hispanic, Harris: chicken and dumplings, steamed rice, black-eyed peas, sliced bread, iced tea.

Jerry Joe Bird, 54, (6-17-91), white, Cameron: double cheeseburger with mustard, mayonnaise, pickles, onions, tomatoes, iced tea.

James Russell, 42, (9-19-91), black, Fort Bend: an apple.

G. W. Green, 49, (11-12-91), white, Montgomery: pizza, coffee and tea. (Didn't eat pizza.)

Johnny Frank Garrett, 28, (2-11-92), white, Potter: chocolate cream.

Nowadays, the average prisoner spends nearly seven and half years on death row before his execution date. James Smith, sentenced to die for a Houston robbery-murder, asked for a lump of dirt for a last meal. It wasn't ordinary prison yard, Walker County dirt that Mr. Smith wanted. He asked for "rhaeakunda" dirt, reportedly eaten in voodoo rituals. Prison officials balked. In the end (6-26-90), Mr. Smith settled for yogurt.

✳ PART III ✳

✳ TEXAS FOLK AND FOLKLORE ✳

***

What's In a Name? Out in Bug Tussle, Folks Aren't Sure

Today, we have naming of parts.

So we turn to that Texan of parts, Fred Tarpley, author of *1001 Texas Place Names.*

Tarpley, a professor of English at East Texas State University, suggested that we play a little game.

Here's how. We'll list ten names of Lone Star places, old or new, current or defunct, along with their counties. You may then try to guess the origin of each name. We'll tell you the true story, according to Tarpley's research, and you can rate yourself as a student of Texas name origins.

1. Buffalo Bayou (Harris County)
2. May West Oil Field (Brown)
3. Nameless (Travis)
4. Cologne (Goliad)
5. Crush (McLennan)
6. Balmorhea (Reeves)
7. Cut 'n Shoot (Montgomery)
8. Dime Box (Lee)
9. Bug Tussle (Fannin)
10. Red Light (Hudspeth)

Origin herewith:

Buffalo Bayou: The bayou on which Houston was built has inspired stories about its naming that involve herds of buffaloes, but the more likely explanation is that it was named for the buffalo fish. Old timers used to tell stories about the days when Buffalo Bayou was so full of buffalo fish that seiners routinely had to dump half their catch to make the remaining load light enough to handle.

May West Oil Field: Although sailors in World War II named their inflatable life jackets for Mae West, the buxom, blond screen star, there is no such influence here. The oil field is located west of May, named for Nathan L. May, one of the first settlers who operated a store and a post office. Instead of taking the usual locational name that would have yielded West May, this oil field was designated May West.

Nameless: The site, first surveyed in the 1850s, attracted numerous settlers by 1852. In 1880, the town applied for a post office, and after authorities rejected six names, a frustrated citizen wrote back, "let the post office be nameless, and be damned." "Nameless" was accepted, and a post office operated with the post mark of Nameless from 1880 until 1890.

Cologne: An educated guess might be that this community was named for the German city. But educated guesses often underestimate the sense of humor behind the naming process in Texas. The settlement was built at a cattle slaughter and shipping center, including a hog rendering plant. The aromatic name was chosen because of the prevailing atmosphere.

Crush: A head-on collision between two unmanned locomotives was staged on September 15, 1896, as a publicity stunt conceived by William G. Crush, M-K-T Railroad passenger agent, for whom the area was named. More than 30,000 spectators, gathered by train from all over the region, watched the two engines speeding toward each other. Contrary to the assurances of mechanics, the steam boilers exploded on impact, killing two persons and injuring others who were struck by flying metal. The event inspired Texarkana-born ragtime composer Scott Joplin to write a tune called "The Crash at Crush."

Balmorhea: It's not a medical problem. In fact, it's a truly pleasant spot. The land promoters who established the town were Balcolm, Morrow and Rhea. Someone figured out a method of honoring all three by combining the first three or four letters of their surnames.

Cut 'n Shoot: Several of the stories agree that there was once a preacher who was much too popular with the women. When charges were made at a church meeting, the men ran to wagons and buggies to get knives and rifles for the melee that followed. Another explanation is that cutting and shooting developed from an argument over the design of a new church steeple.

Dime Box: The name perpetuated the memory of a time when there was a community mailbox, erected by citizens, where teamsters and freighters passing that way carried mail to the residents, asking a service charge of 10 cents for each article delivered. When a nearby post office was planned, efforts were made to call it Brown's Mill, for the proposed postmaster, but confusion with Brownsville made the citizens decide to re-establish it as Dime Box. National publicity came in 1943 when Dime Box was the first U.S. town to "contribute 100 percent" to the March of Dimes.

Bug Tussle: One of Texas' most famous place names identifies a small community in an area once popular with Sunday school classes for picnics. One anecdote describes how swarms of bugs attracted to an ice cream social ruined the party. Another tradition maintains that after the Sunday school picnics, there was nothing to do but watch the tumblebugs tussle. Stories generally agree, however, that the area was a favorite gathering place for both bugs and Sunday school outings. The name is a bumper sticker favorite. The Texas Highway Department has given up placing road signs at the crossroads because they are such prized trophies for dormitories and fraternity houses.

Red Light: If you were hoping for a bawdy origin of this community's name, shame on you. The local explanation is that the settlement was so small that at night when a train passed through, the passengers could see nothing but one red signal light at the depot.

※※※

PHANTOMS PLY TWILIGHT ZONE THAT IS CADDO LAKE AREA'S PAST

If East Texas came in a box, it would have to list a lot of supernatural ingredients.

A somber fog often cloaks spooky Caddo Lake. And ghosts will invade your fancy if you watch the twisting vapors coil about the thick roots and knees of the mossy-haired cypress trees.

Knees. The cypress knobs are called knees. They bob from the water like the heads of drowning men and women going down for the last time.

Many men and women have gone down here, boatloads. Most tragically remembered are sixty passengers lost when the *Mittie Stephens*, a 312-ton steamboat out of Shreveport, burned and sank in these waters on the night of February 11, 1869. But others went down alone. Texas Congressman Robert Potter, revolutionary secretary of the navy, was swimming furiously to escape a gang of feudists when a rifle ball fatally sank him on March 2, 1842. His murder is unavenged.

This lake has claimed a multitude of lives. Indeed, perils are reflected in the very name of the lakeshore village near here. Uncertain, in Harrison County, is the namesake of Uncertain Landing, so called by the leery steamboat captains of yesteryear.

Leaning against Louisiana, this corner of Texas is overpopulated with night bumpers. Take Jefferson, a dozen miles from here. What do you make of a town with 2500 mortals and 15,000 or more graves?

The lovely 150-year-old town in Marion county was once a busy port on Big Cypress Bayou. Now Jefferson teems with specters of its gaudy and gunpowdery past. They're accused of rocking the rocking chairs in dozens of Jefferson antique shops. And they moan when the night wind rubs the antebellum Excelsior House.

A favorite hotel of history buffs and occultists, the Excelsior has frequently sheltered ghosts, Jeffersonians say. The chamber maids know. One maid, who has since resigned, said she saw a headless man stalking the halls. Effects of the Excelsior House are so special that even movie-maker Steven Spielberg experienced weird vibes there.

Once I sat up all night in the Jay Gould Suite, watching, waiting. But I saw nothing more sinister than the capricious door of an armoire that repeatedly swung open—by itself. By itself?

Around the corner at the century-aged Brownhouse, superb actress Marcia Thomas in her Living Room Theater conjures up the late poet Emily Dickinson. Marcia presents in her parlor one-woman performances of "The Belle of Amherst" when she and Emily aren't on the road.

While Marcia easily controls Emily, the actress cannot restrain another roomer, the shade of one of the girls whose giggles once filled the place.

In the long, respectable history of the century-old Brownhouse, Marcia's research revealed a lapse in which the brick building served as a bordello. In her favor, the ghost of the Brownhouse takes dainty steps. But the steps are sometimes a distraction to Marcia's husband, Tater Thomas. And they starch the hair on the family cat.

Marcia will tell you that the trouble with transmogrified tarts is they stay up all night. Old habits die hard.

But Marcia's isn't the most celebrated ghost of a girl gone wrong in Jefferson's past. Nearly everywhere in town are Police Gazette-style pix of Diamond Bessie, a gold-hearted good-time girl done in by her pimp in Jefferson and now buried in Oakwood Cemetery. Bessie is considered restless.

Around the corner from the Brownhouse, at Auntie Skinner's Riverboat Club, Joe Muller plays antique tunes on a rare plectrum banjo. Joe plays background music for a narration of the mystery of the *Mittie Stephens* by Ruby Lang, a marine archaeologist trained by Texas A&M.

Ruby, a Brooklyn girl with a taste for Auntie Skinner's pizza, has been vainly searching for the remains of the steamboat wreck for three years—two years without any funding. Go ahead, applaud. In her research, she did dig up many pix of steamboats that once plied Big Cypress Bayou. Blown up, the illustrations now decorate the walls of Auntie Skinner's.

Ruby believes the wreck is hidden beneath silt in an underwater wasteland of rusting oil well equipment that effectively muddles detection by scientific instruments.

In 1986, on the eve of Ruby's frustrated return to Brooklyn, she was willing to drop a bombshell. The *Mittie Stephens* disaster, she says, may have been a case of arson. Although she's never reported it in her scholarly papers, Ruby, after studying passenger lists and documents in the tragedy, privately conjectures that a murder was done aboard the steamboat on that long-ago February night. She theorizes the *Mittie Stephens* was then torched by the murderer to conceal his crime. "It's a mystery," she says. Her smile is tantalizing.

To confront a genuine, living and breathing will-o'-the-wisp, you need only recross the Harrison County line to Karnack and meet the Caddo Lake Country's most famous citizen—Wyatt A. Moore.

Moore established himself as a ghost while evading revenuers during Prohibition. They never could catch him.

He was famous even before the appearance last year of his autobiography, *Every Sun That Rises*, edited for the UT Press by Thad Sitton and James H. Conrad. The title is Wyatt talking: "I look forward to each day and I feel like every sun that rises is just for me."

Wyatt, eighty-five ("I was born in the Year One"), has been Karnack's most widely known citizen ever since Claudia Alta Taylor moved away and became Mrs. Lady Bird Johnson. But Wyatt is at least as well known as Pee Wee Herman or some candidates for governor.

Since James Michener, writing his novel *Texas*, interviewed Wyatt, he has been handing out business cards that say "consultant." He says "I am a consultant. Mr. Michener had a copy of that book sent to me direct from the publishers as soon as it was out. Three dollars and fifty cents postage on it."

Wyatt told me how to make first-rate booze. "Keep your cooker just under 212 degrees. The alcohol will vaporize and the water won't. You'll get a higher-proof liquor. I like to get strong liquor. The proof is what counts. It's just like octane in gas. If it's weak, it don't push you as far."

And he told how he out-wisped the lawmen during Prohibition. "I kept it down in the lake and I sold it out of a boat. The customers was on their own then. And I wasn't scared out in a rowboat. The law couldn't do nothing. On the ground, I didn't trust nobody. They can hem you up on a one-way road, but that lake's wide open. You can go upside-down out there."

Wyatt could quickly paddle off into the cypress wilderness and no lawman could track him. Caddo Lake is notorious for confusing the orientation of all but experienced swamp rats. One wrong turn can mean an overnight stay in what is unpopularly known as "the Caddo motel."

Wyatt enjoyed moonshining's heyday in the 1920s—when shine would fetch $8 or $10 a gallon—but gave up the trade in the 1930s when the Depression and Repeal combined to drive prices down to $2 a gallon.

"It was costing a dollar to make and it was selling for two. I traded 100 gallons for a car and the car cost $190. It was an A Model Ford. I put sheet metal in the windows because the windows kept breaking out. I put the sheet metal in to keep the weather out. But people thought I had an armored car."

He ran fishing camps, built beautiful boats, worked in the oil fields, and even became a lawman.

"What happened was we didn't have a constable and didn't need one. But the court appointed a man and he started doing things and we didn't need a constable, so I put my name on the ticket and was down at Victoria, Texas, on a drilling rig on election day and I was overwhelmingly elected.

"I stayed on it about eighteen months or three-fourths of a two-year term and I just simply resigned, and we didn't have a constable for eighteen years after that. I got it fixed where it would run itself. I caught bank robbers and handled divorce cases, but I didn't catch any moonshiners."

Wyatt says, "What I done and what I been accused of covers everything, you put 'em both together."

What were we talking about?

Had Wyatt heard that Bob Bowman, in his latest *Best of East Texas* volume, wrote that the best haunted house is at Karnack, where a ghost known as "Oonie" inhabits a house once occupied by Lady Bird Johnson?

"I'm familiar with that ghost story. The late Mr. Frank X. Tolbert used to write about it for *The Dallas Morning News*. The place is just a couple of miles from here."

The place is called the Brick House, an enormous white building with seventeen rooms. It was built by slave labor on a hill in the 1840s for the family of Milt Andrews, a merchant and veteran of the Texas Revolution.

More than a century ago, one of the Adams girls, said to be a belle, was sitting by the fireplace in one of the upstairs bedrooms during a violent thunderstorm. A bolt of lightning came down the chimney and killed her. The story goes that she hasn't yet reconciled herself to her fate.

We drove to the Brick House, which was occupied for half a century by the T. J. Taylor family. This is where Claudia Taylor, now Lady Bird Johnson, grew up. I am told that some members of the Taylor family were aware of Oonie, although I cannot say for sure that Claudia had made her acquaintance.

Today the Brick House is the residence of Jerry and Patricia Jones. They are distantly kin to Wyatt Moore. And Jerry now holds Wyatt's old job of constable.

Mrs. Jones and her eighteen-year-old daughter, Angela, were at home when I visited in 1986. We sat on the veranda and talked about Oonie. Angela, a pre-law student at UT-Arlington, explained that the ghost's real name is "Eunice."

She said that her brother, Jett Jones, a student at Grayson County College, was four years old when he started talking to the ghost. He couldn't quite say "Eunice." It came out "Oonie" and the nickname stuck.

Father, mother, daughter, and son have heard noises they blame on Oonie. Sometimes she calls out names. Sometimes she creates the sound of breaking glass, although no cracked glass is found. The family comprises true believers.

Oonie causes no real trouble. She just wants to be noticed. For example, Angela said, "Once when I was about ten or eleven, I was brushing my teeth when the tube of toothpaste jumped right out of my hand and traveled across the bathroom. Something lifted that tube of Colgate toothpaste right out of my hand."

Oonie?

"Oonie," she nodded.

✳✳✳

Bell County Witchcraft Legend Lives On

We compulsorily educated Texans do not believe in the powers of witchcraft. But we are only about two generations removed from Texans who did.

Kenneth W. Davis can tell you all about it. He grew up in Bell County. Early this century, Davis said, stories about witchcraft and the magical properties of silver bullets circulated in Central Texas. One story blends elements of medieval witchcraft and an ancient taboo. With undertones of Eugene O'Neill's *Desire Under the Elms*, the odd events described by Davis predated the 1924 play by a couple of decades.

It happened in Bell County, near Rogers, a black-dirt farming community a few miles south and east of Temple. All the principle players in the tale are dead, but their kin survive, said Davis, declining to smirch the family name.

In the 1890s, the family migrated from northern Alabama to Texas. Their route was circuitous, passing through Dallas, and stopping for a time in McKinney. Restlessly, they moved to Waco, where they paused before finally buying land and settling near Rogers.

After several cotton harvests, the hard-working patriarch of the family showed he wasn't a man for wasting time grieving when a fever killed his wife of thirty-five years. About a week after he buried her, he married Jane, an eighteen-year-old Alabama girl. She had raven hair and was remembered for "a sallow complexion." She was thirty-eight years younger than her husband, who was fifty-six, and three years younger than her youngest stepson, John, who was twenty-one.

A strapping youth, John was industrious. He farmed his own land adjoining his father's acres. He lived in his dad's house, as did two older brothers. Jane was taken with raising exotic plants from which she saved seeds and leaves for making teas and medicinal potions. And she was taken with John, described by some as "handsome." In time, Jane made advances. John resisted.

John is recalled as an "honorable youth," dedicated fully to farming his land well so he could pay for it. Old-timers said that because of her frustrated love, Jane "sort of lost her mind." For his part, John found her attentions offensive. Without waiting for breakfast, he'd leave the house early, driving his team of mules to work in the dark. He'd carry a lunch—salt pork and biscuits—to avoid returning at noon.

During the late spring, his lunches began to taste spoiled. Although the meat was untainted when he cut it, by noon it was unfit to eat. He began carrying a pistol so he could shoot his lunch—a rabbit or squirrel.

By September, when broom weeds walled the dirt lanes, John started noticing shadowy movements in the brush. He thought he was being stalked by something, a predator, perhaps a wide-ranging panther. He spent a Sunday afternoon vainly hunting tracks. Still, when he drove his mules along the lanes he heard rustling and saw faint movements in the brush. Just wind, he told himself.

But one dark October evening, from the shadows came a scream that sent his mules running out of control a couple of miles. John, disturbed, decided to consult a woman of strange gifts, the subject of much gossip in Rogers. She was a woman never seen in a Rogers church. She never worked but always had money. She was a "conjure woman," nameless in all accounts recorded by Davis. But all accounts agree that she listened with interest as John related the mysterious goings-on.

At length, she told him that he was being "witched" by someone who could take the shape of a panther. The torment could be ended, she suggested, if John would fire three silver bullets at his stalker. She agreed to make the magic bullets if John would pay her two dollars cash and then cross her palm with silver coins for molding into bullets. Cash and silver coins were scarce, but John handed over a fistful. The conjure woman molded three bullets and seated them in cartridges. Thus armed, John awaited an encounter with the unseen. It wasn't long coming.

Early the following evening, John was driving his mules hitched to a wagonload of corn about a half-mile from the farmhouse when he heard a rustling in the brush beside the lane. Quickly, he fired three shots at an eerie movement in the tall broom weeds. The noises abruptly ceased. He was able to calm his mules. He tied the reins to the wagon and got down to investigate. In the weeds, he found only a small puddle of blood and a few faint unfamiliar tracks. But there was no spoor he could follow. After total darkness fell, he gave up the search and drove the wagon to the barn. Entering the farmhouse, he was surprised to find his father and a doctor from Rogers drinking coffee at the kitchen stove.

When John asked who was sick, his father replied that Jane had hurt her "backside." The doctor said it was an odd wound, unlike any he'd seen.

For three days Jane remained in her bedroom. When she emerged, she carried a carpetbag filled with her few clothes and several jars of her dried herbs. She announced to her husband and stepsons that she was returning to Alabama. Befuddled, but never a man to grieve, John's father drove her to the train.

That evening, when John returned from his fields, he saw a large panther cross the lane in front of his team. The skittish mules didn't bolt this time. And the panther made no sound or threatening move. While John groped for his weapon, the graceful cat merely studied the team and driver for a moment, then disappeared into the shadowy brush.

John was rattled. But in the days and months that followed, he found his stalker had apparently gone for good.

Professor Davis said, "This story was still being told around fireplaces on winter evenings as late as 1942, the last time I heard it from a member of the family that had experienced the strange happenings. I was only ten years old then and was scared witless by the sinister details supplied by one of John's elderly cousins.

"I thought no more about the story until I was a senior in high school. By that time, John's cousin had suffered a stroke and was unable to talk or write. I learned that after I'd agreed to write a senior paper on the story for high school English. Since my major source, the cousin, was unable to help, I did field work, of sorts, finding several variants of the story."

Davis continued,"That doctor in Rogers was a man who kept careful records. I was told that in 1911, the year John married, the doctor had quizzed John on his mysterious experiences and wrote John's answers in the ledger."

John died in World War I. And the doctor was dead, too, by the time Davis, as a high school senior, began his research. The folklorist yearned to examine the old ledgers and papers of the doctor. Davis said, "I learned that the ledgers in question had been lost in a fire at the office the doctor had rented from a Rogers druggist. The fire was unexplained. I was told that every scrap of paper in the office was turned to ashes. But the walls, tables, and chairs were barely scorched."

✳✳✳

GRAVES SERVE AS REMINDERS OF WILD WACO

Take a hot McLennan County afternoon when leafy Oakwood Cemetery's dark pools of shadow beckon enticingly to fugitives from August's hardened prairies and softened pavements.

And take Waco historian Roger Conger. He knows where the bodies are buried, particularly the bullet-scarred body of William Cowper Brann. I wanted to see the tomb of Brann, a.k.a. "The Apostle."

I'll visit the tomb of any man who can state his ambition this stingingly: "Would that I could weave of words a whip of scorpions to scourge the rascals naked through the world."

Brann was a slouch-hatted, gun-toting, beer-drinking, woman-worshipping, hell-fire-snorting, scandal-mongering journalist, and, at the end, a casualty in the personal war he had declared on Baylor University.

An itinerant newspaperman from Illinois, Brann briefly glittered as publisher of *The Iconoclast*, a magazine intellectually shocking for its time and place—the 1890s, smack in the middle of gristle-and-guts Texas.

Between 1895 and 1898, *The Iconoclast* gained national and even international readership. Circulation in 1898 reached 120,000.

That was four or five times the population of Waco.

Brann ended up in Oakwood—shot in the back, right where his suspenders crossed—at age 43, one of four men shot to death in a feud triggered by Brann's inked assaults on Waco's Baylor.

Righteous Baylor became an easy target for Brann's editorial rage after a teenaged Brazilian girl, brought to the Baptist bastion for missionary training, turned up pregnant. "A manufactory of ministers and Magdalenes," howled *The Iconoclast*.

Once a Brann admirer, but less so in later life, was Roy Bedichek, the Texas naturalist. Bedichek wrote: "Rationally considered, this bastinadoing of Baylor was based on the commonest of logical errors: that of generalizing not only from too few particulars, but of preferring a wholesale indictment upon a single particular.

"From this one terribly sordid affair, Brann proceeded to damn, to damn utterly and to damn continually, the whole administration of an institution that had been rendering distinguished service to Texas education for half a century."

Brann kindled a shooting war.

Enraged students and Baylor supporters kidnapped Brann, horsewhipped him and strung him up to a tree limb. But they released him after he signed an apology. The Apostle must have had his fingers crossed. Rubbing his neck, he promptly returned to *The Iconoclast* offices to resume Baylor-baiting.

"They have only to notify me where and when they can be found alone, and I'll give the whole accursed mob a show for their money. I can make a shotgun sing *Come to Christ*."

The problem with Baptists, Brann told the world, is they aren't held under water long enough.

Waco was split into bitter factions by the feud. Among those who took Brann's side was McLennan County Judge G. B. Gerald, a quick-tempered Mississippian who was twice wounded as a Confederate officer. He published poisonous handbills on the Brann-Baylor issue.

Judge Gerald was soon cussing the brothers Harris, Jim and Bill, both Baylor backers and both staff members of the *Waco Times-Herald*.

Predictably, the Gerald-Harris fuss ended in a smoking, three-way duel on one of Waco's busiest streets. Gerald braved the brothers' fire to kill them both, but suffered an arm wound and amputation. The judge was so close to Bill Harris that the killing shot ignited the victim's collar.

The Harrises were gunned down by Gerald on November 19, 1897. Then, on April Fool's Day, 1898, the end came for the Apostle. Again, the gunplay was in downtown Waco. Brooding Tom Davis, whose daughter was a Baylor student, caught Brann off guard.

If Davis was gallantly defending the honor of Baylor coeds, including his daughter's, he chose a strikingly ungallant way to do it. He shot Brann in the back.

The Apostle wheeled and emptied his six-gun into Davis. Within a few hours, Davis and Brann were dead and *The Iconoclast* was dying. That courtly Brann would die for smirching any woman's honor was freakish.

Brann's funeral procession was the longest in Waco's history.

Turning into the Oakwood gates, I read a cemetery road sign: "Conger Avenue." I glanced at Roger. "Not me. It's named for my grandfather," he said. "He's buried here." I slowed the car to read the stone:

"Norman Hurd Conger, Aug. 18, 1826, Long Island, New York-Dec. 15, 1876, China Spring." The epitaph said, "They broke the prairie sod." Norman Hurd Conger once bought 28,000 acres at seventy-five cents an acre. That's a lot of sod.

Roger Conger is a former Waco mayor and a former president of the Texas State Historical Association. As a student of the Brann-Baylor feud, Conger surely would have been Brann's biographer, but Charles Carver, a Texan turned New Yorker, beat him to it in 1957. In 1967, Conger edited Brann's *Iconoclast*, a collection that was published by the Texian Press. And in 1973, Conger's talk to the historical association was published: *Insults, Innuendoes and Invective: Waco in 1897*.

Brann's grave is marked with a unique stone: a sculptured lamp inscribed "truth" sits atop a pedestal that bears a carved likeness of the journalist.

"Someone came into this cemetery after the funeral and took a shot at that tombstone," said Roger. He placed a finger in a cavity in the bas-relief head of Brann. "Got him in the temple. Looks like a heavy lead slug did it, a .44 or .45, probably."

As we were leaving, Roger told me that Judge Gerald wanted to keep *The Iconoclast* going, but without brainy Brann there was no way. He pointed to a brown granite stone that was catching a lawn sprinkler's spray. The wet stone was hard to read. I got drenched getting the inscription: "Born 1836-Died Oct. 23, 1918, Omega Gerald. Born 1835-Died Jan. 21, 1914, G. B. Gerald. Husband and wife."

I turned the sprinkler off a moment to read the epitaph, but Roger was reciting it from memory:

"It may be oblivion's dreamless sleep. It may be another and a better life. Quien Sabe? (Note: Who knows?) We are content."

Roger grinned. "I'll tell you something not many people know. The stone says 'husband and wife' but Judge Gerald isn't buried in that grave. The judge was cremated. And he put a provision in his will that required his nephew, Walter Weaver, to go to Galveston and rent a launch and scatter his uncle's remains over a five-mile area of Galveston Bay."

As we started to drive away, Roger quoted Judge Gerald's reasoning: "We'll see if Saint Peter can gather those bones together when the last trumpet blows."

✳✳✳

UT HOLDS "SMOKING PISTOL" TO PA FERGUSON

"A smoking pistol." Historian Don Carleton grinned like a cop who had just cracked a tough case. He nodded at a gray carton of letters on the floor of his glass-walled office at the University of Texas.

Never mind that the case in question was in 1918, three decades older than Dr. Carleton, then the thirty-four-year-old director of the Eugene C. Barker Texas History Center.

What are a few decades to a historian? The ink seems scarcely dry.

"We acquired those letters a few weeks ago. If they don't represent a smoking pistol, they are as close as we'll ever come to find one." Carleton was talking about suspicions of scandal that enmeshed the administration of Texas Governor James E. Ferguson.

Putting the letters in perspective, Carleton talked a bit about Ferguson, who also did business as "Farmer Jim" and, later, "Pa" Ferguson.

Prohibition was a red-hot issue when Ferguson, a banker-lawyer from Temple, Bell County, uncorked his candidacy on the 1914 Democratic scene to defeat in the Democratic primary (237,062 to 191,558) a favored "dry" named Thomas H. Ball of Houston. This was back when nomination by the Democrats was tantamount to election in Texas.

Although he was numbered a "wet," Ferguson actually took the position that too much ink and air had been wasted on prohibition issues in a state that already was mostly dry through local option elections in the counties. But not content, the evangelical Protestants wanted to close down every saloon in the state.

Ferguson promised, if elected, to veto any sort of liquor legislation—pro or anti-pro—that came to his desk. This approach would freeze the status quo like a daiquiri, a dismal prospect for the zealots who wanted to dry out the entire state.

While Ferguson's anti-prohibition posture pulled in the bibulous balloters, it was by no means the only plank in his platform. For example, he called for prison reforms, sharecropper reforms and a countryside measled with little, red schoolhouses. A highbinder to some, Ferguson was a spellbinder to others. Crowds flocked to hear the elegant orator who carefully fertilized his speeches with backwoods expression. Gesticulating and damning every "ism" and "wasm" except Fergusonism, he would mount a cotton bale and sweat through his black suit while appealing to "the man with a hoe"—and a vote.

Although only portions of his platform ever became or survived as law, again in the 1916 primary "Fergusonism" prevailed
(240,561 to 174,611) over another prohibition candidate, Charles
H. Morris of Winnsboro, a comparatively lackluster campaigner.

Since women couldn't vote anyhow, Farmer Jim consistently,
if recklessly, opposed franchising females, although their support openly was being wooed by his opponents. Unlike Ferguson,
normally a crafty candidate, the prohibitionists never underesti-
mated the potential voting power of women. Probably Ferguson
rightly viewed them as an unpolled reservoir of prohibition
voters.

But before his anti-suffrage stance could catch up with him,
the governor managed to stumble into a political minefield right
in his own back yard—the University of Texas.

For whatever reason, UT riled Ferguson. He took a long, cold
look at its operation and he didn't like what he saw. For one thing,
he found the university's administrative officers less than impressed by the absolute authority of the man in the governor's
mansion. Regarding himself as the mandated personification of
the collective citizens of Texas, Ferguson the autocrat resented
the autonomy that the university enjoyed. He wanted to show UT
who was boss.

President William J. Battle, the regent-elected head of UT,
was called by Ferguson to account for the university budget.
Scanning the proposed budget, the governor asked the administrator the name of the professor of sociology listed there. Battle
told him the position had not been filled.

"Let me understand you," Ferguson said.

"Do you mean to tell me that you have come down to this
legislature and told the appropriation committee that you wanted
a professor of sociology in the state university and you wanted to
pay him $3250 a year knowing that you did not have such a man,
that you never did have such a man and that you intended to
divert the money to some other use which you did not disclose to
the appropriation committee of the legislature?"

Not recognizing or not choosing to recognize the difference
between a budget and a payroll, Ferguson began grumbling that
UT was carrying dead men on its books.

Soon the governor was demanding the firing of a half dozen faculty members who displeased him. In addition, he wanted a new president named. And his name turned out to be Robert Vinson, a clergyman who proved as unacceptable to Ferguson as Battle had been.

Many members of the legislature were UT alums. Resolutions began appearing that sought investigations of various Ferguson activities. With a former state attorney general, M. M. Crane, as general counsel, a seven-member committee reported to the house in March 1917 that Ferguson had used public money to buy groceries and other personal articles. The investigators also found Ferguson excessively indebted to the Temple State Bank where he had deposited state funds that failed to draw interest. Even so, the committee decided the matters didn't warrant impeachment.

It was during this period, a time when Ferguson was desperately trying to get his personal finances in order, that he apparently turned to his long-time supporters in the booze lobby. He'd done a number of favors for them. After all, the governor had successfully shot down a proposed prohibitionist plank in the 1916 Democratic platform. And he had fought the prohibitionists throughout his political career.

During his private scramble for cash. Ferguson's public life was going to hell in a hurry. A couple of thousand UT students paraded around the Capitol shouting and carrying anti-Ferguson placards. Bawling his refusal "to be intimidated or bluffed by any mob," Ferguson responded by vetoing the budget of the University of Texas. Across the state and throughout the halls of state, Texas Exes swarmed like enraged hornets.

Once a threat, impeachment was soon to be a reality.

"I am going to be governor as long as I want to be," said Ferguson, announcing for an untraditional third term.

In a preliminary hearing, Ferguson, waving away advice from his attorneys, took the stand in his own defense. In speaking of his affairs with the Temple State Bank, Ferguson casually mentioned how he had borrowed $156,500 from friends to pay off his obligations.

M. M. Crane, who'd been retained as prosecutor, asked "Who were the people from whom you obtained these funds?"

Ferguson said his friends had asked to remain anonymous.

That the governor had something to hide became as clear as gin.

He never wavered and never revealed the source of the money, even though it cinched his impeachment. After all, the loan was gargantuan for a man earning only $4000 a year as governor.

The Texas senators found Ferguson guilty of seven articles stemming from his financial activities, including his recalcitrance in the matter of the loan, plus three more that arose from his dealings with the UT Board of Regents. While the senate considered a penalty, Ferguson, in an effort to avoid punishment, hurriedly resigned from office.

The majority vote in the senate was to remove Ferguson as governor and prohibit him from ever holding another state office. Dismissed professors won reinstatement at UT. Academic freedom seemed restored.Ferguson never did divulge the source of his loan. His silence may have helped defeat him in 1918 for a third term but his acknowledgment of the source certainly would have hurt him more.

Ferguson had little chance anyhow. For the first time, he was facing an incumbent, and a popular one at that, Governor William P. Hobby, who had succeeded Farmer Jim. Then there was the indignity of the impeachment, with its conditions that Ferguson ignored.

Ferguson ran miserably. The outcome was for Hobby, 461,479 to 217,012.

Leaping from 1918 to 1981 returns us to the boxed letters in the Eugene C. Barker Texas History Center and the director's explanation of their importance as evidence in the loan mystery.

Carleton said that even before acquisition of the letters, Dr. Lewis L. Gould, chairman of the UT history department, had known and had written that shortly after the 1918 primary, testimony in an income tax evasion case involving prominent brewers had reflected Ferguson transactions with the brewing interests.

After reading the 200 letters and notes, Gould agreed with Carleton they represented a clinching clue in the case. For example, one letter bears the signature of Louis A. Adoue of a Galveston importing firm, Mistrot & Adoue. Dated January 1, 1917, Adoue's letter addresses R. L. Autrey of the Houston Ice & Brewing Company. Autrey was the leading lobbyist of the wets in Texas in those days. Taken in the context of related correspondence, the letter clearly refers to Ferguson while circumspectly failing to name him:

"I have never written the party in Austin direct regarding this and I don't know whether I should or not. Please take it up direct or send this letter to him advising if I should send the notes to the Temple State Bank for collection, together with the interest coupons."

The Adoue letter is enclosed with a letter from Autrey to Hon. J. E. Ferguson, dated January 2, 1917:

"Dear Governor. Please note attached letter from Mr. Louis A. Adoue about the Bell County land notes.

"You will advise me if these notes must be sent to the Temple State Bank, or through any other bank in Temple or otherwise."

By February 16, Adoue was writing directly to the *party* in Austin:

"Hon. James E. Ferguson . . . I beg to acknowledge receipt of your favor of the 14th and exchange will be sent you under separate cover in the next day or so. . . . I have hopes of coming to Austin shortly, as I want to see you, and really hoped I could be there long before now.

"Assuring you of my willingness to serve you in this matter, and with best wishes, beg to remain yours very truly, Louis A. Adoue."

February 21, 1917, Adoue sent this hurriedly scribbled note:

"Dear Governor—Am sending check for bonds—check endorsed in blank so thought best to register letter—will send interest and write fully tomorrow. Yours in haste, Louis A. Adoue."

If the legislature distrusted Ferguson, at least Adoue had confidence in him, as this February 24, 1917, letter describing the endorsed, blank check seems to indicate:

"Your telegram of the 23rd came yesterday and worried me

no little, as I had endorsed check in blank and mailed to you by registered mail."

No accountant publicly certified is needed to observe that endorsed, blank checks don't commonly pass in the mail.

Other letters involving banking, bonds and financing were written to the governor but there is no admission in writing by Ferguson that he took money from the liquor lobby.

Writing in 1946, one of Farmer Jim's daughters, Mrs. Ouida Ferguson Nalle said: "Suffice it to say that $156,000 that he borrowed . . . was an honest debt and strictly a business transaction. It was well secured and was paid with one of the best black land farms in rich Bell County, Texas."

Nevertheless, in a letter marked "personal," Adoue on March 7, 1917, mixed politics and business:

"Wish to advise that I am sending the bonds by registered mail today and trust they will reach you in due order. I want to thank you for your attention.

"I notice your enemies in the legislature are seeking to persecute you. I want to assure you of my loyal support. This support is extended throughout the state by all of your numerous friends. Your enemies, I am sure, have nothing whatsoever to base their investigation on, probably not even a mistake, which all of us are liable to make, but instead it is being done for their own political profit and personal gratification—not that any of these 'witch-burners' would be charitable enough to appreciate that even the governor of the state might make a mistake, if such were the case in this instance."

Despite Farmer Jim's mistakes, Fergusonism continued as a political force in Texas for years to come.

Ironically, the man who had fought the franchise for women continued as a political power by successfully running for governor his wife, Miriam Amanda (Ma) Ferguson, in the gubernatorial race. She was governor from January 20, 1925, to January 17, 1927, and from January 17, 1933 to January 15, 1935.

Ma ran on the slogan, "Two governors for the price of one."

But detractors like to comment: "Yeah, Jim's price."

※※※

West Texas' Hallie Stillwell Is an Original

More than 1100 species of plants and more than 435 species of birds are found in the Big Bend.

But there's only one Hallie Stillwell.

The tall, blue-eyed grand dame of the grease-wood was ninety-four in 1991. In sunlight her silvery hair glints like old pesos. She's a dainty, poker-playing rancher who once shot a mountain lion smack between the eyes. True to West Texas protocol, she opens conversation with a review of recent rainfall. Right now the desert is splashed with green.

She'd been watching a TV soap, "Guiding Light," when I showed up. She said, "Seeing all the problems of those soap opera folks makes you realize that you don't have any problems at all. Makes you feel good about yourself."

Hallie rules her 22,000 acres of gorgeously hostile land from a modest adobe house in Brewster County. Brewster is Texas' largest county (6200 square miles), a chunk of map big enough to print its own money and declare war.

Maps of the Big Bend country have borne the name "Stillwell" since the century was a teenager—Stillwell Camp, Stillwell Ranch, Stillwell Store. Shut Up Canyon leads to Stillwell Mountain. And to the south, beyond the great blue mountains, is Stillwell's Crossing on the Rio Grande.

Hallie prizes the twilight silences of her ranch on dry Maravillas Creek. She shuns the amenities of her brick house on a lawn-sprinkled, tree-lined street in Alpine, the seat of Brewster County.

Since 1930, she's written chatty weekly columns for the *Alpine Avalanche*. But she won't sit still in Alpine. She prefers the ranch's thorny hills and dagger flats, although she's studied them for seven decades.

In 1918, Hallie Crawford, a Waco-born schoolteacher, said "I do" to a dashing cowboy named Roy Stillwell, who once ranched in Mexico and, as a boy, lived with Indians. Wooing Hallie, he hired musicians to serenade her bedroom window in Marathon: "I'm dreaming tonight of Hallie, sweet Hallie . . ."

The rancher settled his bride in a one-room ranch house, shared by a couple of cowboys. She did a man's work, a cowman's work. She wore pants and rode astride, a jarring sight in those days.

Hallie was twenty, her husband twice that. They survived border troubles, drought, hard times and the Spanish influenza. They raised three children. Then her husband died in a truck wreck in 1948. Hallie took over the ranch.

For fifteen years, until she retired, Hallie was a Brewster County justice of the peace—trying cases, holding inquests and performing marriages. Her precinct was half the size of Connecticut. She enjoyed the job, except for getting up at 2 A.M. to rule on suicides, homicides and motorcides.

For many years, she was returning queen of the world championship Chili Cookoff in Terlingua, a red-hot contest whooped along by Frank X. Tolbert, the late *Dallas Morning News* columnist. Each year, Frank's daughter, Kathleen, fashioned a crown from red and yellow chili peppers for Hallie.

Hallie was a buddy of the late chili czar Wick Fowler, a *DMN* writer and wit. ("Drive friendly. Wave at hitch-hikers.")

A third amigo was H. Allen Smith, the late best-selling humorist (*Low Man on a Totem Pole*). After sampling the Big Bend's chili, he moved from Mount Kisco, New York, to Alpine for good—or maybe not so good. Off the hilarious printed page, Mr. Smith was a practicing curmudgeon.

"He was so smart," Hallie recalled. "He had a mind that wouldn't quit. But he didn't like many Alpine people. And they didn't like him."

Possibly Mr. Smith's widely quoted observations on Alpine contributed to the feeling. For example: "There are more greedy, money-grubbing S.O.B.s per capita in Alpine, Texas, than in any other town I've seen or heard about." Nor was he real keen on Mount Kisco.

Like a reporter, I pried for the secret of Hallie's longevity. Smoke? "No." Drink? "No," she said.

"We have plenty to do out here without smoking and drinking."

What?

"Lying, stealing mostly," she said happily.

Her longevity almost ran out in 1917.

She'd been teaching that year in Presidio, a Texas town on the Rio Grande. Revolution in Mexico splashed across the river. It was a combat zone.

In Presidio, Hallie came to dread both Mexican rebels and drunken U.S. soldiers. Her sister Mabel was teaching in a tiny school at Presidio County's Brite Ranch, a settlement with a store and post office.

The family of T. T. "Van" Neill, the ranch foreman, had invited Mabel and Hallie to the ranch for the Christmas holidays. Hallie wanted to go, but her father, A. G. Crawford, insisted that his whole family gather in Alpine.

At sunup on Christmas Day, about fifty bandidos attacked Brite Ranch. They shot up the place, stole horses, looted the store and killed three people. One bandido was fatally shot.

While the gun battle raged, Hallie was safe off in Brewster County, opening presents with her family. Longevity required some luck.

A sidelight on the Brite Ranch raid is that for many years it was blamed (by stellar historian Walter Prescott Webb, among others) on the gang of Chico Cano, who was best known for the blinding speed with which he switched sides throughout the revolution. But Sul Ross State University Professor emeritus Elton Miles (*Tales of the Big Bend, More Tales of the Big Bend* and *Stray Tales of the Big Bend*) tells me his sources indict another villain.

Dr. Miles of Alpine blames Placido "Pinto" Villanueva. Identity of the ringleader may be historically significant because Pinto's leader was Pancho Villa (who, by the way, later ordered Pinto's execution).

Reacting or overreacting to the Brite Ranch slayings, Texas Rangers rode out and killed fifteen Mexican males. For the bloody work, Texas Rangers Captain J. M. Fox and his entire company were fired. Border troubles continued.

A sure way to deal with troubles is outlive them. On Sunday, October 20, 1991, Hallie celebrated her ninety-fourth birthday by opening the new Stillwell Ranch Museum, a trove of her collected memories.

From Marathon, a crowd drove thirty-nine miles south on U.S. 385 and took FM 2627 six miles east to the Stillwell General Store. Hallie signed copies of her autobiography—*I'll Gather My Geese*. It's from the A&M University Press. The title was a flip retort to her father. He argued against her taking a teaching job in Presidio. He called it a wild goose chase. She replied, "Then I'll gather my geese."

The book takes the reader only to Roy Stillwell's death in 1948. So, there are no Tolbert-Fowler-Smith stories, no adventures of a female JP, and no inside stuff on her poker winnings.

She told me she's now writing the rest of her story, a sequel. What will she call it?

With her girlish laugh, she said, "My Goose is Cooked."

※※※

The Legend of Daredevil Roy Butler

Frozen words of the old daredevil Royal W. Butler rumble in the airy parlor of a Victorian mansion at 313 S. Washington in Marshall. Listen:

"In the spring of 1934 I met this fellow named Art Slye. We got together and we put up this air show. The name of it was Art Slye and His Original Sky Devils. It was a hell of a good show.

"It was accidental that I ever met Art Slye. On the road from Longview into Greggton at that time, on the right side, were these dance halls. There would also be a row of these houses. They were what some people call houses of ill repute.

"So, on this road were several of these houses, then a restaurant or two, then some places where you could buy booze, and then some more dance halls, and so forth. I did go over there occasionally when I had money. There was a place called the Black Cat where I had some friends. Well, one time I started out at the Black Cat and I am not too clear where all I went after that, but I ended up the next morning in the Gregg Hotel with a terrible headache and Art Slye."

Butler's voice comes low and rough across the elegant parlor. Greg Beil and Gail, his wife, own the proud old house, or vice versa. The place was built in 1901 for mercantile tycoon Joe Wiseman. With historical reverence, Greg and Gail restored it as a bed-and-breakfast inn. Greg is a nuclear physicist who became a Harrison County probation officer a dozen years ago. A part-time professor at East Texas Baptist University, he writes papers that are published by the *International Journal of Theoretical Physics*.

Greg is charmed by unified field theory, black holes and other major mysteries of the universe, including characters found in East Texas. He and Gail found Roy Butler at his Riverfront Restaurant in his hometown of Jefferson in Marion County.

They recorded fifteen hours of Butler interviews and were eager for more when he died. Taught to fly at seventeen by World War I ace Eddie Rickenbacker, Butler was an early crop-duster, smuggler and barnstormer.

In Mexico, he narrowly escaped a date with a revolutionary firing squad. In Hollywood, he flew stunts for the movie *Wings*. In China, he flew against the Japanese before Pearl Harbor. Claiming at times both British and American citizenship, Butler was wounded when his Spitfire was shot down during the Battle of Britain. Greg verified most of Butler's past.

Oddly, the 1981 death of the pilot who had survived repeated crashes—some staged for show biz—was from natural causes. He was a ripe seventy-four and still a Sunday pilot. One evening in 1987, Greg Beil played back for me the Butler tapes. Listen:

"We had four planes to start with. Art had a Warner Commander, made in Little Rock, and a Challenger Eagle. I had a Whirlwind Waco and Harry Paag (the ugliest damn man I ever saw . . . a good flier, though) had a Spartan Arts.

"We did about two shows a week. We went all over East Texas and Louisiana and up into Oklahoma. The admission charge was 10 cents. We would rent a pasture near town and have people drive in through some kind of gate. Of course, people could see the show from a distance for free, but we tried to keep most of it down low for the paying customers.

"The day before the show we would have a plane fly over the town and drop circulars. On the morning of the show we would fly low over the town just to drum up business. This got people upset—mayors and councilmen—but it always helped get folks out to the show. Anyway, the show would start about 1:00 or 2:00 P.M. Before the show we would give people airplane rides. For the actual show, we did all kinds of stunts, wing walking, parachute jumps, and trick flying.

"The real star got to be a fellow named Tommy Sullivan or Tommy O'Neal or whatever he was calling himself that day. He was the best wing walker I ever saw. I also think he was an escaped convict. He was a short fellow, but very muscular. I never saw him afraid of anything. Of course, that may have been because he was drunk all the time.

"Sullivan never wore a parachute when he was wing walking. He just didn't give a damn. And he climbed all over the plane. He got down on the landing gear and hung from there. Then he climbed up somehow and grabbed the edge of the back cockpit, swung around, and jumped astraddle of the fuselage. He rode that plane like it was a horse. Sullivan was our best parachute jumper, too. At least when he wasn't locked up in jail. Most of the time he took his pay in whiskey. We kept the rest of his salary to pay his bail. One time in Oklahoma he got ahold of $500. We didn't see him for a month.

"What made it bad was that he always kept his parachutes with him. And they were the only good chutes we had for the show. So when he got locked up, they would lock up the chutes, too. That almost got me killed. I'll tell you about that in a minute.

"We tried to give the people a good show for their money. Sometimes we sat around and thought up new tricks. We did something we called serpentine cutting. You would take a roll of toilet paper up with you, throw it out of the cockpit and let it unroll. Then you would fly back around and try to cut it with the propeller. It sounds easy, but it wasn't.

"And sometimes that paper would catch fire on the hot motor. You would have this burning paper all over the front of your plane. Damn near catch the airplane on fire. You would have to sideslip to put it out.

"Sometimes we would bust balloons that had been let loose. But that was just good flying, which was something I was supposed to be able to do.   What I wasn't supposed to do was parachute jumping. I was a damn fool to ever get started with it. And it all happened because Tommy Sullivan got drunk and thrown in jail in Mansfield, Louisiana. We heard about it the morning of this big show we had in Nachitoches.

"We sent somebody up there with the bail money to get him out. He was supposed to drive right down to the show. Well, it so happened that day that my plane wasn't flying. I had messed up a valve. I knew I wasn't going to have to fly, so I just sat in the hangar and got full of gin. So, it got to be about an hour before the show and Tommy still hadn't showed up. We found out later that he had stopped for a little hair of the dog in Coushatta. It ended up with him and his parachutes getting thrown in jail again.

"Art Slye comes in and says to me that we had a big problem. We had advertised this delayed jump of 5000 feet. He said he guessed we would have to call it off. I don't know what got into me—well, I do know, it was gin—I said, 'Oh, hell, I'll make the jump.' They tell me I wandered out to the microphone. Ben Proffitt usually did most of the announcing for the shows. I took the microphone away from him and said, 'Hey, folks, this here is your chute jumper doing the talking. I use Gordon's dry gin.'

"I don't remember doing that, but I know I did it because the next week the Gordon's distributor from New Orleans sent me a check for $100. They were thanking me for the advertising.... Art was flying the plane. He tapped me on the shoulder and I just sort of fell out of the cockpit onto the wing. I got ahold of one of the struts and held on for dear life. I thought he never would give me the nod. Finally, he did and I just rolled off that wing. I was happy as could be. I felt fine. I felt so good I almost forgot to open the chute. Art had told me to count so far and then pull the rip cord. But I forgot how far he told me to count. So I just kept falling and enjoying myself.

"Finally, I got to noticing that the ground was coming up pretty fast. I wasn't too worried, but I decided to go ahead and pull. I had jumped from 6000 feet. The chute opened at 400 feet.

They told me if I had waited another two or three seconds it would have been too late. Scared all of them half to death.

"But I really enjoyed that jump. The one the next week was the bad one. And I was stone-cold sober. The show the next week was in Alexandria. It was a big one. We had thousands of people there. And, sure enough, Tommy got himself locked up again. He and his good chutes were in some jail, Minden or somewhere, and they wouldn't let them out. So, I had to jump again. Since this was a big show I had to have two chutes. It was a federal rule that for a premeditated jump you had to have an emergency chute. But the only chutes we had were seat chutes. I wore one on my chest and one on my back. That meant the rip cord on the emergency chute, the one in front, was somewhere around in the small of my back.

"I told Art, 'This is a bunch of damn foolishness. I couldn't possibly get to that rip cord.' He said, 'Well, you won't need it anyway. It's just for the Department of Commerce.'

"We had advertised a 6000-foot delayed jump. They took me up to 8000 feet and I was supposed to pull the rip cord at 2000 feet. So, I fell just like I was supposed to. I pulled the rip cord at 2000 feet—and nothing happened. I jerked again and pulled the rip cord plumb out. I looked back and saw that the main chute was hung up on the harness of that damn reserve chute. I looked down and saw the Texas and Pacific railroad track—Shreveport to New Orleans—coming up at me. I got excited. I got to clawing around the small of my back for that other rip cord. I made another turn and it looked like I was almost on that track. I made one last grab. I knew that it was the last chance. I got my thumb on that ring and worked it loose. I pulled—and both chutes came out. I hit the ground after about half an oscillation.

"The perspiration broke out all over me. I was sober for that jump. If I had been under the influence of whiskey, I would have gone plumb through that Texas and Pacific track."

✳✳✳

"Conan" Creator's Life Didn't Match Tales

Here's a weird tale.

Fifty years ago this month, an eerie fictioneer named Robert E. Howard sat down in his car and ended his fantasies with a fatally real slug from a .380 Colt automatic pistol.

Howard's hulking creation, a prehistoric barbarian named Conan, was a star performer in a poor but popular magazine called *Weird Tales*. At the lethal moment, the magazine owed Howard a thousand bucks for past pieces.

But the thirty-year-old master of heroic fantasy didn't kill himself because of accounts unreceivable. By Depression standards in this dusty Callahan County town, Howard was semi-prosperous, despite the failure of two banks that had swallowed big bites of his savings.

Appraisal of the author's earthly goods showed that he left $702 in cash, a postal savings account of $1850, and a bloody Chevrolet valued at $350. That wasn't bad for a young man in a dicey calling during hard times.

For years, townspeople had whispered that the strange man without a job made better money than anybody in town, including the school superintendent. It was perhaps the kindest thing they whispered about Robert Ervin Howard. He was the town's weirdo.

He was aloof. He never scattered wild oats. He didn't chase women. He didn't get likkered up. He didn't smoke or chew. But people noticed that he clung to his overly protective mother like a wet slip.

That tie between adoring son and smothering mother has been advanced as the reason that a little after 7 A.M. on June 11, 1936, Howard's gunshot blew a hole in the silence of the one-story town, forty miles north of Brownwood. Without speaking, the promising writer died in a few hours.

Three days earlier, Howard had watched his mother, Mrs. Hester Howard, sixty-six, sink deep into an irreversible tubercular coma. On the eve of his suicide, he had driven to Brownwood and reserved lot thirteen, block five at Greenleaf Cemetery for three burials. The Baptists had a double funeral for Howard and his mother, who, never regaining consciousness, outlived her son by scant hours.

The third plot was unoccupied until 1944, when Dr. Isaac Mordecai Howard, seventy-three, the country doctor who was Robert's father and Hester's husband, succumbed to a heart attack.

Dr. Howard had spent his final days working for a colleague in the nearby Eastland County town of Ranger. There Dr. Pere Moran Kuykendall ran a little clinic. In his will, grateful Dr. Howard left to Dr. Kuykendall, among other things, the rights to the literary remains of the creator of *Conan*.

All told, Dr. Howard's estate seemed modest. But Mrs. Alla Ray Kuykendall, Pere's widow, and Mrs. Alla Ray Morris, Pere's daughter, do recall that the clinician at rare intervals received a check for a few dollars from some publication.

Only after the deaths of author Howard and Drs. Howard and Kuykendall did *Conan* become a publishing household word. This was due primarily to the work of two men. Glenn Lord of Houston was a longtime fan of fantasy writing, especially Howard's pieces. He studied every scrap of Howard material and pushed for the reprinting of the *Conan* canon. Eventually named literary manager for the Kuykendalls, Lord made it his business to ferret out unpublished Howard manuscripts. The Kuykendalls did well.

Also spurring the *Conan* revival was sci-fi writer L. Sprague deCamp of Villanova, Pennsylvania, whose interest dates back more than three decades, to a time when Howard had been virtually forgotten. DeCamp polished Howard's unsold stories into publishable shape, completed old plot sketches, and even took off with a series of new stories built on Howard's characters. Such works are often called pastiches. And once a market was discovered, Howard pastiches appeared from several authors, including a member of the Swedish air force who was working on his English.

Since the 1970s, Conan has been riding high, once more rescuing maidens (some not so maidenly), slicing up giant slithering things and disemboweling luckless warriors with his quick sword.

Now look around. Millions of *Conan* books are in circulation. Paperbacks and comics are everywhere. A sad note is that not one book written by Howard was published during his lifetime.

Millions have seen two *Conan* movies, starring Maria Shriver's husband, Arnold Schwarzhisname. Another film is optioned.

REH's literary remains turned out to be a gold mine. His stories have inspired a dedicated cult that is fascinated not just by the fiction and poetry of Howard, but anything concerning Howard the Texan.

And this brings us to the weirdest part of this tale.

Touring Texas in June of 1986 were fanatical fantasy fans from all four corners of the Hyborean World, that distant, fictive place inhabited by Conan, REH and their followers.

After nodding to Parker County, where REH was born, they invaded Cross Plains to inspect the little house where he grew up. They took in the Cross Plains Library, where Billie Loving and Jill McCowan had put up an REH exhibit, and they dined on barbecue at the Charles Rodenberger place out in the ranching country where wild turkeys trot along the roads. Rodenberger's wife, Lou, is known for her popular collection of pieces by Texas women writers titled *Her Work*.

The fans visited Greenleaf Cemetery to mourn the loss of REH, who might have been eighty if he had postponed his suicide. And—who knows?—he might have postponed it if he had known something like this was going to happen.

I say postpone rather than cancel because people acquainted with the REH story often suggest that he and suicide were meant for each other. DeCamp has noted that the death of Hester Howard was the *occasion for* and not the *cause of* Robert E. Howard's suicide. I find Howard fans—even those critical of pastiches—who agree totally with deCamp.

High point of the pilgrimage for the fans, who had come from as far away as New Guinea and Switzerland, was a call at Howard Payne University in Brownwood. Howard Payne and Brownwood are significant because REH, having completed the ten grades then offered by the public school in Cross Plains, finished his final two years of high school in Brownwood. He never really went to college, but he did take some typing and bookkeeping courses offered at Howard Payne.

At Howard Payne is the personal library of REH—or what is left of it.

About 300 books belonging to REH were bequeathed to the Howard Payne Library by Dr. Isaac Howard. REH bookplates were placed in these, and unwisely the books were put into general circulation.

By the time librarians sensed the value of keeping the collection intact a few years ago, the damage had been done. Some books had been lost or stolen. Others, worn out, had been thrown away. Only about forty-five volumes from the library of REH could be found. Now they are reserved as a collection for REH scholars. The remaining books range from English classics to Tarzan novels.

Equally bad was the university's loss of the collection of REH's published works, also bequeathed by Dr. Howard after his son's death. This was a huge pile of magazines. One of the librarians at the Baptist school was offended by the lurid covers of such pulps as *Weird Tales*, with their showcasing of imperiled female flesh. She moved them to a corner of the basement.

When Dr. Howard learned of their fate, he reclaimed them, yellowed and crumbling.

At the library, Charlotte Laughlin, former English professor and now president of the Brown County Historical Society, told the sad story to eleven of the true believers. They couldn't believe that REH materials could be treated with such irreverence. Dr. Laughlin had helped rescue the surviving volumes.

Here's the way the fans talk about REH.

Rusty Burke of Houston, an aptitude test administrator: "He was far more than just the writer who created *Conan*. He created an entire field of fantastic literature. His writing can never be duplicated because he was possessed of a unique artistic vision."

Bill Cavalier of Rolling Prairie, Indiana, a graphic artist: "He combined wonderfully concise imagery, poetic prose, and visions of ages only dreamed of to create realistic worlds of adventure."

Graeme Flanagan of Papua, New Guinea, adviser to the Australian Department of Defense: "He was an important figure in American fantasy literature and is accorded only part of the recognition that is his due."

Steve Ghilordi of Zurich, Switzerland, author-publisher: "I have a special interest in American writers of the pulp era. This is a chance for me to look into the roots of one of the best known American writers—in Europe."

Thomas Kovac of Zurich, Switzerland, translator-writer, was suffering from jet lag. William Fulwiler of Duncanville, Texas, a bookseller, wasn't. After some debate, Van Clark of Winter Park, Florida, an aerospace engineer who edits the quarterly fanzine *REH United Press Association,* finally agreed with me that REH was crazy as a coot.

It's true that REH wrote irresistibly thrilling stories. But, let's face it, his life was about as exciting as a bus ride through Kansas. I don't see why people hooked on the stimulation of *Conan* stories would travel great distances—spending $4000 or so, in the case of Flanagan—to examine the extremely private and extremely dull life of REH.

By all accounts, Robert E. Howard was an overly sheltered hot-house flower who spent his brief life in a room typing.

It's weird.

※※※

MURPHY'S WAR DIDN'T END IN THE ARMY

In World War II, Texan Audie Murphy was awarded every U.S. medal for valor that a soldier can win this side of the Distinguished Wooden Cross. But that was only the beginning of the story. At the time he died in a plane crash in Virginia on Memorial Day in 1971, Murphy, once a millionaire, was broke and deep in debt.

Compulsive gambling had driven him to the point of bankruptcy after draining his profits from films and TV. For several years, his associates had included mobsters. He often carried a gun. Murphy had worked behind the scenes to get labor racketeer Jimmy Hoffa released from prison. Indeed, Murphy, in his last year, had called on President Richard Nixon in Hoffa's behalf. And, in late 1971, Nixon reduced the sentence of Hoffa, freeing him. Hoffa vanished in 1975.

Although Murphy shunned booze and hated dope, he was an insomniac who became hooked on Placidyl, a sleeping drug. It slurred his speech and sometimes gave him a sleepy or drunken look. Hollywood sources remember that Murphy's deceptively angelic features concealed a womanizing devil.

In 1988, Don Graham gave me the lowdown on Murphy in an interview in Austin. Behind the medals (more than two dozen of them) was "a little Irish runt—real proud and real smart—from a family that had no standing." Author Graham, a UT-Austin English professor, has researched Murphy's life for years and has written an eye-opening book, *No Name on the Bullet: A Biography of Audie Murphy*.

The Audie Murphy story has tragic overtones. Graham quoted the hero as saying the Army treated its dogs better than its soldiers because the Army retrained the dogs before returning them to civilian life.

At the time Murphy died at age forty-six, American patriotism hung at half-staff. Most Americans were fashionably nursing wholesale guilt from the court-martial revelations of another soldier, Lt. William Calley, who'd just been convicted of killing Vietnamese civilians. It was a sad season for military heroes.

Murphy, once a poor, pint-sized grammar-school dropout in Hunt County, had won glory in World War II and a dazzling career in TV and movies. In contrast, Calley had been an anti-hero in a war lacking glory. Murphy personified an American dream; Calley, a nightmare. In death, Murphy was neglected. But Graham now senses a shift in the nation's mood. After twenty years, he believes Americans are ready to give Murphy the attention he deserves.

Graham can't remember when he wasn't fascinated by Murphy.

"When I was a kid, growing up in Collin County in the 1940s, the three big heroes in my part of Texas were Bonnie and Clyde and Audie Murphy." Farmersville and nearby Princeton, both in Collin County, embraced Murphy as a native. But Graham says that Celeste, in Hunt County, has a better claim because Murphy went to school there for four of the five years he went to school. His other school year was at the Hunt County town of Floyd.

"Murphy was born at Kingston, which is nothing but a wide spot in the road in Hunt County. And he wasn't even born in Kingston, but outside Kingston. His was a farm family, share-croppers. Farmersville had a mayor named Beaver, whose first name I forget. Anyhow, Mayor Beaver was eager to claim Murphy. So, Farmersville staged one of the first big Audie Murphy appreciation celebrations in 1945."

"Today, Farmersville has a downtown monument to Murphy. Murphy's dad had drifted off somewhere and his mother had died, leaving an orphaned teenager to scratch out a living and yearn to get into a war. Murphy was turned down by the Marines because of his size. He joined the Army in Greenville, the Hunt County seat," said Graham. Today, the Greenville Public Library has an Audie Murphy Room. There's another at Hill County College in Hillsboro, where the military historian Colonel Harold Simpson authored a 1976 book on Murphy's combat.

Other Murphy shrines are scattered around the state. An eight-foot statue of the five-seven warrior (who actually grew a couple of inches and put on weight during World War II) can be found at a San Antonio veterans hospital. Baylor University has a trove of Murphy material, as does West Point.

"Murphy came home to a lot of celebration," Graham said. "Texans were proud of him. Actually, he'd left no sweetheart behind when he went to war, but you can bet *Life Magazine* found him one for their picture layout. Everyone wanted to give Murphy something. For example, someone told me that George Bannerman Dealey (the late publisher of *The Dallas Morning News*) offered to pay all of his expenses for four years at the college of his choice.

But what's a guy with a fifth-grade education going to do in college? He decided to go to Hollywood. Along the way, Murphy managed to educate himself. He read a lot and observed people closely. He became well-informed and sophisticated. Somewhere there's a recording of Murphy reciting Shakespeare. I couldn't find it."

Murphy's first big civilian success was the publication of his combat autobiography, *To Hell and Back*. Spec McClure, a stringer for Hollywood gossip columnist Hedda Hopper, did most of the writing. McClure later recalled his response when Murphy, after a few bit parts, said he wanted to become a movie star: "I told him he couldn't act. But he said: "Look at those other guys. They can't act either."

Actually, Graham says, Murphy had talent. With more than forty films to his credit, Murphy had a career that outlasted those of most stars. And he continued successfully in B Westerns long after other cowboy heroes had hung up their spurs.

Beyond that, Murphy had a few roles in which he was "brilliant," according to Graham. Without debating whether Murphy played himself convincingly in *To Hell and Back* (1955), one can argue that he was perfect as the redneck racist in *The Unforgiven* (1960).

In contrast, Murphy's most memorable role was probably as a Yankee soldier in *The Red Badge of Courage* (1951), directed by John Huston. Both gamblers, Huston and Murphy hit it off.

When Murphy was asked to endorse John F. Kennedy for the presidency, he replied that he would do it only if JFK would agree to make John Huston treasury secretary—"because he's the best poker player in the world."

Graham interviewed Huston a few months before his death. Huston noted that Murphy not only owned thoroughbreds but bet on them. He called that a dangerous combination. The director called Murphy "a gentle little killer."

In the 1960s, Murphy was betting as much a $30,000 a day on horse races, said Graham, who added, "Huston called him the worst gambler he ever saw." Graham believes that Murphy, who didn't smoke, usually shunned booze because his father, a drifter, drank heavily. After Murphy became famous, reporters would occasionally dig up his father for interviews. "At one time the father was running a drive-in movie out at Abilene. Can you imagine? He could look up on the screen and see the son he'd abandoned. Now, that's poignant."

Murphy lived a sort of secret life, said Graham. Bored after the war, he was always seeking excitement. Haunted by combat nightmares, he'd spend sleepless nights cruising with Los Angeles policemen, who were glad to have a one-man army along for the ride. When Graham obtained Murphy's FBI files, he confirmed that Murphy had worked undercover, reporting to the FBI on his conversations with certain mobsters.

Murphy married a red-haired starlet, Wanda Hendrix. They made a movie together, *Sierra* (1950). Did romance blossom on the set? "More like it ended there," said Graham, chuckling. "The marriage only lasted about a year."

Murphy later married a Braniff flight attendant, Pamela Archer. They had two sons. Graham said Audie and Pamela remained at times tenuously but always officially married until Murphy died. "She was what he needed, but Audie liked action," said Graham.

In Hollywood, Graham said, Murphy got in fights and carried a gun. He was known as a lady-killer. "I tracked down a few of his women," said Graham. "They saw his baby face and found in him a vulnerable quality." Vulnerable?

This one-man army, who once single-handedly, ignoring wounds and almost certain death, chased six German tanks and 200 infantrymen from the field? This GI who lovingly honed his bayonet before battle? Vulnerable?

Call it Audie Murphy's greatest acting role.

※※※

OLD SALTS REMEMBER SAM DEALEY'S VALOR

Sam Dealey was a Dallas boy who smiled easily when he wasn't studying math. At the U.S. Naval Academy, he bilged out—as midshipmen say—in his first year. But he bounced back, trying harder. He mastered Annapolis math, won a commission, and became one of the most decorated U.S. submarine heroes of World War II.

Hearing old salts talk about Commander Dealey, I concluded that, math aside, he was a flawless hero and well-liked by everyone he encountered—except the crewmen of enemy warships and merchantmen. He was the first and only skipper of the *Harder*, a U.S. submarine generally credited with sinking more than a score of Japanese vessels. Sixteen kills were officially documented.

After combat patrols that sent more than 54,000 tons of enemy shipping to the bottom, Harder's bold career ended in 1944 when Japanese depth charges blasted the boat, killing Commander Dealey, age thirty-seven, and all hands.

Harder, with her crew of seventy-nine, was lost August 24, 1944, south of Lingayen Gulf on the west coast of the island of Luzon in the Philippines. The skipper earned the nation's highest award for valor, the Medal of Honor, and too many other medals and citations to count here. But among them were four prized Navy Crosses and even an Army Distinguished Service Cross The Navy named a destroyer escort for him, the Naval Academy named a room for him in Memorial Hall. Unexplainably, Dallas has no real monument to Sam Dealey.

Landlocked Dallas was an unlikely hometown for a deep-diving torpedo marksman. But similarly landlocked was the high, dry hometown of his boss in the Pacific, the nation's last five-star admiral, Chester W. Nimitz of Fredericksburg. Inland origins of blue water heroes are among the mysteries of the deep.

Fredericksburg's old Steamboat Hotel, with its simulated seaworthy facade, built by the Nimitz family, is now the flagship of the Admiral Nimitz State Historical Park and Museum of the Pacific War. About 600 historians, military buffs, and members of Sub Vets groups gathered in rocky, arid Gillespie County in May 1989 for "Up Periscope," a symposium on submarine warfare in the Pacific, 1941-1945.

The program was dedicated to Sam Dealey. But adventures were recounted of all seven WW II submariners who won Medals of Honor. Remarkably, four were aboard. USN retired, yes, but walking on their own sea legs, were Vice Admiral Lawson P. Ramage, Rear Admiral Richard H. O'Kane, Rear Admiral Eugene B. Fluckey and Captain George L. Street.

An exhibition was installed to recall Commander Dealey's sea battles, that included his photos, citations, saber and medals. In addition, a plaque on the museum's wall of honor was un-veiled at a ceremony for U.S. crews of fifty-two subs lost in WW II.

The events drew more than fifty kinfolks of the skipper, who was the son of the late Samuel David Dealey and Virgie Downing Dealey of Dallas. Young Sam was the nephew of George Bannerman Dealey, the late publisher of *The Dallas Morning News*. The commander's children, David Dealey of Santa Monica, California, Joan Ewen of Houston and Barbara Batterman of Grand Junction, Colorado, and their children and grandchildren, were celebrities, along with Sam Dealey's only living sibling, Mrs. Margaret Dealey Royal of Meridian in Bosque County.

Commander Dealey's widow, Edwina, survived her hus-band several years but never really recovered from his loss, Joan Ewen told me. "My mother was a casualty of the war."

Rousing cheers greeted another submarine hero, a visitor from Boca Grande, Florida, retired Rear Admiral Chester W. Nimitz Jr., son of the sailor who gave his name to the museum. Chester Jr. was a buddy of Sam Dealey and skipper of the *Haddo*, one of the subs in Commander Dealey's last wolf pack.

"I'm the last living person to have talked with Sam Dealey," revealed Rear Admiral Nimitz, who's credited with sinking more than five enemy ships.

Of his old friend, Rear Admiral Nimitz said, "Peacetime prediction of who would or would not become an aggressive wartime commander is still, in my opinion, a highly uncertain gamble. I submit Sam Dealey's case as an example. He was one of the greatest skippers of our initial submarine officer pool, although he was certainly not so recognized before the war."

Sam Dealey proved a brilliant fighter. In one patrol, the Texan killed five enemy destroyers in about as many days, his comrade said. "I last spoke to Sam about 11:00 P.M. on August 23, 1944. We lay to [surfaced] side by side, my *Haddo* and his *Harder*, about five miles off the west coast of Luzon, some twenty miles north of Manila.

"I pointed out the lights and activity in a small coastal indentation directly inboard from us, where the Japs had tried to tow and beach the remains of a destroyer whose bow I had blown off early that morning. I being out of torpedoes, Sam said, 'Leave it to me.' He sent me off to an advance base to get more torpedoes. *Harder* was lost the next morning as she approached the beach submerged. Subsequent intelligence information indicated that *Harder* was depth-charged repeatedly, at successively greater depths, by Japanese Patrol Boat No. 102—which was ironically, the old four-piper USS *Stewart*. As part of the combined Dutch-American striking force, *Stewart* was badly damaged in action, and placed in drydock in Surabaya (Indonesia). There she was further damaged by Japanese bombs, and then captured as the Dutch East Indies fell. The Japanese rebuilt her—and she destroyed one of our greatest submarine skippers and his crew."

The two-star son of a five-star father talked about the Pacific war: "U.S. submarine operations in the Pacific in WW II can quickly be put in dramatic perspective. Some 15,000 submariners, a minute fraction of the U.S. Naval personnel in the Pacific Theater, with 288 submarines, sank two thirds of Japan's merchant fleet and a third of its navy.

"And they did it with losses of only an approximate fifth of their people and submarines—a remarkably favorable comparison to the horrendous losses incurred by German WW II submariners, who waged a similar campaign in the Atlantic. They lost 28,000 of the 41,000 men they sent to sea—a sixty-eight percent casualty rate."

He noted that U.S. successes were achieved despite scandalously unreliable torpedoes. Indeed, "Damn the torpedoes," acquired new meaning among U.S. submariners. But enough torpedoes worked to cripple Japanese shipping.

Rear Admiral Nimitz said: "The war with Japan was the perfect opportunity for unrestricted submarine warfare—an island enemy, poor in natural resources, with widely scattered bases and supply sources, not to speak of a vulnerable code."

U.S. cryptographers became so fluent in the codes of the Imperial Japanese Navy that U.S. submariners sometimes complained when an enemy convoy was late for a date.

The retired admiral told Texas Sub Vets and others: "Submarines weren't very useful when or where they were denied the element of surprise. In the presence of determined enemy forces, concentrating on a specific objective, such as a landing at Balikpapan (Indonesia) or Lingayan Gulf, submarines cannot stand and oppose to keep the enemy from achieving his objective. Sink a few ships, yes. But drive them off, no.

"Nor could they defend Midway against a carrier strike force and landing attack group. Nor could they force a fanatical Japanese government to throw in the towel. But I will aver that in the performance of their primary mission, interdiction of supplies to Japan, U.S. submariners accomplished their important assignment in a manner that has to be rated outstanding. In short, although you didn't win the war singlehandedly, you almost certainly eliminated any Japanese chance to win, and contributed greatly to their predisposition to quit."

Ancient submariners talked tactics for hours and told war stories into the night. A favorite among his peers of the periscope, Captain Slade Cutter of San Antonio, credited with sinking more than twenty enemy ships, paid concise professional tribute to his friend, Sam Dealey:

"He was damn good."

✳✳✳

MEMORABILIA REVEALS THE LIPSCOMB LEGACY IS ALIVE

A hundred dollars may sound like a high price for a book about a man who used to pick and sing all night for a buck or two. But collectors and musicians are signing up to get first editions of the biography of Mance Lipscomb.

For the first sixty-five years of his eight-decade life, Mance Lipscomb was a songster who, for the most part, was widely unsung. "Songster" was the term the black sharecropper and musician used in speaking of himself. He liked that word because it didn't pin him down to a single category: bluesman, folk singer, composer or master of the guitar.

His admirers say he was all of those—and more. Nevertheless, he wasn't always popularly celebrated for his picking, singing or, by his own admission, his farming.

From his youth, Lipscomb's name was a farm-household word along the rich bottoms where the Brazos and the Navasota rivers form a Y in Grimes County. But he wasn't recognized outside his "precinct," as he called it, until the 1960s when, discovered by "white folks" with a tape recorder, he became the darling of blues lovers and, later, a favorite of the flower (or deflowered) generation. As early as 1961, he was playing concerts for audiences of more than 40,000. He performed on eight record albums. Then oblivion almost reclaimed him.

In 1976, several hundred people turned out for his funeral in Navasota and an obituary in *The Dallas Morning News* noted " . . . he wasn't forgotten after all." Today, Lipscomb is still not forgotten. Moreover, his music and his personality, interlaced as they were, seem destined for a resurgence of interest.

In 1981, for example, the Barker Texas History Center of the University of Texas at Austin produced a program and exhibit dedicated to Lipscomb. The program was called "The Texas Blues."

Hundreds showed up to view Lipscomb memorabilia, a forty-five-minute film (*A Life Well Spent* by Les Blank and Skip Gerson) and to hear friends of Lipscomb talk about his style, his philosophy and his life.

The program was timely.

Don E. Carleton, director of the museum, and Harold Billings, UT's director of general libraries, are campaigning to attract more attention of the general public to the museum, a Texana treasure trove that in the past primarily has attracted scholars.

The Lipscomb event marked the acquisition by the museum of notes, documents, manuscripts and recordings gathered by Lipscomb's biographer, a thirty-three-year-old guitarist and singer named Glenn Myers.

Myers spent nine years assembling the material for his book. In the course of the work, he taped about sixty hours of interviews and transcribed around 1000 pages from the tapes. He transcribed the lyrics of about 100 of Lipscomb's songs (Lipscomb claimed a repertoire of 350). In addition, Myers accumulated photos, maps and documents.

Living for months near Lipscomb's farm, Myers learned to pick like Lipscomb, talk like Lipscomb and, from neighbors, to learn many of the Lipscomb legends from the sharecropper-musician's early days.

Myers tells rollicking stories of Lipscomb during the years he played for "Saturday night suppers"—an institution that lingered for years among many Texas blacks in cotton picking seasons when there was money available for drinking, gambling, barbecuing whole hogs and dancing until dawn.

Once, as a youth, Lipscomb was sitting on a windowsill picking and singing for dancers at a Saturday night supper when a celebrating cotton picker began firing a six-shooter. Young Mance's hat flew off and Mance toppled out of the window into the darkness. Myers says witnesses, certain that Mance had been shot through the head, broke the tragic news to his mother, who promptly became hysterical, howling the loss of her son. While friends tried to comfort her, others began searching the darkness for the corpse of the young musician. The tragic scene had gone on for several minutes, Myers relates, when someone heard a noise beneath the farmhouse. In a moment the boy came crawling out of his hiding place. His mother was stunned for an instant, says Myers, and then became outraged. She proceeded to administer to her son a severe tongue-lashing for embarrassing her by permitting her public display of bereavement when he wasn't even hurt, not to mention dead.

From Lipscomb's repeated use of the phrase in conversation, Myers calls the biography *I Say Me for a Parable: the Life and Music of Mance Lipscomb.*

✳✳✳

THEY'RE PICKIN' GRASS IN NACOGDOCHES

Steve Hartz's Old Time String Shop on the square in Nacogdoches is an East Texas shrine for bluegrass pickers. One Saturday afternoon in 1988 when "Foggy Mountain" was exquisitely breaking down, a play-by-play commentary was uttered by Ab:

"A fast, driving, high-speed race of music and time," Ab called it. "Now the banjo's leading the pack, then the fiddle, then the mandolin, and then in the climactic beauty of a great chase, they all cross the finish line, neck and neck, together."

Don't envy a music critic unless you happen to dig post holes for a living. Music can defy words. But with a bass fiddle or with words, Ab's a virtuoso. He's played Texas music all over the world and written or edited so many books that he's about lost count.

Everybody in Nacogdoches knows Ab—Francis Edward Abernethy, Shakespeare professor at Stephen F. Austin State University and J. Frank Dobie's successor as secretary-editor of the Texas Folklore Society. Statewide, Ab spurs Texans' interest in the arts—both the fine kind and the unrefined kind. In the Piney Woods, he tries to elevate East Texans' appreciation of outhouse architecture and locally bottled moonlight. He is a founder of the East Texas String Ensemble, a band that includes SFA professors Tom Nall, history and banjo; Stan Alexander, English and guitar; and, of course, Ab, English and doghouse bass. Ronnie Wolfe, a fiddling high school math teacher from the

Shelby County town of Timpson, completes the Strings. Around here, String Ensemble is always pronounced "Strang In-symbol" to avoid possible confusion with a group from Budapest. Both groups will sell record albums and travel the world. But the one from Hungary doesn't play video store openings or motorcycle weddings. The East Texas Strings are ready for anything. Be it admitted, Ab and those who have exceeded the half-century mark sometimes complain, "Man, I'm too old for this damn foolishness." That happens only after hard traveling or a hard gig, when they are putting up their instruments and breaking down their sound system.

You don't need me to tell you that bluegrass is best without a sound system. And I mention the East Texas String Ensemble mainly because they typify electronically enslaved musicians who abandon their amps to become bluegrass purists when they haunt Steve's shop.

Many of the best pickers and grinners in the Piney Woods regularly find their way to Steve's. An example is fiddler Charles Gardner, SFA geology professor, retired from the Ensemble a couple of years ago. He shows up at Steve's to saw some lovely bluegrass passages. Young musicians and old ones hang out at Steve's. Superb banjoist and composer Paul Buskirk, a veteran master of every style and technique, drops by to impart bits of wisdom to Kelly Lancaster, a guitar prodigy who, at twenty, is starting a career in music.

Of a Saturday, you'll find them or others sitting in or standing back to listen. In mild weather, you may find the pickers on the sidewalk in front of the shop. They keep the music going. It's like a barracks crap game whose players drift in and out. A concert begins unpromisingly with a musician or two trying to tune up. They gripe about real or imagined damage inflicted by humidity, barometric pressure or a poor night's sleep. After endless tuning and retuning, someone will say, "Gimme some E" or "Gear of G" or whatever. In a flash, they're gittin' down on "Columbus Stockade Blues" or "Roll in My Sweet Baby's Arms."

Musicians come from all over. Tom Nall was impressed by the cosmopolitan completeness of the place after an Okinawan came in with a ukulele a couple of weeks ago. "He had it in a case. It was a Martin. I'd never seen a Martin ukulele in a case before."

While some of the boys mourned over "The Banks of the Ohio," I watched some honest-to-Ned potential customers come in. For a few minutes, they looked around the room, which was jammed with the jamming musicians. Finally, without a word, they wandered out the door. No one offered to sell them anything. Steve Hartz, owner and no-pressure salesman, was sweetly plucking his mandolin.

You can actually buy strings at the String Shop, if you're truly deserving, plenty patient, and do not step on the big dog, Maydelle, who is forever trying to find elusive sleep or improved acoustics in various corners of the shop.

In addition to Black Diamond strings, Steve offers an array of musical musts—guitar straps, kazoos of unbreakable plastic, stringwinders and pickholders. What's a pickholder? Well, if you carry your picks in a pickholder, you will avoid the telltale sounds of picks loosely rattling around in your pocket. Landladies will not suspect that you are a musician when you rent a room.

My impression is that most of the revenue at the String Shop is generated by the instrument repair work that goes on in the back room. Stringed instruments of every sort can be seen in all stages of perfection and destruction. I don't know why people break fiddles, but those who do butter the parsnips of Steve Hartz.

At thirty-seven Steve has owned the String Shop for a decade. He took an SFA degree in agriculture in 1969. The ag curriculum apparently included no courses in salesmanship because you can enjoy a melodious Saturday afternoon at the String Shop without spending a nickel. There's no cover and no minimum. You cannot buy a sandwich. No one tries to sell you a beer. If you want a Dr Pepper, you have to go next door to the fire station to get one from the machine. The musicians are as orderly and abstemious as if they were in church. The String Shop has no dance floor and I'll bet no one ever picked up a girl in the joint.

"I encourage the public to drop in," Steve says.

Walking in off the street, you'll wonder for a moment what exactly is the meaning of this strange layout with its almost reverential air. Then away they go—banjo, fiddle, mandolin, guitar, doghouse bass and, strung through it all, a melancholy tenor voice high-squalling, "In the pines, in the pines, where the sun never shines . . . "

Then you know.

✳✳✳

CHEROKEE JACK LOOKS THE PART, AND HE'S APT TO PLAY IT

Hollywood's Slims, Chills, Smileys, Gabbys and Fuzzys have ridden off into the sunset. Now, riding out of Sunset (pop. 200) is Cherokee Jack Glover. You can find a leading man on any street corner. But who're you going to cast as his sidekick? Yep, Cherokee Jack. He could bring back Westerns.

Spitting image of old coontailed Arthur Hunnicut, pony-tailed Cherokee Jack speaks as clearly as Laurence Olivier wif sumfin in his mouf. Yep, it's unspeakable Copenhagen. "Tell 'em to expect me at that Kim Dawson Agency in Dallas," said Jack, a warning to get out the spittoon because Jack will saunter by on Tuesday, maybe. He reckons the agency is looking to manage the career of a genuine cow-country character who can act like one. And listen, if he ever reaches a movie set, no fancy director will need to tell Jack his motivation. It's money. Jack needs scratch for his sure-fire gold mine in New Mexico. He's been talking about that mine all summer.

Jack's story is familiar. He had a piece of a Taylor County foundry that was making him richer than cowlot dirt. Then the foundry foundered in cheap oil. Well, Jack's a good painter and sculptor whose works fetch top dollar. He's author of a dozen books. One is *The Sex Life of the American Indian*, which went through several editions before getting scarce. He's an expert on another thorny topic, "bobbed" wire. And his latest book for barb collectors is *The Bobbed Wire Bible VII*, published by the Cow

Puddle Press of Sunset, a firm that is owned by Jack and really likes his stuff. But life is short and art takes too long. The sculptor-painter-writer refuses to become a robot on an artistic assembly line. So show biz must fund the gold digs.

Jack's an experienced performer, having already worked on several movie sets. But he acted only briefly before the cameras. Mostly, he did chores and built wigwams. This time it'll be different. This time he's motivated. He can smell that gold.

Many people might recognize Jack as the model who posed variously as cowhand, soldier or Indian for many paintings by Arlington artist Joe Grandee, paintings that became covers on Western magazines. Jack looks exactly right.

And, in three decades, thousands of West Texas travelers have met him and toured his occasionally open museum—the Sunset Trading Post, on U.S. 287 between Alvord and Bowie. He hopes it'll be "the Smithsonian of the Southwest." To step inside is to step into the past, and, for the remainder of the day, to live in the past—or at least to be an hour or two late. Both the exhibits and mustache-twirling Jack have stories to tell.

"My great-great-granddaddy had to leave the old place because of his beliefs. He believed they was gonna hang him so he left. He was one of Jean Lafitte's pirates before he got into the fight for Texas independence. Here's his picture, Henry Journeay." Jack, half French and half Cherokee, counts among his kinfolks Will Rogers and Sam Houston.

"I'm about the only member of my family for five generations who wasn't born in Texas. My mother took a trip and I was born in North Carolina. I'm a double cousin to Temple Houston," said Jack, referring to the wild son born to Sam Houston when he was past sixty and in the Texas Governor's Mansion. "I've got some of Temple's belongings. Here's his six-shooter." Jack displayed a Colt .45, serial number 87034.

"My father said it was the one Temple used in a saloon shoot-out in Woodward, Oklahoma, to kill Ed Jennings."

Ed Jennings was the brother of Al Jennings, the Oklahoma outlaw who went into show biz after he got out of prison, but never found a gold mine.

"I've got Temple's bed, his divan, his hall tree, and a mounted goat head. There's his whiskey cabinet," said Jack, pointing to a dark piece of furniture that tippling Temple Houston found functional to excess.

Nodding at a massive piece of wood and glass, he said, "That secretary belonged to Will Rogers." And pulling out a drawer filled with forks and spoons, he said, "Woodrow Wilson's silver." Picking up a beaded stick, he said, "Geronimo's cane."

When I admired an old bed in one of the rooms back of the museum, Jack showed me a notorized statement:

"The brass bed came from the 'Old Homestead,' a bawdy house in Cripple Creek, Colorado. This house was closed in 1954 after nearly seventy-five years of operation.

The curator of the Sunset Trading Post is a Cherokee Jack of all trades—sheetmetal worker to dairy farmer, which is harder than show biz. He said he logged 2,000 hours as flight engineer aboard B-17s during World War II. The Dodgers wanted him to pitch, he said, when they were in Brooklyn. And he used to do a little rasslin'.

But mostly, he's been married for more than forty years to Wanda, a woman who is about half Cherokee and about half tolerant. "I was over in eastern Oklahoma huntin' with some friends and I was about nineteen. I saw this girl sittin' on a log. She was nekkid as a jaybird, eatin' grubs, and I thought, 'Man, that ol' girl would be easy to keep,' so I just brought her home and married her."

Tolerant, yep.

Jack said, "On the ranch, when I was growing up, we used to do a little rodeoing. But that was just something we'd do if we didn't have enough money to go to the picture show." He really oughta be in pictures.

STALKING THE ELUSIVE BUCKAROO

We've all been told that the last real cowboy rode off into the sunset many moons ago (a scene since colorized). Well, what's a real cowboy, anyhow? The popular notion of a real cowboy probably never got within Winchester range of reality. At some turn in the trail, romance unhorsed reality.

I was saddled with these heavy thoughts at the big Texas Tech Cowboy Symposium in Lubbock in 1989. More than 250 authorities on the cowboy talked and sang about his image, solitary spirit, zest for danger, respect for womenfolk, capacity for hard work, capacity for hard liquor and you name it. A sort of unwritten agreement was reached by the authorities that the real cowboy survives, although he is extremely rare and often limps.

Moreover, you may not recognize him—or care to. Beyond the various shadings of unreal cowboys—urban cowboys, rhinestone cowboys, transcontinental trucking cowboys, etc.—is the real cowboy, a genus of two living species. One species of the mounted herdsman is the Texas style cowboy-cowboy, a decreasingly familiar figure. The other is the even more exotic cowboy-buckaroo.

My amigo, Dr. Lawrence Clayton of Abilene, Dean of Arts and Sciences at Hardin-Simmons University, says the distinction is important. The genus is tiny, but seems larger because its members move around a lot. Describing the shrinking world of the nomadic cowboy and buckaroo, Lawrence told me about Rick Taylor, a buckaroo who lives in Elko, Nevada. "Rick writes poetry. I met him at a poetry reading. When I saw him recently, he was wearing a neck brace. He told me he'd broken his neck in Arizona on a ranch where he was herding cattle. Rick and two others were riding together when Rick's horse stumbled in a badger hole.

"Later, back in Texas, I was talking to a cowboy over in Shackelford County and mentioned the badger hole. The Shackelford County cowboy knew all about it. It turned out that he was one of Rick's two companions on that Arizona ranch when the horse fell.

"They move around," said Lawrence, adding: "Incidentally, cowboys and buckaroos don't always work well together." Explaining differences in style, he said:

"Mexican herders were a powerful shaping influence on the Anglo herdsmen on the Texas coastal plains. But the Texas cowboys modified their gear and techniques of working cattle.

"The buckaroo is found mostly in the Intermountain West of Nevada, Idaho, western Utah, Washington, Oregon and northern California and on up into Canada. He was influenced by the Mexican herders of southern California, from whom he got his gear, his working methods and his name. The word buckaroo is an Anglicization of vaquero. His cattle originally came from stock grown by settlers in Washington and Oregon rather than from the Texas Plains. Indian treaties cut off the supply route of Texas cattle in 1867, a crucial time in the development of ranching in the Intermountain West. Later, Texas cattle were driven into the area in large numbers, but the buckaroo tradition was already established.

"The buckaroo's hat will usually have a narrower brim than the cowboy's. The buckaroo's crown may be pushed up to its full height with three or four vertical creases. Or it may be brought down flat on top with a one-inch rim raised around the edge. The brim will usually be flat but may be pulled down slightly in front and back." That's in contrast to the Texas cowboy's familiar broad-brimmed, high-crowned hat with the brim rolled up on the sides.

"The buckaroo's saddle shows more Mexican influence than the Texas cowboy's. The buckaroo's spurs are bigger and his chaps are shorter than the cowboy's. The buckaroo's rope," Lawrence said, "will range between 50 and seventy feet, more than twice the length of that preferred by the cowboy.

"The cowboy's lariat often has a loop built into the end that is tied to the saddlehorn to facilitate a roping and tying method called 'hard and fast.' Recently, dallying—wrapping the rope around the saddle horn—is becoming more common," Lawrence said. He explained that dallying is properly a buckaroo practice that dates back to the days of rawhide ropes, or riatas. They couldn't absorb without damage the full sharp shock of an animal hitting the end of the rope.

Other differences between cowboys and buckaroos are vivid, Lawrence said. For example, you never see a cowboy carrying a quirt. But more similarities than differences exist. They both work cattle. No matter how you slice your steak, working real cattle isn't a glamorous calling.

Novelist Clay Reynolds of Denton, author of *The Vigil, Agatite,* and *Franklin's Crossing,* encountered a couple of real cowboys in a Wilbarger County pizzeria.

Clay said: "My wife and I were visiting my home country. We stopped at a Pizza Hut to have dinner with a high school chum of mine, who is a farm implement dealer in Vernon. As we chatted and munched our pepperoni our reunion was interrupted by the entrance of two men. One was lanky and tall, and the other was stocky and short. Both were covered with the red clay of the region, and both were so bowlegged they could hardly stand upright. Both men were clad in well-worn, high-heeled, spur-scarred boots, denim trousers and plaid shirts. Neither had shaved in several days, and both had skin burned nut brown and wrinkled beyond ironing. Their hands were calloused and stained, and they moved toward the counter in a casual gait that could only be described as a saunter. Each man removed a huge, wide-brimmed hat, covered with dust, and held it politely down to his side while the waitress approached them."

"Who are they?" Clay's wife asked.

"They're cowboys from one of the Wilbarger ranches. Probably just got off," said Clay's friend, who knew them.

He explained that neither cowpoke had a lot of education or enough money to own a house, buy a new car or to consider marriage and family.

Meanwhile, the novelist was reading the cowboys like a book:

"Although the ranch where they worked was probably run by computer, there was no doubt that they were as familiar with tack, animals and the working-cowboy routine as anyone who had dealt with bovines in the West for the past century. Likely, neither man would ever see Paris, New York or even Houston,

216 A Month of Sundays

unless he was employed to go to one of those places for a stock show. They were bachelors who spent their active lives working cattle, hoping that injury or disease would avoid them, and that at some point they could retire and be pensioned off on a reasonable income that would permit old age to be as painless as possible. They lived in mobile homes on the ranch. They owned Sunday clothes for weddings and funerals. They doubtlessly had color TVs and VCRs, maybe a satellite dish. But either would trade all of it for a fancy saddle or a good horse. I sat there, listening to their 'yep' and 'nope' responses to the counter girl and I had the feeling I was looking directly into the past."

✳✳✳

"DOVE" STILL RUFFLING A LOT OF FEATHERS

Lonesome Dove refuses to roost.

Everyone's still talking about Larry McMurtry's big book and its TV adaptation. And millions of readers and viewers remain puzzled by the Hat Creek Cattle Company's damnable Latin motto. We'll get to that.

First, we'll hear from Lewis C. Rigler, who has a bur under his saddle. *Lonesome Dove's* chief characters are three old Texas Rangers. Rigler also happens to be an old Texas Ranger.

Retired in Gainesville, Rigler, 74, is more literary than the next Ranger because he helped his daughter-in-law, Judy Rigler, write his biography, *In the Line of Duty*. Ranger Rigler wrote me in 1989:

"Kent, I first became acquainted with the Texas Rangers in 1921. Through the years I have known very well Tom Hickman, Manny Gault, Frank Hamer, Jay Banks, Alfred Allee, M. T. (Lone Wolf) Gonzaullas, Clint Peoples, Lester Robertson, and Johnny Klevenhagen.

"None of those mentioned would be proud to claim *Lonesome Dove*. I can't imagine a Ranger captain of that time having $50. Further, I never heard of a Ranger captain paying a prostitute for her favors."

Lewis, I wouldn't touch that last line with a borrowed badge.

Other Rangers at Fort Fisher in Waco, I hear, have questioned fictional Captain Gus McCrae's sidearm. They observed his Walker Colt on TV but they never saw him toting around its necessary impediments—caps, powder flask, patches, balls and molds.

True, the cap and ball six-gun displayed by Gus may seem oddly out of place among cowmen armed with cartridge-firing Henry repeating rifles. But McMurtry knows all that. I believe he consciously armed Gus with the antique weapon to underscore his character. Gus is a throwback to an earlier time.

For a few critics, *Lonesome Dove* is a sitting duck. Any book of nearly 1000 pages makes a fat target. But a lot of this carping is nonsense. Take David Braun, Texas director of The Nature Conservancy. He sounded off to *The Washington Post*:

"McMurtry subjects our heroes to a fantastic series of natural disasters: floods, dust storms, lightning, hailstorms, two snake bites, a grasshopper invasion, etc. Any one of these oversized events might happen once in a decade but not all in one year on one trail drive."

Braun is all wet. Any West Texan can set him straight. Texas weather will do anything to get into print or on TV as often as possible. So will snakes. Clearly, McMurtry selected dramatic incidents from fact and folklore recounted by old-time trail drivers. He had hundreds to choose from. Trail drivers and their cows always suffered hardships, frequent and oversized.

In the *Houston Chronicle*, curmudgeon H. B. Fox, the Cowhouse philosopher, takes sharper aim:

"What, I got to wondering, would the late J. Frank Dobie, that ridiculer of unauthentic writing about cow country, have said if he had read about a bull that bays in Larry McMurtry's *Lonesome Dove*? That's right. McMurtry writes about a bull that bays all night. I can report, however, that there's no dog in the book that bellows or lows." On the cover of the *Chronicle's* magazine, *Texas*, a cartoonist drew a bull baying at the moon.

You can almost hear Gus saying, "Welcome to fiction, girls."

But even in fiction, county courthouses and city halls aren't interchangeable. And that's my only kick about *Lonesome Dove*.

McMurtry can't decide whether July Johnson is sheriff of Sebastian County, Arkansas, or city marshal of Fort Smith.

A puzzler for some readers is how blood poisoning in one of Gus McCrae's legs proved contagious to the other leg. But that requires no leap of faith for a true believer. And I'm one.

The thing that has people tossing all night is that vexed Latin motto. Not knowing it would become his epitaph, Gus wrote on his sign for the Hat Creek Cattle Company and Livery Emporium: *"Uva Uvam Vivendo Varia Fit."*

By now, every seminarian, law clerk and classics professor in the nation has had a go at translating the thing. Nothing seems to Fit Varia Mucho. I summoned my expert, Ernestine P. Sewell of Commerce, a fastidious scholar and a retired English professor.

Ernestine helped me with a column a couple of years ago in which I called *Lonesome Dove* the *Gone With the Wind* of the American West. She liked it, too. Her remarks about the Pulitzer Prize-winning Western sparked an exchange of letters with McMurtry. Her analysis was published in a learned journal, *Western American Literature*, for fall 1986.

For McMurtry's readers, Ernestine explained:

"In *Lonesome Dove* the Cowboy-God is a Freudian composite of the three old Rangers: (Woodrow) Call is Super-Ego; Gus (McCrae), Ego; and Jake (Spoon), Id. Taken as one, the three embody the idea of Cowboy, the man on horseback, full of the joy of life, accepting the tragedy of life, brave, daring, hard-working, loyal, reliable, proud, stoic, often ascetic, straightforward, restless, independent, and not without a sense of humor.

"Each of the Rangers is consistent within the Freudian concept. When Jake the Id dies, nothing seems to go right anymore. When Gus' tempering Ego is gone, Call becomes a confused old man. . . .

"That the three-in-one figure is by authorial intent is strengthened by the motto Gus painted on the sign . . . which may be translated: 'The cluster of grapes—many sides, parti-colored, diverse—through living, begets one grape.' The three, like a cluster of grapes, so various are finally, after much ripening by the vagaries of life, one, the Cowboy-God."

I conspired with Ernestine's husband, Charles Linck, an ETSU English professor, to filch copies of a couple of her prized McMurtry letters. Responding to the column, McMurtry wrote her on December 14, 1986:

"... I was particularly interested in the translation quoted of the Latin proverb—it is somewhat more elaborate than the ones I worked from. I found it in Gurney Benham's *Putnam's Complete Book of Quotations*, New York 1927. There the proverb is translated as 'The grape changes its hue (ripens) by looking at another grape.' There is a reference to a Persian proverb, very similar (One grape gets color by looking at another grape) and to *Juvenal, Satire 2, 81*: 'And the grape gains its purple tinge by looking at another grape.'

"Those are the translations I worked from—missing, of course, is the sense of clusters which seems to be important to your reading of the novel."

Then, on February 19, 1987, he wrote:

"Thanks a lot for writing and sending your essay, which I thought was excellent. I grew up an Empsonian and am comfortable with as many meanings as possible. . . .

"I see what you mean about the possibilities of the motto. I'm trying to remember more about when I got it. *LD* was a movie script first—done in 1971 for (John) Wayne, (James) Stewart, (Henry) Fonda, but never made. The sign was in the script, but I think not the motto. I think I added that during the sporadic composition of the first draft of the novel."

McMurtry went on to note that his script was archived at the University of Houston, "and I'm not sure if I tried more than one motto or not. It's possible."

Speaking of the motto, Professor Linck told me:

"I suspect that McMurtry was spoofing. Being an 'Empsonian' puts him into a very modern literary criticism school. And I think he was doing William Empson's thing—'seven types of ambiguity.'"

Linck explained that Empson's seventh type is ambiguity that arises from error. And, apparently, McMurtry allowed Gus McCrae to err in copying the sign's Latin motto. Linck added that

among the book's clues to McMurtry's spoof is the comment of a
fairly educated character in the book (cattleman Wilbarger):
"That's a damned amusing sign." The professor went on:
"McMurtry refers Ernestine to his source for the Latin proverb as
Putnam's Complete Book of Quotations (G.P. Putnam's Sons, NY,
1927.) There one finds:

"*Uva Uvam videndo varia fit.* The grape changes its hue (ripens)
by looking at another grape. (Note: It is a saying in Persia that one
plum gets color by looking at another.) But the all-important
'looking' of the verb *VIDENDO* is different from McMurtry's
VIVENDO—living.

"McMurtry goes on to say his source was also *Juvenal, Satire
No. 2*, line 81: 'And the grape gains its purple tinge by looking at
another grape.' He doesn't reveal his edition or translation for
this version or variation. Actually, all tranlators say it differently,
but the operative word *VIDENDO* (looking) is still there.

"So, McMurtry gave this much about his source, pointing out,
'. . . missing, of course, is the sense of clusters which seems to be
important to your reading of the novel.' And he adds, 'I chose it
mainly for its euphony'—which I, Charles Linck, take with a
grain of salt.

"Now, let us go to *Juvenal's Satire No. 2*, lines 80-81, where the
accepted editions give us this Latin line: '*uvaque conspecta livorum
ducit ab uva*' and these translations: 'Just as one bunch of grapes
takes on its sickly color from the aspect of its neighbor,' (*Juvenal
and Persius*, with an English translation by G. G. Ramsay, London:
Heinemann, 1920); 'Or the touch of one blighted grape will blight
the bunch,' (*Juvenal: the 16 Satires*, translated with an introduction
and notes by Peter Green, Harmondsworth: Penguin Books Ltd.,
1967).

"In a note—Note Number Seven—Green, in quibbling about
a choice of words, refers to the 'proverbial' *UVA UVUM VIDENDO
VARIA FIT*—which isn't found at all in the *Juvenal* text but is
found only in that note. No doubt McMurtry got his phrase from
the note and not from Juvenal itself. However, he changed that
word *VIDENDO* (looking) to *VIVENDO* (living etc).

"But I should mention one other translation: 'A rotten apple spoils the whole barrel,' (*Satires of Juvenal*, translated by Rolfe Humphries, Indiana University Press, 1958)—a version by a non-grape man.

"There are dozens of these translations," said Linck. "McMurtry said the motto probably wasn't in the original movie script of 1971 and probably was added when he was composing the first draft of the novel. He was doing 'sporadic composition' and perhaps feeling ornery, reading the satirical writings of Juvenal and picking up on the name Laronia (for his Lorena), which is found there.

"Maybe he was reading St. Paul's Letter to the Corinthians for (chef) Bolivar's clanging cymbals and for notions about the degrees and variations of love, and Lord know what else for 'influences' and more and more symbolism for scholars like Ernestine to investigate or any good Empsonian to admire."

But, professor.

"Right, we still haven't found the original of the motto with the *VIVENDO* word which changes the whole meaning of the proverb from *seeing* to *living, ripening, evolving* or *melding into one*. And that's crucial to Ernestine's interpretation and holistic reading.

"Well, my answer is that McMurtry is a sharpie and he is pulling our collective legs. He gives us a clue in Wilbarger's remark—'That's a damned amusing sign'—and there are other oblique comments. Once people become suspicious, they begin to give a considerable amount of attention to the motto. Ernestine immediately picked up on that.

"I think she hit upon what McMurtry was all about. In fact, at the fall 1987 meeting of the Western Literature Association in Lincoln, Nebraska, McMurtry mentioned the 'classicist' at ETSU, who had given the appropriate interpretation to his novel. She wasn't at the meeting, but her friends heard it and reported back to her.

"McMurtry invented the motto. It cannot be found anywhere in the form he used. He did this on purpose to prove the novel's theme."

Whew. No wonder McMurtry's been dodging interviews

lately. Not even Gus McCrae knew what the motto meant.

Readers of Simon & Schuster's *Lonesome Dove* will remember this conversation:

"So what's it say, that Latin?" Call asked.

"It's a motto," Agustus said. "It just says itself." He was determined to conceal for as long as possible the fact that he didn't know what the motto meant, which anyway was nobody's business. He had written it on the sign—let others read it.

Call was quick to see the point. "You don't know yourself," he said. "It could say anything. For all you know it invites people to rob us."

Agustus got a laugh out of that. "The first bandit that comes along who can read Latin is welcome to rob us, as far as I'm concerned," he said. "I'd risk a few nags for the opportunity of shooting an educated man for a change."

Who, at this point, could argue with Gus McCrae's sentiment?

And if his Latin motto's all that damned amusing, Larry McMurtry must be laughing all the way to the bank.

✳✳✳

ACE REID COULD ALWAYS DRAW LAUGHS

Ace Reid. Didn't he ramble?

The cowboy cartoonist rambled all over the map. And his conversations (really monologues) rambled all over the universe. I'll get to that.

A good artist may at decent intervals exhibit his works in a one-man show. But Ace, for as long as I knew him, *was* a one-man show.

He created those Cow-pokes cartoons you see published in West Texas newspapers and taped to cafe cash registers. But he was at his best in the ample flesh, holding forth. With a big crowd or a lone listener, Ace captured all eyes and ears. Nearly everything he uttered was funny. I guess he couldn't help it. His gift must have been a curse when he tried to be serious, if ever.

Everything he said came out droll as the stockman's line in one of his cartoons: "To think, all this ranch is mine—15,000 acres of land, no grass, five miles of creek and no water." That was the millionaire cartoonist's manner when he spoke of his own Draggin' S Ranch in the hills near Kerrville. The Draggin' S is only about 250 acres (enough for plenty of deer and four or five cows in that country).

Ace's biographer John R. Erickson (*Ace Reid: Cowpoke*) told me, "Those 250 acres would be about five sections if you mashed them flat."

Ace got his mail at the ranch where he lived with Madge, a Wichita County physician's daughter he wooed and wed forty-three years ago. At the time, a career in cartooning appealed to Ace because it could be conducted in the shade. I'm not going to tell you the doc was ecstatic about all this.

"We eloped," said Madge, her tone suggesting a high-speed chase.

They have a talented son, Stan Reid (and two grandchildren). Madge and Stan will go on providing about 300 newspapers with Cow-pokes cartoons although Ace died in November, 1991. Those of us who took Ace for a Texas landmark won't accept his death right away.

At sixty-five, Asa E. Reid had survived World War II combat, horse wrecks, excruciating arthritis, heart attacks and diseases among the worst known to man or woman. His recovery from leukemia thirty years ago made the medical journals. When he developed a stomach ulcer not long ago, he checked into a San Antonio hospital. Madge said he caught a staph infection. The infection became fatal when it involved a heart-valve implant he'd received several years ago, she said.

I once wrote that Ace had longevity in his jeans. But maybe sixty-five is longevity for someone who'd lived through as much as Ace.

He leaves a dozen collections of his work in book form. And he illustrated several others. One is a 1991 publication, *Horsing Around*, edited by Lawrence Clayton and Kenneth W. Davis.

For me a vivid memory is Ace razzing a bunch of writers at Kerrville's YO Hilton one evening half a dozen years ago. The YO

Hilton was Ace's home away from the Draggin' S. He hung out there. The tourists gathered around the pool were members of the Western Writers of America. A few of them knew Ace, and the others won't forget him.

Ace sat with his buddy Charles Schreiner III, then sole owner of the 50,000-acre YO Ranch. Charles III was dressed as if he'd just fallen off a fast freight. Ace was lubricating his tonsils from a tall glass with a lime in it.

After a while, he stood up on the red-tiled steps, a heroic beer-bellied figure in rainbow-colored suspenders. He appraised the writers with distaste. When at last he spoke, he began cussing them up and down for being a no-good bunch of transcontinental liars.

In the group were front-rank novelists such as Elmer Kelton and distinguished historians such as C. L. Sonnichsen. Those two knew Ace, so it was OK. They knew Ace might call you a worthless old SOB as an endearment. But most of the two dozen or so writers didn't know him. I wish you could have seen their faces. Laugh?? I thought I'd choke.

Ace boomed: "Why in hell don't you ever write about sheep-herders? Nobody writes about the pore old sheep-herder, sittin' in his little old wagon reading *Shakespeare*, with only three damn dogs out there watching 10,000 head of sheep."

His talk rambled on, then returned to the unsung sheep-herder who needed to be written about. He boomed: "Naw, you won't do that. You gotta write about some glamorous cowboy. I'll tell you about that glamorous cowboy. He gits up about four o'clock in the morning, eats some cold beans and goes out to the pen in the dark and throws a frosty saddle on the back of some old horse that he knows damn well is gonna try to kill him.

"And then he throws a rope on an old cow, and she's gonna try to kill him, too. And if I was that cowboy and I had a six-shooter like you always give him, the first thing I'da done is kill that horse and the second thing I'da done is kill that damn cow.

"See, you-all are going about this thing in the wrong damn way. But you already knew somethin' was hay-wire, didn't you?"

He rambled on. He spotted biographer Erickson, who lived in the Panhandle town of Perryton. Ace loudly advised Mr. Erickson to go home and drown himself if he could find any water in Ochiltree County.

In those days, the YO Hilton had an Ace Reid Suite. A hotel staffer told me, "It was quite popular." Ace complained because they wouldn't let him stay there. The suite went for $250 a night. If Ace moved in, there was a large risk that he might claim squatters' rights on it—if not Divine Right.

Madge told me that Ace had asked that his ashes be scattered over the Hill Country that he loved. It seemed fitting. In a manner of speaking. Old Ace could ride the Texas wind and go on rambling forever.

What a glorious way to go.

$$***$$

John Henry Faulk Looms Tall Over Texas

Part I

Years ago, when I met the late John Henry Faulk, aka Don Quixote with a twang, I knew he was crazy about me because he kept calling me "My Dear." Later, I was a bit crestfallen to learn that John Henry bestowed wholesale endearments equally on women, children, men and stray dogs.

For example, in 1987, everyone was "Honey" during the run of "J. Frank Dobie" at Black's Opera House in the Caldwell County seat of Lockhart. Dobie was an earthy echo of the granddaddy (1888-1964) of Texas letters. ("Hell, I'd rather have VD than a Ph.D.") John Henry co-wrote that show with a fellow Austin author-actor, Cactus Pryor, who took the title role. Both Cactus and John Henry looked robust, but folks whispered that John Henry was dying.

A tumor the size of a goose egg had been found in his sinuses.

A year earlier, I had seen him at a gathering of the Tejas Storytellers in Denton. He consistently addressed them as "Loves."

The Tejas group gave John Henry two standing ovations and
an award for his contributions to Texas storytelling. But John
Henry's cancer had flared up. Several storytellers privately expressed surprise that John Henry was alive, much less able to spin
yarns. Appealing to liberal funny-bones, John Henry had named
his cancer "Bork," after the unsuccessful nominee for the U.S.
Supreme Court, conservative Judge Robert Bork. The scene
warmed the old tale-monger, known for his books (*Fear on Trial*
and *The Un-censored John Henry Faulk*), his spots on TV's "Hee
Haw," and his lifelong identity with liberal causes. (Best remembered line: "Why don't they leave Lyndon alone and let him fight
his war in peace?")

When the old storyteller took the stage, he was equal to the
occasion, telling his "Loves": "I enjoy you all more than safe sex."

After Denton, John Henry carried on, presenting one-man
shows and reaping good notices until again the cancer struck him
low. He had surplus foes from 1983, when the lifelong liberal
Democrat ran a bitter, losing race against Senator Phil Gramm.
The Dallas Morning News' conservative columnist, William
Murchison, is one who doesn't dig John Henry. He wrote:

"I live in expectation that one day, in an un-guarded moment,
John Henry Faulk will say something funny." Defying description, John Henry's style often defies newspaper or news-cast
translation. He owns dozens of stage characters. But the characters generally ramble through stories, tortured with digressions,
to reach some distant point.

Early in 1987, Cactus told me that John Henry was responding to chemotherapy. A plum-sized tumor had been reduced to
the dimensions of a grape. In June, he was well enough to accept
the James Madison award of the Freedom of Information Foundation of Texas at the group's meeting in Houston.

The Associated Press reported: "It's fitting that an award
named for the founding father James Madison will be presented
to a once-blacklisted humorist who can recite Madison's handi-
work without pause." John Henry recites the Bill of Rights like his
Social Security number.

John Henry was born August 21, 1913, in south Austin, son of a lawyer with socialist leanings. He earned   bachelor's and master's degrees from the University of Texas, where he studied under J. Frank Dobie. John Henry's master's thesis was a collection of sermons by black preachers. It established him as a Texas folklorist.

During World War II, after Army rejection for bad vision, he served in the Merchant Marine and later with the American Red Cross in Egypt. In 1944, when the Army relaxed vision standards, he was accepted as a medic. On leave in 1945, he visited New York, where CBS execs liked his folksy manner. By 1951, he was a radio performer on WCBS in New York, where he emceed the one-hour John Henry Faulk Show five days a week. He seemed fated for stardom. Besides his New York radio show, he did guest spots on network radio and TV. His show wasn't supposed to be on the network, but in Austin, KLBJ Radio's Cactus Pryor accidentally-on-purpose broadcast John Henry's show "by pressing the wrong button sometimes."

In 1956, John Henry was targeted by a powerful right-wing watchdog group that called itself AWARE Inc. The self-appointed Communist fighters had ruined the careers of several entertainment figures by charging they were reds or Communist sympathizers. AWARE's bulletin, freighted with innuendo and falsehood, was routinely sent to broadcasters, sponsors and advertising firms. Victims were professionally blacklisted. John Henry had publicly denounced blacklisting.

He was tarred in a series of false charges. Taking one, for example: "According to the *Daily Worker* of April 22, 1946, 'Jack Faulk' was to appear at Club 15, 13 Astor Place, NYC—a favorite site of pro-Communist affairs." Never mind that John Henry wasn't pro-communist and hadn't been to Club 15. Moreover, he wasn't Jack Faulk. The "Red Scare" was afoot.

Despite support from newscaster Edward R. Murrow and others at CBS, John Henry was dropped by the network. He soon found that he'd been blacklisted by the entire industry.

Retaining attorney Louis Nizer, he sued AWARE. In 1962, he won a record $3.5 million judgment. But AWARE turned out to be all mouth and no money. The judgment was reduced to

$500,000. Finally, John Henry was able to squeeze only $175,000 from AWARE's backers. Half went to his attorneys. Half went to his creditors. He'd been out of work for six years.

John Henry's trial ended widespread acceptance of blacklisting. He wrote a best-selling account of his ordeal—*Fear On Trial*. And in 1975 there was a two-hour TV movie based on his story. Ironically, it was shown by CBS.

Friends conjecture that John Henry would be a big TV star had he not been smeared. But there's no conjecture about his being a big star in his hometown. He owned Austin. In letters an inch tall, the *Austin American-Statesman* called John Henry the "National Treasure of Texas." Mayor Lee Cooke presided at the dedication of a star honoring John Henry in the Sixth Street sidewalk in front of the historic Driskill Hotel. Singer Willie Nelson's was the only other star.

A $200-a-plate banquet in the Driskill in 1987 drew 130 fans. A rousing tribute to John Henry followed at the Paramount Theater. The twenty-five-dollar-per-ticket event had the feel of a liberal political rally. Billed as "A Texas Tribute to John Henry Faulk," the show benefited the Live Oak Theater.

Ann Richards got in the spirit of the testimonial evening, joined by Chicago's Studs Terkel (*Hard Times: An Oral History of the Great Depression*), Austin's Jaston Williams (*Greater Tuna*) and California lawyer-movie producer Barbara Boyle. Stage and screen veterans of the blacklisting years, Ossie Davis (*Purlie Victorious*) and Lee Grant (*Peyton Place* and *Shampoo*) paid dramatic tribute to their hero. Mr. Davis remembered, "John Henry stood like steel." Ms. Grant's figure of speech was, "John Henry flew like a flag."

Mr. Terkel said "John Henry's probably the best storyteller since Mark Twain." The blowout was as Texan as an ice chest of Shiner Bock beer. Pickers and grinners, notably Steve Fromholz, provided a tuneful background. And Jerry Jeff Walker brought the house to its feet with "This Land Is Your Land." Its late composer, Woody Guthrie, used to hang out with John Henry.

You'd think John Henry might have overdosed on adulation. But he said "God isn't ready for me in heaven yet and the devil's afraid to have me in hell."

If he never gets heavenly stars in his crown, John Henry, who died in 1990, will always own a star in the Sixth Street sidewalk down in Austin.

Part II: Bennie Augustus "Peavine" Jeffries

It was Geography Awareness Week, 1991.

A couple of miles south of North Zulch (est. pop. 100) are the ruins of South Zulch. Never mind that. Finding North Zulch is plenty of Geography Awareness for one week. But strangers alighting in North Zulch always ask about South Zulch. They wonder where's the rest of the town. Here's what happened.

South Zulch was once just plain Zulch. A post office called Willow Hole, dating to 1870, was renamed Zulch in 1903. Zulch wasn't much. Worse, when the railroad missed Zulch, most Zulch burghers picked up and relocated along the shiny tracks. The new community became North Zulch. Old Zulch, meanwhile, dwindled. Old Zulch then became South Zulch (est. pop. 50 in 1949). And South Zulch became South Zilch. Nada, in Tex-Mex. (Geographical Awareness reminds me that Nada is actually in Colorado County. And Nada's est. pop. of 165 has zoomed ahead of all Zulches.)

Zulch was named for Dr. Julius Zulch, a local healer. On the face of the map, North Zulch is a bit of a zit, one of those tiny towns you've never heard of. North Zulch is soooo small it doesn't have a town drunk. Folks have to take turns. And having a local celebrity can be a problem. In recent years, it's been Peavine's turn. Peavine Who? Bennie Augustus "Peavine" Jeffries, an old retired carpenter-farmer and semi-retired celebrity, is who. He lives with his wife Phynia a few miles south of North Zulch on an unpaved road known only to the geographically aware.

Peavine was discovered (invented?) by the late Texas humorist John Henry Faulk in the middle 1970s. An all-natural wit ("half-wit," he corrects), Peavine became a perfect foil and patsy for John Henry.

John Henry avoided the personal shame of many an outrageous line or marginal joke by pinning it on Peavine, who became mildly famous. He took Peavine to Nashville a couple of times to

film television's "Hee Haw," a show whose ratings must over-
come the reluctance of viewers to admit that they watch it. John
Henry was a regular until he died in April, 1990.

"Going to Nashville was just fine," said Peavine. "Especially
for somebody like me—who has no known talent. I can't even
play a radio." "Hee Haw" producers paid all Peavine's expenses,
gave him a pair of overalls and paid him $400 to boot. He balked
when they asked him to think up fifteen jokes. "It's hard to think
up fifteen jokes in a row," he said. A hard row, indeed. But he
allowed that what passes for a joke on "Hee Haw" is usually
several country miles short of hilarity. "And none of them folks
can tell a joke worth a flip," he said.

"I don't remember much of the stuff that Johnny and I did.
Well, let's see. There was one, something about me being in the
doghouse and not liking it because I didn't enjoy living with
somebody who was smarter than me."

Even in the re-telling, Peavine filled the room with gales of
silence. Peavine met John Henry when Jubal Richard Parten,
Madison County's New-Dealing, Fair-Dealing, wheeling-deal-
ing oillionaire angel of liberal causes, placed the two in charge of
his private fishing hole, Patterson Lake.

Peavine and John Henry required sportsmen to sign in and
out when they used the lake. "That way we'd know how many
drowned," Peavine explained. Their register resembled the roll
call of a political rump meeting. Every liberal politico from
Austin showed up. And the register bore autographs of writers
such as Ronnie Dugger, Molly Ivins, Cactus Pryor, and then-
journalist Jim Hightower (later Democrat Texas Agriculture Commissioner defeated by GOP State Representative Rick Perry).

"Ann Richards used to fish with us. She was just an old
country girl back then. She even helped clean fish," Peavine
recalled.

Peavine is hard to figure. When he tells about his Uncle Will,
who wore size-sixteen shoes and had to fight the battle of the
Argonne Forest with his feet wrapped in burlap bags, you believe
him. Uncle Will Jeffries was six-feet-ten. Peavine was six-feet-

three the last time he straightened up—which was before he came down with the Parkinson's disease that dogs him.

When he was diagnosed, Peavine asked the doctor: "How long did old Parkinson live after he got this disease?"

The doc shrugged, "He may still be living for all I know."

Big guys run in Peavine's family. Another of Peavine's relatives was Cousin Jim—James J. Jeffries, the heavyweight champ. But Peavine believes that with a little training, his papa, the late Gus Jeffries, a big strong Madison County farmer, could have whipped Cousin Jim.

Peavine is trying to spike the rumor that he climbed out a schoolhouse window and both literally and figuratively dropped out of the third grade.

"It was the fourth grade," he said primly.

But he learned his numbers. He can count, for example, ten grandchildren. He and Phynia raised two sons and a daughter. The daughter, Etta Rush, is co-owner of Etta Jean's Pout House Ceramics. Although Etta's residence is miles away, the Pout House sits on Peavine's farm.

What's a Pout House? She explained, "When my partner Jean May and I would go there to work, everyone always said we must have fought with our husbands and went to that little house to pout." Pouting or not, they cook up some appealing ceramic pieces.

Peavine feels his wit is vastly overrated. But properly set up, he can get off a line. Like the time a few years ago when he was doing some cabinet work at the home of his dentist. The dentist wasn't home, and the dentist's wife was supervising the job.

"I came across a fifth of vodka in that cabinet. Whenever she'd leave the room, I'd take me a nip. All afternoon we was wisecracking back and forth. Finally, she says, 'Peavine, if you was my husband, I'd give you poison.'

"I says, 'If you was my wife, I'd take it.'"

I says, "Hee Haw."

J. EVETTS HALEY: "SORT OF AN ALAMO"

Southerners would be better off today if the Confederacy had won *The War*.

Texans would be better off today if their ancestors hadn't formally joined the United States.

Texans would be better off if they clearly understood that their state remains sovereign to the federal government.

Everyone probably would be better off if Texas had acquired Mexico long ago.

Democracy is nothing but mob rule unless it's moderated by the protections to the minority provided by the restrictions of a well-designed republic.

Outrageous talk?

It came straight from a leading historian of Texas.

You may not agree with what J. Evetts Haley had to say, but he'll defend to the death—yours or any other mother's sons—his own right to say it. His eyes are as darkly serious as shotgun muzzles when he talks politics. Then he takes a sip of Rebel Yell bourbon and his eyes turn good-natured again, wrinkling at their corners in grin-lines.

This mean old man, in the view of some, this lion of the desert, in the view of others, can be downright neighborly. He is by habit as hospitable and polite as a southern gentleman from long ago. And he's a hard-sell, welcome wagon for this forsaken land that has more sand hills than windmills and more windmills than people. That's symbolic. Haley, unyielding as the hardpan that lies just below the sand, has spent a lifetime with windmills— erecting them, greasing them and, moreover, quixotically jousting with them.

Like any Bell County-born country boy, he talks of the weather—about 30 inches of rain in five years—and quotes an old-timer: "God's in His heaven. He damned shore ain't around here."

Haley cusses with the conviction of a true believe.

Haley is a cowboy.

He's a proudly confessed bow-legged, busted-up cow puncher.

Disturbing to some people, he's also a thinker.

Whether he thinks deeper than a troublesome gopher hole or a deregulated gas well depends on where you stand—and Haley stands somewhere off the right margin of this page.

"Riding this country gives you time to think." And some of Haley's thoughts may seem as wild as the country he rides. Perhaps the silence, uncluttered by claptrap conversation, encourages contemplation.

This ranch—the JH—is 10 miles long and its silence is deafening, except for some distant gas drillers and the occasional stirring of a roadrunner or rattlesnake. A nephew was killed by a rattler. Maybe that's one reason Haley is never far from a loaded .38 caliber sixgun. He often drives through towns with the worn-blue Smith & Wesson on the dashboard of his Oldsmobile just as casually as some motorists carry along a box of Kleenex.

The list of Haley's literary works is as long as a lariat. His *Charles Goodnight: Cowman and Plainsman* is an undisputed masterpiece of Texas history. ("And who, nowadays, is going to spend 20 years writing a book?") His *The XIT Ranch of Texas and the Early Days of the Llano Estacado* is widely admired. (Who but Haley in an "authorized biography" of a business like this one could generate nearly a dozen libel suits? His explanation: "I called damn outlaws 'outlaws' and I won in court.")

Outside courtrooms and classrooms (he's a historian and never a teacher), he has won variously both the unbridled academic respect and the withering political scorn of critics and scholars.

In 1964, he infuriated the liberal press with his *A Texan Looks at Lyndon*. He tried to nail President Lyndon Johnson's skin to the barn door. "The lawyers told me, 'Hell, Evetts, there's libel on every damn page.' So I published it myself with $20,000 I'd saved up. I even went to the publishers and mailed cartons of 100 copies or so all over the country before they could get a court order against its distribution. It was the only one of my books that really ever made any money to mention."

It was also the book that came close to costing him his credentials as a historian of repute, although he insists that the book was carefully documented. The liberal critics climbed the walls. LBJ just winced. No lawsuit resulted except an unexpected one, the widow of a San Antonio journalist sued Haley for copyright infringement. Haley argued that he had properly cited the work, but settled the case out of court with a payment to the widow.

Don't be misled by the out-of-court gesture to the widow. Make no mistake, Haley can be as tough as a dollar steak. ("Sure, I had to shoot a man up on the Canadian. But I didn't kill him. And he was trying to steal my car. I don't want to talk about it.")

Haley can also be as tender as the veal at Gianni's, a Midland restaurant he favors—when he's not out in the wilds cooking up sourdough biscuits and mountain oysters. "Look here at these wild buttercups. Pretty things."

His political notions are as rigid and thorny as a well-built—if at points rusty—barb-wire fence.

But he never let political arguments alienate him from his old, long-gone pals like J. Frank Dobie, Roy Bedichek, Walter Prescott Webb and John Lomax, all giants of Texas literature.

Haley is an unsettling individualist, a patriot who consistently has battled the federal government in comment and courtroom while privately lamenting all the while that he was too young for World War I (when he tried to fib his way into uniform) and too old for World War II.

He is a sort of an Alamo in search of a besieging army. In fact, that old fortress' mission bell is enshrined at the Haley Museum in Midland, an impressive conservatory of cow country culture. How the bell ended up in the Nita Stewart Haley Memorial Library and the J. Evetts Haley History Center is a tale of liquor, loans and lofty ideals that would make a book, a book that Haley wrote and titled *The Alamo Mission Bell*.

Pretty Nita Haley died in 1958 after bearing him a son, J. Evetts Haley, Jr. The senior Evetts, whose eye for a well-turned ankle is as keen as his ear for a well-turned phrase, married his present wife, a slender blonde named Rosalind.

A Carolinian who sometimes yearns for magnolias and slaps on a plastic dust mask against the gritty wind of the plains, "Ros" finds the elder Haley unterrifying.

"Take off your hat in the House, Evetts," she commands. "You know you never wear your hat in the house unless you're in a slovenly mood."

His response is to comply meekly and proceed to cuss all disco cowboys and the much-to-be-detested rhinestone cowboys who *never* remove their hats under a roof in the gentlemanly manner of old time cowpokes.

A Confederate Doodle Dandy, Haley was eighty years old on July 5, 1981. With the posture of a surveyor's rod he still rides through the clawing mesquite to herd his cattle and inspect his land. He has ownership or interest in thousands upon thousands of acres of this arid dirt he loves. He has reason for loving it. Much of it has multiplied many times in value since he began buying it for $15 an acre as a $30-monthly-salaried cowhand.

He has houses and bunkhouses scattered throughout West Texas like a small chain of motels, but he and Ros spend most of their time in thriving Midland when they're not at the ranch eighty-five miles away in Loving County, a lonely county named for an early traildriver and then forgotten by all but those who in its 650 square miles manage to survive. That's about 100 people, if you count the census taker.

It's a country that shapes tough people. Most of Haley's major bones have been busted a time or two by his horned herd or in car wrecks or horse wrecks or—you name it. He's been gored dangerously but insists he prefers working horned cattle because they don't "bunch up."

Forty or fifty cows have walked over his face, now well repaired by plastic surgery, an uncharacteristic concession to his personal beauty. He has written of trail herds numbering thousands of cattle that moved through the countryside without disturbing a bird's nest on the ground. He laughs: "Cattle haven't always been that discriminating with me."

Men, politically enraged, also have tried to walk on his face— but without much effect.

His arms are as scarred as his old pair of chaps from fighting the bedeviling brush and cactus that struggle to live in this wasteland beyond the Cap Rock—the Staked Plains' geological ruffle that the Comanches used to call the "Eyebrow" and which Haley later aptly described as an angry one.

As a historian acquainted with the rape of the South by the Republicans after the Civil War, how can Haley reconcile his decision to become a Republican?

"There's been political change. The Republicans now offer the best path for effective government." (Read: lack of government.) Of the Republican Party, the member of the Methodist Episcopal Church South grins: "Isn't everyone entitled to a little Christian redemption?"

Of the Democratic Party, he sadly shakes his head: "They may be beyond redemption."

After Midland High School, West Texas State and the University of Texas (B.A. and M.A.), Haley became field secretary of the Panhandle-Plains Museum at Canyon. But that was after his work as a member of the UT history department from 1929 to 1936. He's still sore about that job. "I was fired because of my vigorous fight against the insidious invasion of socialistic federal power."

He went on perfecting his knowledge of the cattle business, collecting valuable interviews with old timers of the range.

In 1946, in Amarillo, Wick Fowler, the late journalist and champion of chili, watched a fine fist fight between Haley and a supporter of then gubernatorial candidate Homer P. Rainey, whose campaign had been ignited by the required reading at UT of *USA*, a novel by John Dos Passos (which was admired by Rainey forces and is to this day unread by Haley).

"This stranger in the crowd called me a paid propagandist of the Republicans and I called him a God damned liar," Haley recalls. The two men were well on the way to vigorously slugging out their differences when they were finally separated.

But there were more fights ahead for Haley. In 1956, when he ran for governor as an archly conservative Democrat, he was known as "two-fisted Haley" and was soundly beaten. His platform typically included promises of such things as calling out the Texas Rangers to defend the state from desegregation-enforcing U.S. marshals. "I finished third in a field of five, but I got what I really wanted. I got a damn forum."

Haley is still enraged about one old battle. When bureaucrats learned that Haley's son had failed to register before planting about sixty acres of wheat on a farm in which the elder Haley had an interest in Sequoyah County, Oklahoma, the bureaucrats wanted to inspect the farm. The elder Haley told them to come ahead and he'd be there to welcome them, "Winchester in waiting."

The U.S. Department of Agriculture agents merely flew over the farm to observe the wheat. Presumably, the elder Haley had no anti-aircraft gun "in waiting."

The upshot, after a legal crusade that went to the U.S. Supreme Court, was that the Haleys finally in 1963 had to pay a $506 fine for raising wheat on their *own* land to be fed to their *own* stock. The old cowboy still unleashes a charge of electric language every time he recalls that battle. U.S. District Judge T. Whitfield Davidson of Dallas even apologized to the Haleys for levying the Supreme Court-ordered fine.

Looking over his shoulder at the dust of eight decades, does Haley have any regrets?

"Hell, yes. I wish I could have won more of those damn fights."

Haley's newest book is *The Diary of Michael Erskine*, a cattleman's recollections that Haley edited and to which he added historical notes and an introduction.

Liberals may be relieved to learn that he presently has no major works in progress.

※※※

Chili vs. Steak Feud Could Get Powerful Hot

In 1977, Texas lawmakers, after fiery oratory, decriminalized chili and adopted the hot stuff as our state dish. It's the law. But scofflaws scoff. And I hear stomach rumblings of dissent. No less than Mary Faulk Koock, the toast of Austin cookery, has floutingly declared that chicken-fried steak—not chili—holds the top spot on cafe menus from the Panhandle to Eagle Pass. And Panhandle menus have more spots on them than a spade flush.

James Ward Lee rants about the "the thousands of paper napkin cafes that have made the succulent chicken-fried steak the national food of Texas—not chili, as some misguided propagandists like the late Francis X. Tolbert (of *The Dallas Morning News*) have asserted." Scholars will find Professor Lee's outburst in the foreword to a book called *EATS—A Folk History of Texas Foods* (TCU Press) or in a collection of his essays and speeches titled *Texas, My Texas* (University of North Texas Press). It's no typo. I heard him say as much a couple of years ago, but he was cautiously standing with one foot in Louisiana at the time.

A dangerous precedent. Who can say how Frank Tolbert would respond? Would the author of *A Bowl of Red* smite the separatists? Or would he coolly shrug? After all, his namesake restaurant in Dallas' West End serves the best of both chili and chicken-fried steaks.

Professor Lee should be wary. Mr. Tolbert's chili crusades spawned a lot of, well, hot heads. And chili fiends are extremely dangerous when cornered in paper napkin cafes. I kid you not. A killing in Alpine a few years ago was the upshot of an argument between two men over how to cook chili. The feud was brewed at a chili cookoff in the Brewster County ghost town of Terlingua. CFS eaters lack that kind of passion.

But Dr. Lee's attack is a significant thrust at the powerful chili trust. His gustatory reputation is solid. He teaches English at the University of North Texas, but never with his mouth full. Moreover, Dr. Lee, the author of *Classics of Texas Fiction* and *1941: Texas Goes to War* is director of UNT's Center for Texas Studies, a responsible institution.

EATS was co-authored by Ernestine Sewell Linck of Commerce and Joyce Gibson Roach of Keller. Dr. Linck is a retired literature professor. Mrs. Roach teaches Southwestern literature at TCU. They talked with me in Fort Worth.

Dr. Linck's grandfather ran a Dallas cafe that he advertised as the only restaurant in town where a gentleman would want to bring a lady. He thus lost a lot of business. Anyhow, she inherited from him a trunk filled with cookbooks.

Mrs. Roach's grandmother worked in a Fred Harvey railroad restaurant. Right, she was one of the MGM-celebrated Harvey Girls on the Atcheson, Topeka and the Santa Fe. But she wasn't Judy Garland. Mrs. Roach's notion of good food is what she finds at her neighborhood 7-Eleven. She denies that she's the one you've seen there, sitting on car fenders, smoking cigarettes. Actually, in several precincts, she is known as a high-toned woman.

Without gnawing the chili-CFS bone of contention, the writers offer a full plate of the state's finest and folksiest recipes—Billy Archibald's Black-Eyed Peawheels to Yucca Flower Soup. Where you gonna find a good recipe for pig's feet? Or, say, slang jang (which is a sort of picante)?

Many of the recipes have an authentic tang. But missing is the original formula for chili recorded by Mr. Tolbert in *A Bowl of Red*. That concoction—free of all fruits and vegetables except peppers—is a tasty but tedious day's work. Instead, the authors serve us Pedernales River Chili:

"Four pounds chili meat, one large chopped onion, two cloves garlic, one teaspoon oregano (wild marjoram), one teaspoon ground cumin seeds, six teaspoons chili powder, two sixteen-ounce cans of tomatoes, salt to suit you, and two cups of hot water.

Put the meat, onion, and garlic cloves (finely chopped) in a large skillet and sear until light brown. Add the other ingredients, bring to a boil, lower the heat, and simmer for an hour with the cover on the skillet. Skim off the grease. This will serve twelve." The writers told me that this chili was standard at the LBJ Ranch, where Lyndon B. Johnson decided that chili should be named the state food of Texas.

Without paper napkins, here's the CFS recipe from *Eats*:

"Take one round steak about one-half inch thick. Cut it into four pieces. Pound it with a meat pounder, beat it, stretch it, then pound it some more, until it is as thin as a thin pancake. In a shallow dish, beat two large eggs and two tablespoons of milk. In another plate, mix one-fourth cup of flour with salt and pepper. Dip each steak first into the egg mixture, then into the flour mix. Melt two tablespoons of margarine, stir in two tablespoons of flour. Cook and stir until blended. Add 1 cup of milk slowly, sprinkle with salt and pepper. Cook slowly and stir constantly until the gravy is smooth and is not-too-thin and not-too-thick consistency. This will make a cup of gravy. Double the recipe if you want more. With more gravy you can stretch the meat and add a guest at the table."

That the title of "state dish of Texas" should go to chili is supported by those who agree with Mr. Tolbert's contention that chili was invented in Texas. Although chili is commonly considered a Mexican dish, researchers find early references to chili in San Antonio.

No one can successfully claim that chicken-fried steak is a Texas invention, although it may have reached perfection here. My guess is that the first chicken-fried steak was a minor accident involving a Wiener schnitzel.

The CFS-chili competition will remain lively, I guess. But many Texans would agree with Mike Kingston, editor of *The Texas Almanac*, published by *The Dallas Morning News*:

"I don't have a problem with either one."

The contest could become louder and more complicated if Texas barbecue enthusiasts make a serious bid for the state title. That's unlikely. Texans will never agree on a definition of barbecue. Texas barbecue is sometimes hard to identify—as toxicologists know.

✳✳✳

Texas' Carl Hertzog: Typography as Fine Art

Carl Hertzog speaks modestly of his vast talent as if it were a mixed blessing, if not a curse. But his overpowering drive for perfection in fine printing and book design has produced nearly 300 titles prized by collectors around the world.

While they sometimes pay thousands of dollars for a rare edition bearing the "CH" mark and refer to the initials' owner as "a master," Hertzog calls himself "a damn nitpicker."

When I interviewed him in 1979, at the age of seventy-seven, he'd gathered just about all the honors any book designer could want. The silver-haired, fanatical, typographical artist enjoys kicking back his recliner chair in his sunny parlor, lighting a cigarette and laughing about one remaining ambition—that of growing into "a dirty old man."

If he does, you can bet the dirty old man will be an exasperatingly impeccable one.

Like many people nowadays, Hertzog frequently becomes irritated when he reads a newspaper. But unlike most readers, who are disturbed by bad news, Hertzog is bothered by what his eye perceives as occasional blunders of layout and typeface. He admits, "I can't help it." Instinctively and critically, his spectacled eyes hawk any block of print.

"I have a theory that would apply to the craftsmanship in any design. Every design should be balanced and well proportioned, but there's another element involved, too. That is tradition.

"Let me mention an example. You could build a house of, say, Spanish design that might have balance and symmetry and seem perfect in every way. But if you put a perfect English gabled roof on it . . . well, actually, by design, the house may be all right. But the tradition would be all wrong. The same applies to printing. That's why I'm so often horrified by things that I see. The printing might be good mechanically—well spaced and well balanced, but there are certain traditions regarding typefaces and harmony that are often violated in modern printing. I'm afraid what I'm saying sounds kind of high hat. Well, it is, in a way."

The compulsion for perfection began in his youth. He might have been just another good printer if, while studying printing at Carnegie Tech in Pittsburgh, he hadn't come under the influence of a fastidious man named Porter Garnett, who was then establishing his Laboratory Press in the fine arts department. On a campus primarily directed toward industrial efficiency, Garnett became famous for producing fine printing and fine printers.

What's fine printing? Hertzog likes to quote his late mentor:

"Fine printing, sir, is printing that is free from errors, blemishes and imperfections. Fine printing is done on a hand press, with hand-set type on hand-made paper."

When Garnett went around saying things like that, the up-shot was eyebrows. Other teachers were instructing in fast pro-duction, as Hertzog recalls—"good craftsmen though not inter-ested in art or literature." That's why they put Garnett in the fine arts department. (That's where Hertzog would later be assigned when he began teaching and printing at what is now the Univer-sity of Texas at El Paso.)

The exacting Garnett is fondly remembered by the exacting Hertzog. "In 1942, about twenty years after leaving Carnegie Tech, I finally produced a little book which I thought was good enough to send the maestro. In acknowledgement he said it was good but, 'Why didn't you put the folios closer to the page?' (Referring to the page numbers in relation to the text on each page.) I rushed to look at the book. Why didn't I? The page numbers were too far into the bottom margin and looked spotty.

"In the same letter Garnett said, 'I am sending a little book just because it should belong to you. You will understand when you get it.'

"So when the postman brought the small package, I was all curiosity. The first thing I saw under the wrapping was an old vellum binding, then brass locks and then, lettered on the spine, '1496.' Laid inside the book, neatly typed and centered, was a slip with this inscription: "This volume, printed at Venice in 1496 by Johannes Hertzog, presented to Carl Hertzog, printer of El Paso, Texas, by his friend and well-wisher, Porter Garnett.'"

Hertzog knew he had arrived.

In 1934 Hertzog had established the Press of Carl Hertzog after eleven years of printing for other people in El Paso. "A guy died and his shop was run down and in bad shape . . . I could get into it for $1,000."

The Paso del Norte Hotel had ordered some menus. Hertzog had heard that Tom Lea, a first-rate artist, had returned home to El Paso. Talking mostly about things other than money, Hertzog persuaded Lea to do the covers.

It was not only the start of a friendship, but the start of a collaboration that would produce several major books. (Even the menu covers eventually grew into a book: *Calendar of Twelve Travelers Through the Pass of the North.*)

Hertzog's reputation grew. He did the El Paso Centennial Museum's catalog of a showing of Lea's drawings for J. Frank Dobie's *Apache Gold and Yaqui Silver*. He began designing and printing for Neiman-Marcus.

(About 1979, he designed and produced for miniature book enthusiast Stanley Marcus' Somesuch Press of Dallas a 300-page new edition of the first novel about Texas printed in miniature, an 1831 publication titled *Little Manuel the Captive Boy* by Barbara Hofland. Red-leather bound, gold-stamped, with pages smaller than a playing card, the seventy-two-page book sold for $50. Hertzog damns the cramped requirements of miniatures and says he'll never do another one—even if Marcus did send him a copy of his *Quest for the Best* inscribed to one who has achieved the best.)

Hertzog also did books for the University of Texas at Austin Library and the Texas Folklore Society. In 1946, *Calendar of Twelve Travelers* was published to the applause of critics. (Lon Tinkle wrote in *The Dallas Morning News*: "The mere existence of such a book is a reprimand to the slipshod and a challenge to the aspiring. . . .")

The long delay had resulted from Hertzog's frustrations in finding backing. "I went to two of the richest men I knew. One couldn't read and the other one already had a book. So, I put the project aside."

When Hertzog did *Peleilu Landing*, an account of the World War II battle written by Lea and illustrated with his combat drawings, the designer wanted to cover the book with the cloth of Marine fatigues. He wrote to every official he could think of in trying to get a wartime priority for the material. He couldn't get one. Finally a Marine officer told him that with no authority to issue a priority, he could suggest that Hertzog approach the contract supplier of fatigues. The manufacturer didn't need a priority.

Hertzog recalled: "I reset half the book by hand to get better spacing, mortised letters, made plates over and so on. Then I stood over the pressman and sweated blood."

(Hertzog had a mixed reputation with pressmen, printers and bookbinders. He laughs, "I know they say 'It looks all right to me, but that crazy sonofabitch wants to print it over. One binder finally just ran me off.' On the other hand, anyone in the printing game knew to be flattered that Hertzog had chosen him for a project. A confessed nitpicker, he has managed not to bring this habit home with him, probably one reason that his marriage to Vivian has lasted more than half a century.)

Peleilu Landing was a hit. So were other Lea-Hertzog collaborations—especially 1957's *The King Ranch*. (Lea, speaking of his amigo, says, "Carl Hertzog has an almost morbid attention to detail. He's the best damn typesetter around.")

In 1947 Hertzog had produced *Aboriginal America: The Journey of Three Englishmen Across Texas in 1568* for E. DeGolyer of Dallas. This work ignited his imagination for a subsequent "period design," so called by Hertzog because he imported type and paper to suggest the historical flavor of the narrative's time.

The following year, Cleve Hallenbeck's manuscript of *The Journey of Fray Marcos de Niza*, a telling of the travels of a Franciscan friar in search of the Seven Cities of Cibola in the time of Coronado, was accepted by Allen Maxwell, director of the Southern Methodist University Press. Maxwell (book editor of *The Dallas Morning News*), eager to publish a book of exceptional quality, turned to Hertzog.

What followed was more than a year and a half of creative agony for the two men, and ultimately by the ecstasy of seeing their work exhibited as one of the American Institute of Graphic Arts' 50 Books of the Year 1949. The SMU publication of the tale of "the lying monk" also won the Texas Institute of Letters design award that year. (Charlotte T. Whaley's account of Hertzog's struggle for perfection and Maxwell's constant encouragement appears in the 1979 winter issue of *Southwest Review*.)

William R. Holman, professor of history and art of the book at UT/Austin, has called Fray Marcos "one of the most beautiful and well-proportioned page layouts ever achieved by any designer."

Hertzog was the first winner of the Dallas Museum of Fine Arts Award for the best designed book of the year, an award he's won six times since 1949.

Two years ago Al Lowman, research associate at the Institute of Texan Cultures in San Antonio (which has offered a Hertzog exhibition), lectured at the opening of Hertzog's exhibit in the Fondren Library at Rice University. Pointing out Hertzog's influence on quality printing in the Southwest, Lowman spoke of an Austin protege of Hertzog:

". . . Bill Wittliff, whose Encino Press has bestowed typographical distinction on most of its publications, expressed his own feeling about Carl's contribution. Wittliff observed that J. Frank Dobie was the first man of letters to plant his feet firmly on Texas soil and to declare it as legitimate a place to write about and from as any on earth, so long as one was not provincial. In that same sense Hertzog was the first to establish Texas as a legitimate place from which to create quality books. Thus they made it valid for younger writers and printers to come, or to stay, and do likewise.

"Wittliff [said that] Hertzog was, in his own way, interpreting the subject matter through carefully thought-out design, paper choice, typeface selection and binding materials. The result was, in Wittliff's phrase, 'a satisfying whole, every element fitting, complementing, building an atmosphere for the author's words.' He is entirely correct in saying that typographically these books will never become dated; they are timeless. . . ."

Hertzog's favorite of his book designs is a reissue edition of *Interwoven*, an early-day history of West Texas' inter-married Reynolds and Matthews families, first published in 1936 and brought out by Hertzog with two-color typography in 1958. Illustrated by E. M. Schiwetz, it's a lovely volume, printed in large type on natural laid paper, bound in cloth with gold-stamped title and brands on the cover.

Hertzog has designed dozens of cow country books, including works by J. Evetts Haley and C. L. Sonnichsen. Although identified with the Southwest, Hertzog's work has been diverse. He's done half a dozen books for his friend Alfred Knopf ("A great publisher") and only one of them—John Graves' *Goodbye to a River*—was a Southwestern book.

The book designer is almost apologetic about not being a born

Texan. But the truth is that Jean Carl Showalter Hertig McElroy Hertzog was born in France. Carl's father (like his grandson, now working as a psychologist in Waco Veterans' Hospital) was named "Carl." The study of music had drawn the elder Hertzog to Europe, where he played first violin for the Berlin Symphony. But both mother and father were Americans. They'd met while attending Hiram College outside Cleveland. (Before marriage Hertzog's mother was courted by Harold Bell Wright, who later became a best-selling novelist.)

The Hertzogs returned to the U.S. because of the father's tuberculosis, which would kill him when his son was only two years old. The tot's mother later married a high school English teacher from Boston, who may have shaped the boy's career when he was nine by providing him with a small hand press and a case of type. There was a print shop near their home in Pittsburgh where the kid would go for an occasional nickel's worth of ink. Young Carl was soon setting type. By the time he left high school, he was a first rate typesetter.

After working his way up to the job of layout man for a larger printing firm, Hertzog saw an ad for a layout job in El Paso. He sent along samples of his work and landed a job with McMath, a border printing firm, in 1923.

After gathering experience with several other firms and, later, his own press, Hertzog began teaching and established the college print shop that would grow into the Texas Western Press at what is now UTEP (whose library houses his archives and a complete collection of his titles.) The first title from that press was *The Spanish Heritage of the Southwest*. Hertzog, of course, wanted to capture the subject of the book in his cover design. So, the covers of the hardbound edition were fashioned by printing them from adobe bricks. When a piece of adobe brick broke during the printing, disclosing an unmistakable bit of horse manure, Hertzog noted that it was the first time in history of printing that the crap was found on the outside of the book.

Until a decade ago, he continued running the press and, at times, teaching. He still keeps his hand in as a consultant.

Hertzog says that great strides in the technology of printing are bound to come. Traditional printing was the process of pushing ink into the paper or, as he says, "the ink is supposed to become one with the paper." Offset printing has changed things dramatically. But Hertzog likes to quote Tom Lea on that subject: "Tom says, 'Hell, I don't like that damn offset. It looks like you could scrape it off the paper.' But the big thing now is a photo-computer. You haven't got anything you can put your fingers on. You can't see anything. It's like music on a record, a memory bank and all that stuff. It requires an entirely different concept of how to proceed. I have trouble thinking in those terms. But it's bound to come because it's so fast and there are a lot of things you can do with it—like a lot of the things I used to do myself, like shaving letters and mortising them and making better connections. Now you just have to punch a key on the computer and move things around.

"My real craft is a thing of the past now, but the principles of design are still there."

Looking back on his long career from the recliner chair in his hillside home, Hertzog muses about fate. He should be a religious man, if not a preacher. He holds honorary doctorates from both Baylor University and SMU.

"I'm a Presbyterian, but I'm not sure about predestination. I have noticed, however, through the years things have happened to me that could only be attributed to some kind of *Great Spirit* or something of that nature. When I recall the events of my life, I find a sort of design."

A grand design in the life of a nitpicker?

He smiles, "I work on Michelangelo's principle that trifles make perfection, but perfection is no trifle."

✳ Index ✳

Abernethy, Francis Edward (Ab), 207
Aboriginal America: The Journey of Three Englishmen Across Texas in 1568 (DeGolyer), 244
Ace Reid: Cowpoke (Erickson), 223
Adoue, Louis A., 182
Agatite (Reynolds), 215
air show, 187-91
Alamo, 23-25
Alamo Mission Bell, The (Haley), 234
Aldrich, Bob, 65
Alexander, James M., 72
Alexander, Stan, 207
Allee, Alfred, 216
Allsup, Thomas, 77-78
Almonte, Juan, 40
Alpine Avalanche, 184
Alpine, Texas, 184, 185
Alverson, Virginia, 124
Anderson, Wilson, 121
Andrews, Milt, 169
Annexation of Texas, 4
Anthony, Susan B., 83, 84
Antrim, Billy. *See* Billy the Kid
Antrim, Henry. *See* Billy the Kid
Antrim, Kid. *See* Billy the Kid
Antrim, William, 116
Apaches, 17
Apache Gold and Yaqui Silver (Dobie), 243
Archer, Branch T., 5, 33
Archer, Pamela, 200
Armstrong, John B., 112
Army life, 71-77. *See also* Buffalo Soldiers; Laundresses in Army
Arson. *See* Fires
Askew, Harrison, 124
Auntie Skinner's Riverboat Club, 167

Austin American-Statesman, 228
Autrey, R. L., 182
Avers, Austin, 149
AWARE, 227-28
Bailey, Harvey, 134-37
Ball, Thomas H., 178
Balmorhea, Texas, 164
bank robbery, 134-37, 141-45
Banks, Jay, 216
barb wire, 210-11
Barber, Christina, 153
Barber, Robert Hugh, 152-55
Barlow, Billy, 118
Barrow, Blanche, 146
Barrow, Buck, 146
Barrow, Clyde, 146-47, 150
Barrow, Rube, 122-26
Barry, Buck, 100
Bass, Sam, 120
Batres, Jose, 32
Batterman, Barbara, 202
Battle of Dove Creek. *See* Dove Creek, Battle of
Battle of Little Bighorn. *See* Little Bighorn, Battle of
Battle of San Jacinto. *See* San Jacinto, Battle of
Battle of San Jacinto, The (Pohl), 26
Battle, William J., 179
Baylor, John Robert, 62-63
Baylor University, 174-76
Beauchamp, Jenny, 83
Bedford, Bit, 143, 144
Bedford, H. G., 99
Bedichek, Roy, 175, 234
Beil, Gail, 188
Beil, Greg, 188
Benko, Alexander, 74

Bessie. *See* Diamond Bessie
Best of East Texas (Bowman), 169
Bewley, Rev. Anthony, 58-59
Big Bend, 184
Big Tree (Chief), 49, 50, 54, 55
Billings, Harold, 206
Billy the Kid, 114-18
Black Jack. *See* Pershing, John J.
Black Seminoles, 79-82
Black soldiers. *See* Buffalo Soldiers
blacklisting, 227-28
Blank, Les, 205
Blanton, Annie Webb, 86
Blasengame, (Mrs.) B. P., 142
Blasengame, Frances, 142
Bluebellies, 64
Bluegrass, 207-10
Bobbed Wire Bible VII, The (Glover), 210
Bogie, W. L., 147
Bollaert, William, 39
Bonney, William H. *See* Billy the Kid
Bonnie and Clyde, 146-49, 150
Book of Knaves, The, 92-96
Border (Metz), 133
Bork, Robert, 226
Bounty Hunter (Miller), 111, 114
Bowen, Neal, 112, 113
Bowie, Jim, 4
Bowl of Red, A (Tolbert), 238, 239
Bowman, Bob, 169
Boyle, Barbara, 228
Brackenridge, Eleanor, 84
Brann, William Cowper, 174-77
Braun, David, 217
Brick House, 169-70
Brite Ranch raid, 186
Brogdon, Veda, 51
Brooks, David B., 89
Brown, Charles L., 157
Brown, Jim, 122
Brown, Roger, 81
Brown, Rube, 44, 45

Brownhouse, 166-67
Brushy Bill. *See* Roberts, Ollie L.
Buchanan, James, 74
Buckaroos, 213-16
Buffalo Bayou, Texas, 163
Buffalo Soldiers, 75-79. *See also* Army
    life
Bug Tussle, Texas, 165
Bullis, John Lapham, 81-82
Bullock, Richard, 35
Burke, Rusty, 195
Burleson, Edward, 32
Burleson, Rev. Rufus, 22
Burnet, David G.,
    in Houston-Burnet feud, 12-13
    as Houston-hater, 19-20
    as Republic president, 8, 9
Burnett, Warren, 154
Burrow, Jim, 124
Burrow, Joel, 124, 125
Burrows, Bill, 122
Busch (Calhoun sheriff), 47
Buskird, Paul, 208
Butler, Roy W., 187-91
Butterfield Overland Mail, 68, 72
Byrd, James W., 108, 109, 110
Byrd, Joe, 156
Cabell, Ben, 125
Caddo Lake, 165-70
Cahill, F. P., 116
*Calendar of Twelve Travelers Through
    the Pass of the North*, 242, 243
Calley, William, 197
Cambern, Thomas, 99
Cambern family massacre, 99
camels, 43
Cameron, D. R., 104
Campaign speeches, 12–15
Canby, Edward Richard Sprigg, 63
Canvassing districts, 14-15
Carl, Prince of Solms-Braunfels, 43
Carleton, Don, 177, 178, 181, 206

Carlshaven, Texas, 43. *See also* Powderhorn Bayou
Carlton, Perilee, 50
Carmichael, George, 143, 144
Caro, Ramon Martinez, 28, 39
Carpetbaggers, 64
Carroll, John M., 65
Carter, Jefferson Davis, 126
Carter, R. G., 100-01
cartoons, 222-25
Carver, Charles, 176
Caston, Ellie, 128
Cavalier, Bill, 195-96
Chadbourne, Theodore, 68
Charles Goodnight: Cowman and Plains-man (Haley), 233
Cherokee Jack. *See* Glover, Jack
Cherokee War, 18
chicken-fried steak, 237-40
Childress, George C., 7, 9
chili, 237-40
    cookoff, 185, 238
    Pedernales River recipe, 239
Chiquito, Juan, 102
Chirac, Jacques, 34
Christian, George, 38
Cisco bank robbery, 141-45
Citizens at Last (Taylor), 85
Clark, Van, 196
Classics of Texas Fiction (Lee), 238
Clayborne, Peter, 77
Clayton, Lawrence, 213-16, 223
Cleary, John, 37
Clements, William, 34
Clemmons, Joe, 128
Clemmons, Tom, 129
Cliett, Oscar, 143
Coleman, Robert M., 21-22
Collins, Michael L., 50-51
Cologne, Texas, 164
Comanches, 17, 42, 69, 81, 98
Comer, Laverne, 142, 145

Conan, 192-96
Confederate graves, 60-64
Conger, Norman Hurd, 176
Conger, Roger, 174, 176, 177
Connally, John, 55
Conrad, James H., 168
Constitution (Texas), 8
Convention of 1836 (Texas), 3-9
Cooke, Josh, 129
Cooke, Lee, 228
Coronado, 244
Corry, Thomas F., 32
Courtright, Jim, 111
cowboys, 213-16
Cox, O'Byrne, 103
Crain, William, 46
Crane, M. M., 180
"Crash at Crush, The" (Joplin), 164
Crawford, A. G., 186
Crawford, Hallie (Mrs. Roy Stillwell), 184-87
Crawford, Mabel, 186
Creasy, Sir Edward, 26
Creek tribe, 16-18
Crime Book, The, 92-96
Crockett, David, 4, 23-25
Cross, Mollie, 114
Cross Plains, Texas, 194
Crush, Texas, 164
Crush, William G., 164
Cry Unheard, A (Marshall), 99
Culberson, Charles A., 10
Cunningham, Minnie Fisher, 84, 86
Custer, George Armstrong, 64-67
Custer in Texas (Carrol), 65
Cut 'n Shoot, Texas, 164
Cutter, Slade, 204
Daggett, Ephraim, 59-60
Dallas Morning News, The,
    columnist Murchison, 226
    investigating hospital conditions, 155

on suffrage, 84
on train robberies, 124
reporting crimes, 149-51
Dalton, Bill. *See* Dalton, William
Marion
Dalton, Bob, 127
Dalton, Emmett, 127, 130
Dalton, Frank, 127
Dalton, Grat, 127
Dalton, William Marion, 126-30
Danforth, Grace, 83
Davidson, T. Whitfield, 237
Davis, E. J., 54
Davis, Jefferson, 62
Davis, Kenneth W., 171, 173-74, 223
Davis, Louis, 143-45
Davis, Ossie, 228
Davis, Tom, 176
Dealey, David, 202
Dealey, Edwina, 202
Dealey, George Bannerman, 198, 202
Dealey, Samuel David, 201-04
Dealey, Virginia Downing, 202
death penalty, 89-96
Death Row, 156-60
death warrant, 156
DeCamp, L. Sprague, 193, 194
Declaration of Independence (Texas)
adoption of, 3
missing, 9-12
DeGolyer, E., 244
De La Pena, Jose Enrique, 23-25
Delgado, Pedro Francisco, 28, 39
Denman, F. J., 73
Diamond Bessie, 107-11, 167
*Diamond Bessie Murder and the Roths-
child Trials, The* (Russell), 110
Diary of Michael Erskine, The (Haley),
237
Diaz, Porfirio, 96
Dickinson, Emily, 166-67
Dime Box, Texas, 165

Dobie, J. Frank
and J. Evetts Haley, 234
as author, 243
on Texas, 245
on unauthentic writing, 217
as teacher of John Henry Faulk,
227
and Texas Folklore Society, 207
Dooley, Tom, 132, 133
Doolin, Bill, 127, 130
Dos Passos, John, 236
Dove Creek, Battle of, 68
Driskill Hotel, 228
dueling, 13-14
Dugger, Ronnie, 230
Duncan, John Riley (Jack), 111-14
Duncan, Simeon, 111
Dunston, W. O. 129
Durham, George, 94, 95, 97
Dutchman's Hog Ranch, 70
Eagle Heart (Indian), 55
Earhart, J. B., 101
Earle, Ronnie, 154
East Texas String Ensemble, 207-08
EATS—A Folk History of Texas Foods
(Linck and Roach), 238
Editors Make Way (Reynolds), 56-57
El Paso Stage Line, 69
electrocution, 157
Elkins, Jane, 102-04
Ellis, Richard, 6
Empson, William, 219
Encyclopedia of Western Gunfighters
(O'Neal), 117, 127
Erath, George, 39
Erickson, John R., 223
Every Sun That Rises (Moore), 168
Ewell, T. T., 105
Ewen, Joan, 202
Excelsior House, 166
Factor, Pompey, 81-82
Fannin, James Walker, Jr., 5

Farmer Jim. *See* Ferguson, James E.
Father of Texas, 5, 7
Faulk, John Henry, 225-31
Fear on Trial (Faulk), 226, 228
Fenoglio, Melvin, 51
Ferguson, James E., 85, 178-83
Ferguson, Miriam, 142, 143, 183
feuds
    Brann-Baylor, 174-76
    chili-steak, 237-40
    Houston-Burnet, 12-13
    Mitchell-Truitt, 105-07
    Sutton-Taylor, 112
Fifteen Decisive Battles of the World
    (Creasy), 26
Filisola, Vincente, 27
Finnigan, Annette, 84
fires, 56-58. *See also* Lynching
Fischer, Rudolph, 101
Fisher, Bill J.
    Army life research, 72-75
    Fort Chadbourne research, 69-71
Fisher, King, 96-98
Fisher, O. C., 97-98
Flanagan, Graeme, 196
Fluckey, Eugene B., 202
Folsom, Mariana, 83
Forbes, John, 31-34
Fort Chadbourne, 67-71
Fort Concho, 69
Fort Phantom Hill, 71-72
Fort Worth Gazette, 124
Fossett, Henry, 68
Fowler, Sue, 41
Fowler, Wick, 185, 236
Fox, H. B., 217
Fox, J. M., 186
Franco-Texienne Bill, 35
Franklin's Crossing (Reynolds), 215
Fromholz, Steve, 228
Fulwiler, William, 196
Galveston, Texas, 49

Gardner, Charles, 208
Garner, John, 100
Garnett, Porter, 241-42
Garrett, Pat, 115
Gault, Manny, 216
Gentry, Tiana Rogers, 19
Gerald, G. B., 175-77
Gerald, Omega, 177
Geronimo, 212
Gerson, Skip, 205
Ghilordi, Steve, 196
Gibson, Forrest, 149
Glorieta Pass, 60-64
Glover, Jack, 210-12
Glover, Wanda, 212
Gonzaullas, M. T. (Lone Wolf), 216
Goodbye to a River (Graves), 245
Goodnight, Charles, 100
Goodnight-Loving Trail, 69
Gould, Lewis L., 181
Gouldy, Isabella, 109-10
Graeter, Frances, 119
Graham, Don, 197-200
Gramm, Phil, 226
Grandee, Joe, 211
Grant, Lee, 228
"Grave of John Wesley Hardin, The"
    (Sonnichsen), 133
graves. *See* Confederate graves
Graves, John, 245
Gray, William Fairfax, 5-6
Greater Tuna (Williams), 228
Green, Peter, 220
Greene, A. C., 122
Gunn, June, 103
Guthrie, Woodie, 228
Haddo (U.S. submarine), 202, 203
Haley, J. Evetts
    as biographer of Bailey, 134-37
    as historical author, 135, 232-37
Haley, J. Evetts, Jr., 234, 237
Haley, James L., 15, 17-18

Haley, Nita Stewart, 234
Hall, Lee, 48
Hallenbeck, Cleve, 244
Hamer, Frank, 216
Hamilton, Raymond, 149, 150, 151
Hamilton, Robert, 9
Hancock, Leonard, 154
Handbook of Texas History, 96, 102
Haneman, Albert, 67
Hanging, 157. *See also* Lynching
    of Wild Bill Longley, 119-22
    of women, 102-04
Hanna, Ebenezer, 60-61, 64
Harder (U.S. submarine), 201, 203
Hardin, John Wesley
    capture of, 111-14
    grave of, 131-33
    as gunfighter, 44, 120
Hardin, Wes, 113
Hard Times: An Oral History of the Great Depression (Terkel), 228
Hare, Luther, 65
Harris, Bill, 176
Harris, Jim, 176
Harris, Woodrow Wilson, 144-45
Hart, Loss, 130
Hartz, Oma, 52
Hartz, Steve, 207-10
Hatch, John P. 101
Hay, Jess, 154, 155
Hayes, Rebecca Henry, 83, 84
Hays, Michael, 72-73, 74
"Hee Haw," 226, 230
Hefner, Bill, 118
Hefner, Bob, 115, 117, 118
Helms, Henry, 141-45
Hendrix, Wanda, 200
Henson, Jake, 64
Henson, Margaret, 27–30, 38
Hertzog, Carl, 240-47
Hertzog, Johannes, 242
Hertzog, Vivian, 244

Her Work (Rodenberger), 194
Hickman, Tom, 145, 216
Hightower, Jim, 230
Hill, Robert, 143-45
Hilton, Conrad, 141
Hinton, Ted, 146
Hobby, William P., 86, 181
Hoffa, Jimmy, 197
Hofland, Barbara, 243
Holliday, Doc, 111
Holman, William R., 244
Hoover, Adeline, 124
Hopper, Hedda, 199
Horse, Billy, 53, 55
Horsing Around (Clayton and Davis), 223
Houston Chronicle, 85, 217
Houston Displayed: Or Who Won the Battle of San Jacinto? (Coleman), 21-22
Houston, Sam
    baptism, 22
    boyhood, 19
    Creek war wounds, 18
    as father of Temple, 211
    in Houston-Burnet feud, 12-13
    and Indian-Mexican conflict, 15-18
    marriages, 19, 22
    opium use, 18, 20, 21, 22
    penal code, 89
    in the Runaway Scrape, 8-9
    Sins of Sam, 18-22
Houston, Temple, 211, 212
Howard, Hester, 192-93, 194
Howard, Isaac Mordecai, 193, 195
Howard, Jack, 129
Howard, Robert E., 192-96
Huckabee, Bob, 71
Hunnicut, Arthur, 210
Hunt, Frazier, 116
Huntsville Item, 156

hurricanes, 42, 45-49
Huston, John, 199
Hutton, Paul Andrew, 23
I Am Annie May (Winegarten), 85
I Say Me for a Parable: the Life and Music of Mance Lipscomb (Myers), 207
ice, imported, 43
Iconoclast, The, 174-77
I'll Die Before I'll Run (Sonnichsen), 46-47
I'll Gather My Geese (Stillwell), 187
Indian Place-Names (Rydjord), 52
Indian purification ritual, 53
Indian raids, 49-51
Indian-Mexican conflict, 15-18
Indianola Railroad, 43
Indianola, Texas, 41-48
Indianola—the Mother of Western Texas (Malsch), 46
Insults, Innuendoes and Invective: Waco in 1897 (Conger), 176
Interwoven, 245
In the Line of Duty (Rigler), 216
Ivins, Molly, 230
Jackson, Andrew, 18, 29
Jackson, Joe, 125
Jaggars, Fred, 114
James, Frank, 111
Jefferson: Riverport to the Southwest (Tarpley), 110
Jefferson, Texas, 166-67
Jeffries, Bennie Augustus (Peavine), 229-31
Jeffries, Gus, 231
Jeffries, James J., 231
Jeffries, Phynia, 229, 231
Jeffries, Will, 230
Jenkins, John H., 21
Jennings, Al, 211
Jennings, Ed, 211
Jennings, Gary, 103

John Selman: Texas Gunfighter (Metz), 131
Johnson, Lady Bird, 168, 169, 170
Johnson, Lyndon, 233-34, 239
Johnston, Harold, 70
Johnston, Joe, 68
Jones, Angela, 170
Jones, Jerry, 170
Jones, Jett, 170
Jones, Patricia, 170
Jones, Tom, 145
Joplin, Scott, 164
Journeay, Henry, 211
Journey of Fray Marcos de Niza, The (Hallenbeck), 244
Juvenal: The 16 Satires, 219, 220
Karnack, Texas, 168-70
Kelly, George (Machine Gun), 135, 136
Kelton, Elmer, 224
Kemp, Louis Wiltz, 9-10
Kennedy, John F., 199
Key, Francis Scott, 19
Kickapoos, 68-69
Kid, Billy. *See* Billy the Kid
Kimble, H. S., 6
King, C. Richard, 123
King Fisher. *See* Fisher, King
King Fisher: His Life and Times (O. C. Fisher), 97
King Ranch, The (Lea), 244
Kingston, Mike, 240
Kiowa, 49-51, 53-55, 69, 98
Klevenhagen, Johnny, 216
Knopf, Alfred, 245
Koock, Mary Faulk, 237
Kosiuszko, Tadeusz, 40-41
Kovac, Thomas, 196
Kuykendall, (Mrs.) Alla Ray, 193
Kuykendall, Pere Moran, 193
Labadie, Nicholas Descomps, 31
Lacy, Charles, 129
Lafferty, Oscar, 147

Lafitte, Jean, 211
Lale, Max S., 30
Lamar, Mirabeau B., 31, 90
Lancaster, Kelly, 208
Lang, Ruby, 167-68
Laughlin, Charlotte, 195
Laundresses, in Army, 70. *See also* Army life
Lavaca Wave, 42
Lea, Margaret, 22
Lea, Tom, 242, 243, 244, 247
Learn, Charles, 129, 130
Leatherwood, John, 51
Lee, James Ward, 238
Lee, Robert E., 67, 74
Legendary Ladies of Texas (Underwood), 103
Lehmann, Herman, 101
lethal injection, 157
Lewis, Henry, 124
Life Well Spent, A, (Blank and Gerson) 205
Linck, Charles, 219, 220, 221
Linck, Ernestine Sewell, 238. *See also* Sewell, Ernestine
Lindsey, Seldon, 130
Lipscomb, Mance, 205-07
List of Fugitives From Justice, A, 92-96
Little Bighorn, Battle of, 64, 67
Little Manuel the Captive Boy (Hofland), 243
Littleton, Vance, 142, 143
Littrell, Barbara, 61
Lomax, John, 234
Lonesome Dove (McMurtry), 216-22
Long, Nathan, 51
Longley, James, 121
Longley, John, 121
Longley, Neill, 121, 122
Longley, Wild Bill, 119-22
Lord, Glenn, 193
Lott, John, 4-5

Louis Philippe of Orleans (king of France), 35
Louse, Willie Walla, 52
Loving, Billie, 194
Low Man on a Totem Pole (Smith), 185
Lowman, Al, 245
Lubbock, Francis, 14-15
Lynching, 56-60. *See also* Hanging; Fires
Ma Ferguson. See Ferguson, Miriam
Mabry, Thomas, 117
McCallum, Jane Y., 11, 84-85, 86
McCarty, Henry. *See* Billy the Kid
McClure, Spec, 199
McCormick, Harry, 150
McCowan, Jill, 194
McCracken, J. C. (Charlie), 50
McCulloch, Ben, 13-14
McDonald, Archibald, 73-74
McDonald, Walter, 73
McGuire, James Patrick, 79
Machine Gun Kelly. *See* Kelly, George
Mackenzie, Ranald, 69, 101
McLean, Thomas F. M., 100-01
McMurtry, Larry, 216-22
McNelly, L. H., 95, 97
McQueen, J. W., 129
Madam Walker. *See* Walker, Madam
Malsch, Brownson, 46, 47, 49
Malsch, Louise, 46
Marcus, Stanley, 243
Marshall, Doyle, 99
Marshall News-Messenge, 30
Martin, C. W., 52
Mason family massacre, 99
Masoner, George, 49-51
Mast, Milton, 122
Matagorda Bay, 41, 43, 45
Matthews family, 245
Maxwell, Allen, 244
May, Jean, 231
May, Nathan L., 164

May West Oil Field, Texas, 163-64

Meanest Man in Texas, The (Umphrey), 147-48

Memorial and Biographical History of Dallas County,Texas, 104

Metz, Leon Claire, 131, 133

Mexican prisoners. *See* prisoners of war

Mexican War, uniforms, 68

Michener, James, 168

Miles, Elton, 186

Miller, Cyrill, 57

Miller, Rick, 111, 114

Miller, Verne, 135

Mitchell, Bill, 105-07

Mitchell, Cooney. *See* Mitchell, Nelson

Mitchell, Jeff, 105

Mitchell, Nelson, 105-07

Mitchell, William, 95

Mittie Stephens, 166, 167-68

Mobley Hotel, 141

Montague, Daniel, 52

Montgomery Advertiser, 125

Moody, Dan, 11

Moonshining, 169

Moore, Wyatt A., 168-69

More Tales of the Big Bend (Miles), 186

Morgan, Charles, 43

Morgan, Emily, 37-38

Morgan, James, 29, 39, 40

Morris, (Mrs.) Alla Ray, 198

Morris, Charles H. 179

Morrison, William V., 117

Most Excellent Sir (Haley), 15

Mow-wi (Indian), 101

Muckleroy, Matt, 129

Muller, Joe, 167

Munden, Jerry, 129

Murchison, William, 226

Murphy, Audie, 196-200

Murrow, Edward R., 227

Murry, Ellen, 13

music, 205-10

Myers, Glenn, 206-07

Myre, Paul E., 153

Nalle, (Mrs.) Ouida Ferguson, 183

Nall, Tom, 207, 208-209

Nameless, Texas, 164

Nash, Frank, 135

National American Woman Suffrage Association, 83

National Intelligencer, 19

Navarro, Jose Antonio, 8

Negro Army units. *See* Buffalo Soldiers

Neighbors, R. S., 100

Neill, T. T. (Van), 186

Neiman-Marcus, 243

Nelson, Willie, 228

Newton brothers gang, 137-40

Newton, Doc, 137, 140

Newton, Jess, 137

Newton, Joe, 137-40

Newton, Willis, 137-40

Nimitz, Chester W., 201

Nimitz, Chester W. Jr., 202-04

Nite, Big Asa, 128, 129, 130

Nite, Jim, 128, 130

Nixon, Richard, 197

Nizer, Louis, 227

No-Ko-Wat (Chief), 69

No Name on the Bullet: A Biography of Audie Murphy (Graham), 197

Nolan, Nicholas, 78-79

Noose for Chipita, A (Smylie), 102

O'Kane, Richard H., 202

Okla-hombres, 127, 130

Old Time String Shop, 207-10

Oldham, Billy, 57

Olney, Richard, 10

Olson, Marion, 144

1001 Texas Place Names (Tarpley), 163

O'Neal, Bill, 117, 127

O'Neal, Tommy. *See* Sullivan, Tommy

Oonie (Eunice), 169-70
opium
    as medical treatment, 22
    use by Houston, 18, 20, 21, 22
    use by Santa Anna, 22, 39
Outlaw: Bill Mitchell, Alias Baldy Russell
    (Sonnichsen), 95
Outlaws, 89-160
Overton, W. P., 104
Owl Prophet (Indian), 54, 55
Pa Ferguson. *See* Ferguson, James E.
Paag, Harry, 188
Palmer, Joe, 149
Pancho Villa, 186
Parker, Bonnie, 146-49, 150
Parten, Jubal Richard, 230
Patrick, George M., 28
Payne, Isaac, 81-82
Payton, Donald, 103
Peak, Wallace, 57-58
Peckerwood Hill, 53
Pedernales River Chili, 239
Peleilu Landing (Lea), 243
penal code, 89-96
Peoples, Clint, 216
Peralta, Battle of, 62
Periwinkle, Pauline, 83-84
Perry, James Hazard, 20-21
Perry, Rick, 230
Perryman, Austin, 51
Pershing, John J., 76
Peticolas, A.B., 63-64
Phillips, William Hallett, 10
Pierce, Robert, 55
Pig War, The, 34-37
Poe, E. J., 144
Pohl, James W., 26-27
Port Lavaca, Texas, 49
Porter, Giles, 74
Potter, Robert, 3-4, 20, 166
Potterizing, 3-4
Powderhorn Bayou, 41, 43

Powell, Shana, 51
Prince, Bill, 76
prisoners of war, 27-30
Proffitt, Ben, 190
Prohibition, 178-79
Pryor, Cactus, 225, 226, 227, 230
Pryor, Charles, 56
Purification ritual, 53
Putnam's Complete Book of Quotations
    (Benham), 219, 220
Rainey, Homer P., 236
Ramage, Lawson P., 202
Rambie, Margaret, 140
Ramsay, G. G., 220
Ranger's Bible, 92-96
Ratliff, Marshall, 143-45
Reagan, John H., 104
Reconstruction, 66
Red Badge of Courage, The (film), 199
Red Light, Texas, 165
Redheaded warriors, 98-101
Reed, Hiram, 133
Reid, Asa E., 222-25
Reid, Don, 156
Reid, Lee, 60
Reid, Madge, 223, 225
Reid, Stan, 223
Republic of Texas, 3-9
Reynolds, Clay, 215-16
Reynolds, Donald, 56-58
Reynolds family, 245
Rhodes, George Fred, 42, 47
Rhodes, Marion, 47-48
Richards, Ann, 228, 230
Rickenbacker, Eddie, 188
Rigler, Judy, 216
Rigler, Lewis, 216
Ritch, W. G., 116
Roach, Joyce Gibson, 238-39
Robbing Banks Was My Business (Haley),
    135
Roberts, Barlow, 134

Roberts, Ollie L., 117-18
Robertson, Lester, 216
Robinson, Emma May, 142, 145
Rodenberger, Charles, 194
Rodenberger, Lou, 194
Rodriguez, Chipita, 102-03
Rogers, Texas, 171-74
Rogers, Tiana Gentry, 19
Rogers, Will, 19, 211
Ross, Reuben, 14
Rothschild, Abe, 108-11
Royal, Margaret Dealey, 202
Ruiz, Francisco, 8, 24-25
Rush, Etta, 231
Rusk, Thomas Jefferson, 15-18
Russell, Baldy. *See* Mitchell, Bill
Russell, Traylor, 110, 111
Rydjord, John, 52
Saldigua, Apolinario, 24-25
Saligny, Comte Alphonse Dubois de,
    35-37
Salt Creek Massacre, 54
*Samuel May Williams: Early Texas
    Entrepreneur* (Henson), 27
San Jacinto, Battle of, 25-34
San Jacinto: The Sixteenth Decisive Battle
    (Wharton), *26*
Sanderlin, Eva, 98
Santa Anna, Antonio Lopez de
    capture at San Jacinto, 27
    escape attempt, 28-29
    as Mexican dictator, 4
    as Napolean of the West, 4
    release as POW, 29
    surrender at Alamo, 23-25
    Yellow Rose story, 37-38
Santa Claus bank robbery, 141-45
Satank, 54
Satanta, 53-55
Savage, John, 102
Schiwetz, E. M., 245
Schreiner, Charles III, 224

Schwarzenegger, Arnold, 194
Selman, John, 114, 131-32, 133
Seminoles. *See* Black Seminoles
Sesquicentennial, 12
Seven Cities of Cibola, 244
Sewell, Ernestine P., 218, 219, 221. *See
    also* Linck, Ernestine Sewell
Sex Life of the American Indian ,The,
    (Glover), 210
Shannon, Boss, 136
Shepard, Seth, 10-11
Sherman Daily Democrat, 134, 135
Sherman, Martha, 100
Sherman, Sidney, 31
Sherman, William Tecumseh, 54
Shirley, Myra Maybell, 111
Short, Luke, 111
Shriver, Maria, 194
Sibley, Henry Hopkins, 61-63
Sierra (film), 200
Silvera, Juan, 102, 103
Simpson, Harold, 198
Sitting Bear. *See* Satank
Sitton, Thad, 168
Sketch-writing, 93-94
Slaton, Alvin D., 152-55
Slaughter, Gabriel, 44
Slavery, 4, 8, 56-60
Slye, Art, 187-91
Smith, H. Allen, 185
Smith, Henry, 3
Smith, (Mrs.) Tom, 135
Smith, P. A. 134
Smylie,Vernon, 102
Somervell, Alexander, 32
Sonnichsen, C. L.
    and Ace Reid, 224
    and Carl Hertzog, 245
    and Hardin's grave, 132, 133
    as author, 46-47, 95, 105, 107, 133
    Mitchell-Truitt feud, 105
Southwest Review, 244

Spanish Heritage of the Southwest, The, 246

Spears, Alex, 143

Specklemeyer, Charles, 126-29

Spielberg, Steven, 166

Spradley, A. J., 106

Stanberry, William, 10-20

Stanley, David S., 70

Starr, Belle. *See* Shirley, Myra Maybelle

Steele, William, 113

Stillwell, Hallie, 184-87

Stillwell, Roy, 184-85

Stout, Nancy, 103

Stray Tales of the Big Bend (Miles), 186

Street, George L., 202

Stroebel, Freda. *See* Weiser, Freda

Suffragists, 82-86

Sullivan, Tommy, 189-91

Sutton, Laura, 44-45

Sutton, William, 44

Sutton–Taylor feud, 44-48

Sweitzer, Alonzo, 14

Tales of the Big Bend (Miles), 186

Tarpley, Fred, 110-11, 163

Taylor, A. Elizabeth, 85

Taylor, Billy, 44-48

Taylor, Claudia Alta (Lady Bird Johnson), 168, 169, 170

Taylor, Jim, 44, 45

Taylor, Rick, 213

Taylor, T. J., 170

Tecalot, 100

Teer, Claud, 11

Tehan, 101

Tehauno, Patsy and Vernon, 55

Ten Texas Feuds (Sonnichsen), 105

TERA. *See* Texas Equal Rights Association

Terkel, Studs, 228

Texan Looks at Lyndon, A (Haley), 233

Texas (Michener), 168

Texas Almanac, 27, 30, 31, 33, 240

Texas Association Opposed to Woman Suffrage, 85

Texas Bar Journal, The, 110

Texas County Government, Special Districts, and Authorities (Brooks), 89

Texas Equal Rights Association (TERA), 83, 84

Texas Exes, 180

Texas Monthly, 23

Texas, My Texas (Lee), 238

Texas Rangers, 48, 92, 216

Texas Women: A Pictorial History (Winegarten), 85

Thomas, J. M., 148

Thomas, Marcia, 166-67

Thomas, Tater, 167

Thompson, Ben, 97

Thompson, Clyde, 148-49

Thornton, Roy, 146-49

Tinkle, Lon, 243

To Hell and Back (film), 199

To Hell and Back (Murphy), 199

Tolbert, Francis X., 169, 185, 238, 239

Tolbert, Kathleen, 185

Tragic Days of Billy the Kid, The (Hunt), 116

Train robbery, 122-26, 137-40

Travis, William B., 4

Truitt, Ike, 105-07

Truitt, James, 105-07

Truitt, Perminter, 105-07

Truitt, Sam, 105-07

Tunstill, William, 118

Turner, Martha Anne, 39

Twain, Mark, 228

Tyler, Ron, 102

Typography, 240-47

Umphrey, Don, 147-48

Uncensored John Henry Faulk, The (Faulk), 226

Underwood, Marylyn, 103

Unforgiven, The (film), 199
University of Texas, 177, 179-81
Up Periscope symposium, 202
Urrea, Don Jose, 4-5
Urschel, Charles, 136
USA (Dos Passos), 236
Uva Uvam Vivendo Varia Fit, 218-22
Val Verde, 62
Van Pelt, Peewee, 138
Vigil, The (Reynolds), 215
Vigilance committees, 56, 57
Villanueva, Placido (Pinto), 186
Vinson, Robert, 180
Waco, Texas, 175, 176
Walker, Jerry Jeff, 228
Walker, Madam, 83
Walker, William R., 132
Walla Walla, 52
Wallace, Houston, 128, 130
Wallace, Jim, 128, 130
Wallace, Lew, 115-16
Ward, Beverly, 81-82
Ward, Dorothy, 81-82
Ward, John, 74, 81-82
Ward, Latoya, 81-82
Warren, Henry, 54
Washburn, Betty and Kenneth, 55
Washburn, Hattie, 114
Washington, George, 41
Washington-on-the-Brazos, 3
Watson, Margaret, 83
Watts, H. Oram, 42
Weaver, Walter, 177
Webb, Charles, 112
Webb, Walter Prescott, 186, 234
Weird Tales, 192, 195
Weiser, Freda, 141-45
Welborne, John, 129
Wells, Jim, 85
Wells, (Mrs.) Jim, 85-86
West, Emily D., 38-40
Whaley, Charlotte T., 244

Wharton, Clarence, 26
Wharton, William, 5, 9
Whiskey and politics, 15
White, Rev. R. M., 57
White Bear. *See* Satanta
Wild Bill Longley. *See* Longley, Wild Bill
Willa Walla, 49, 51, 52
Williams, Alfred, 50
Williams, C. A., 57
Williams, George Washington, 50
Williams, Jaston, 228
Williams, Noland G., 147
Willis, Bill, 99
Willow Wallow, 52
Wilson, Bernice, 119
Wilson, Chunky Joe, 51
Wilson, Woodrow, 119-22, 212
Winegarten, Ruthe, 82, 85
Wiseman, Joe, 188
witchcraft legend, 171-74
Wittliff, Bill, 245
Wolfe, Ronnie, 207-08
Women's Christian Temperance Union, 83
WPA Dallas Guide and History, 104
Wright, Harold Bell, 246
XIT Ranch of Texas and the Early Days of the Llano Estacado, The (Haley), 233
Yellow Rose of Texas, 37-40
Yellow Rose of Texas, The (Turner), 39
Younger brothers, 111
Zavala, Lorenzo de, 8, 27, 40
Zulch, Julius, 229